John L. Davies

Spiritual Apprehension

Sermons and papers

John L. Davies

Spiritual Apprehension
Sermons and papers

ISBN/EAN: 9783744743365

Printed in Europe, USA, Canada, Australia, Japan

Cover: Foto ©Lupo / pixelio.de

More available books at **www.hansebooks.com**

SPIRITUAL APPREHENSION

Sermons and Papers

BY THE

REV. J. LLEWELYN DAVIES

M.A. CAMBRIDGE; HON. D.D. DURHAM; VICAR OF KIRKBY LONSDALE
AND ONE OF H.M. CHAPLAINS

London
MACMILLAN AND CO., Limited
NEW YORK: THE MACMILLAN COMPANY
1898

All rights reserved

PREFACE

THE sermons and articles contained in this volume form a somewhat miscellaneous collection, but their general object is to promote that inward action towards things invisible and visible which I have sought to indicate by the title "Spiritual Apprehension." In the expressly theological portion which is placed first, I have advocated the principle that our spiritual faculties, which may be summed up in faith and hope and love, have by the Creator's appointment the chief authority in our nature, and that by these we are intended to have a real knowledge of the incomprehensible Being who awakens and attracts them. I have pointed out that these spiritual faculties assert their dominion irresistibly in human life, and that the intellect, which claims to be supreme and to govern, finds itself baffled and confounded in ways that surprise it. And I have inferred from these facts that we do rightly and wisely in yielding ourselves to the lead of the spirit, and that the understanding has to follow and serve the spirit as best it can.

All the better and truer theology of Christendom, from the New Testament onwards, has represented our knowledge of God as personal and living, such as can be improved by acquaintance and experience, rather than as a matter of intellectual or verbal definition. Nothing is more evident in the Gospels than that our Lord deliberately put back all statements about His own nature until He could be spiritually known by those who had opportunities of observing Him, and that He cared for no confession but such as sprang inevitably from a matured reverence. What St. John tells of Andrew and Simon suggested to Keble the lesson—

> First seek thy Saviour out, and dwell
>   Beneath the shadow of His roof,
> Till thou have scanned His features well,
>   And known Him for the Christ by proof;
>
> Such proof as they are sure to find
>   Who spend with Him their happy days,
> Clean hands, and a self-ruling mind
>   Ever in tune for love and praise.
>
> Then, potent with the spell of Heaven,
>   Go, and thine erring brother gain,
> Entice him home to be forgiven,
>   Till he, too, see his Saviour plain.

So, in Matthew Arnold's words, "We shall find ourselves more and more, as by irresistible viewless hands, caught and drawn towards the Christian revelation, and made to desire more and more to serve it."

Preface

If some of the special experiences of our age are driving us back upon this Scriptural method, we may hold that it is Divine Providence that is strengthening our distaste for the so-called dogmatic theology, of which the Commination called the Creed of St. Athanasius is the unpleasing representative. The divines who have expressed reverence for the theology of the *Quicunque vult* have laboured with some success to explain away its damnatory clauses; but when the attention is thus drawn from these stumbling-blocks to its definitions of the Divine Nature, it will be the more generally felt how unlike these are to the theology of the Gospels and Epistles. Not only have they no nourishing quality, but they tend to obscure the one grand idea of the New Testament theology, the filial unity—the unity dependent on the relation between the Son and the Father—which gives its life to our own relation towards God. There is a peculiarly infelicitous disregard, not to call it a contradiction, of this truth in one of those "Proper Prefaces" which are the least valuable portion of our Book of Common Prayer, that for Trinity Sunday, which makes us say that "what we believe of the glory of the Father, *the same* we believe of the Son, and of the Holy Ghost, *without any difference* or inequality." This language outdoes that of the *Quicunque vult*, but was probably one result of its influence. The method which we are being taught to prefer to this is so to dwell on the significance of the Divine names, the Father, the Son, the Breath of the Father and the Son, as to be drawn into a sense of an inconceivable Unity in the Eternal Nature.

The Athanasian Creed has some qualities which have given it favour for a time even with such an evangelical teacher as Maurice :—it defies the common rationalism, whilst it is itself the consummate flower of the orthodox theological rationalism ; it turns into heresy any doctrine which assumes that the mind of the Son towards sinners is different from the mind of the Father ; it implies that right conduct, the doing of good, is dependent on the right spiritual apprehension of that which is above us. But if the method of the lines I have quoted from Keble gains upon the general Christian mind, there will hardly be rest in our Church until we are relieved from the saying or singing of this dogmatic canticle in our public services, if not by legislation, then by a general consent of the authorities to its disuse. Already, according to a recent statement of Canon Gore, there are many churches in which the Athanasian Creed is never heard.

CONTENTS

		PAGE
1.	THE WISDOM OF MEN AND THE POWER OF GOD .	1

"My speech and my preaching were not in persuasive words of wisdom, but in demonstration of the spirit and of power; that your faith should not stand in the wisdom of men, but in the power of God."—1 CORINTHIANS ii. 4, 5.

2. THE TRINITY 16

"The Spirit Himself beareth witness with our spirit, that we are children of God: and if children, then heirs; heirs of God, and joint-heirs with Christ."—ROMANS viii. 16, 17.

3. THE PERMANENCE OF THE SPIRITUAL AFFECTIONS   26

"Now abideth faith, hope, love."—1 CORINTHIANS xiii. 13.

4. THE CONVICTING OF THE WORLD . . . 40

"He, when He is come, will convict the world in respect of sin, and of righteousness, and of judgment: of sin, because they believe not on Me; of righteousness, because I go to the Father, and ye behold Me no more; of judgment, because the prince of this world hath been judged."—ST. JOHN xvi. 8-11.

Contents

                                            PAGE

5. THE CHRISTIAN INTERPRETATION OF THE TEN COMMANDMENTS.—I 54

> "Thou shalt love the Lord thy God with all thy heart, and with all thy soul, and with all thy mind. This is the great and first commandment."—ST. MATTHEW xxii. 37, 38.

6. THE CHRISTIAN INTERPRETATION OF THE TEN COMMANDMENTS.—II 68

> "Remember the Sabbath day, to keep it holy."—EXODUS xx. 8.

7. THE CHRISTIAN INTERPRETATION OF THE TEN COMMANDMENTS.—III 81

> "Thou shalt love thy neighbour as thyself."—ST. MATTHEW xxiii. 39.

8. MORALITY PROGRESSIVE 93

> "This I pray, that your love may abound yet more and more in knowledge and all discernment."—PHILIPPIANS i. 9.

9. LAW AND REVELATION 104

> "Ye are not under law, but under grace."—ROMANS vi. 14.

10. BROAD CHURCH TEACHING 118

11. THE HIGHER LIFE: HOW IS IT TO BE SUSTAINED 128

12. "THE ETHICS OF EVOLUTION" . . . 161

> "The creation was subjected to vanity ... in hope."—ROMANS viii. 20, 21.

13. THE CHURCH AS THE FLOCK OF CHRIST . . 175

> "I am the good shepherd."—ST. JOHN x. 11.

Contents

	PAGE
14. THE NATURE OF THE CHURCH CATHOLIC	188
15. REUNION	204
16. THE BIBLE AND THE CHURCH	217
17. CHURCH PRIDE	227

"Since ye are zealous of spiritual gifts, seek that ye may abound unto the edifying of the church."—1 CORINTHIANS xiv. 12.

18. THE MORAL USE OF MONEY 244

"Make to yourselves friends by means of the mammon of unrighteousness; that, when it shall fail, they may receive you into the eternal tabernacles."—ST. LUKE xvi. 9.

19. PEACE AND WAR . . . 269

"If it be possible, as much as in you lieth, be at peace with all men."—ROMANS xii. 18.

20. PUBLIC SPIRIT 289

"Not looking each of you to his own things, but each of you also to the things of others."—PHILIPPIANS ii. 4.

21. THE NATURE OF JUSTICE: AN EXPOSITION ADDRESSED TO WORKING MEN . . . 301

22. JUBILEE ADDRESSES, 1897 (1) 319

"Out of them shall proceed thanksgiving and the voice of men that make merry: and I will multiply them, and they shall not be few; I will also glorify them, and they shall not be small. . . . And their prince shall be of themselves, and their ruler shall proceed from the midst of them; and I will cause him to draw near, and he shall approach unto Me. . . . And ye shall be My people, and I will be your God."—JEREMIAH xxx. 19.

		PAGE
23.	JUBILEE ADDRESSES, 1897 (2)	329

> "Then Samuel took a stone, and set it between Mizpeh and Shen, and called the name of it Eben-ezer (*i.e.* the stone of help), saying, Hitherto hath the Lord helped us."—1 SAMUEL vii. 12.

24.	"RECKONINGS" IN 2 CORINTHIANS X.	337
25.	ST. PAUL'S "GRACE"	343
26.	THE "MANY MANSIONS" AND THE "RESTITUTION OF ALL THINGS"	348

I

THE WISDOM OF MEN AND THE POWER OF GOD[1]

" My speech and my preaching were not in persuasive words of wisdom, but in demonstration of the spirit and of power; that your faith should not stand in the wisdom of men, but in the power of God."—I CORINTHIANS ii. 4, 5.

IT is a matter of course that in addressing you this morning, my Christian brethren, I should keep in view what is in all our minds—that gathering of Churchmen which is to take place this week in your town. The purpose of the Church Congress is to give Churchmen an opportunity of consulting together upon dangers and openings and duties that are of interest to us at the present moment as members of the Church. We are led to consider how the Faith by which we live is now standing with reference to the ways of thinking and the demands of our time.

Now as I reflect from this point of view upon what is most modern and characteristic in our age, it seems to me that we are being emphatically warned

[1] Preached at St. Mary's, Nottingham, on the Sunday before the meeting of the Church Congress, 1897.

to fall back upon the old position taken up by St. Paul as a preacher of the Gospel. The method to which he firmly adhered was to proclaim the good news of the crucified and risen Son of God, without regard to any wisdom of men. The wisdom of men, he perceived, was against him: so much the worse, he held, for the wisdom of men. He paid no timid deference to that wisdom, made no attempt to conciliate it; his business was to deliver the message from heaven with which he was charged, whatever might be his hearers' opinions about it. In our day there is a very earnest desire amongst Christians, more general, I am inclined to think, than ever before, to reconcile our Christianity with the wisdom of men. There is so much that is manifestly good in this desire that we can hardly refuse to regard it as a Divine inspiration. But the desire, if it has a high Christian motive, and some good appointed end, may yet be a dangerous one. No such reconciliation is at present possible—none that is more than partial or superficial: Christianity cannot be brought into a really satisfying agreement with science. And if we were induced to adhere to Christianity because of its being rational, that might not be in accordance with the intention of God, who would have us hang on the Divine will revealed in Christ, and surrender ourselves to it in thankfulness and trust, and walk as children, not of this world, but of that which is above and to come.

  The scientific investigation of Nature which has had such triumphs in our time finds before it two infinities, those of Space and Time. Our whole solar system is a very small thing amongst the

and the Power of God

bodies which science can see and measure in the space which is immeasurable: how infinitesimal man is in the universe of which no bound is known, words and numbers fail to make perceptible to the mind. As the men of science look back to the past of things on this speck of a planet, its present state is seen to have grown out of millions of years of antecedents. Everywhere growth, gradual and natural growth, is increasingly recognised. The world as it is, including the human race, has grown by degrees from elements of which no beginning can be touched, through the constant pressure of a force which in the animated and organised departments of existence shows itself as a struggle for self-preservation and self-gratification. Sometimes science asserts the altogether non-moral character of this evolution; at other times it seeks to explain how a working morality, involving a certain control of self, has been naturally produced by care for self. In the universe thus surveyed by science all kinds of grandeur and wonderfulness awe the imagination and stimulate the ardour of inquiry. But it has been increasingly felt in recent years that the universe thus regarded affords no ground of duty, and exhibits men as atoms casually produced by the general creative force. Mr. Herbert Spencer has confessed that "contemplation of a universe which is without conceivable beginning or end, and without intelligible purpose, yields no satisfaction."[1] Mr. Huxley, who had argued triumphantly that man is an automaton moved by the natural forces, in his later years declared his conviction that

[1] Quoted by Mr. F. Harrison in *The Positivist Review* for August 1895, p. 140.

men were bound to fight against nature, in order to save morality. More recently, a striking protest has come from the small body of men who call themselves Positivists. The Positivists, as some of you will know, are followers of a French man of science, Auguste Comte, who not only co-ordinated the sciences, but also founded a religion. The deity of this religion is Humanity, and the social duties are prescribed by it with religious warmth and stringency. Mr. Frederic Harrison, writing in the name of the Positivists, looks the scientific scheme of the universe in the face. "The infinity in space, in time, and in proportion, which science reveals . . . is alien," he declares, "to the very basis of religion, of duty, and of activity, in so far as it reduces humanity to the level of the worm, and converts man's earthly abode into a casual atom. In killing theology, science has paralysed religion; for the noblest attributes of the human spirit, the inspiration to active conduct, and the power to frame synthetic conceptions, are all alike endangered. The scientific specialist says, 'That is no affair of mine, see thou to that!' but religion and philosophy both feel the dilemma."[1] Referring to the admissions of Mr. Herbert Spencer, he calls them "very honest, very pathetic, very significant words." He does not question—"we fully adopt," he says,—"the conclusions of science as to our being but infinitesimal bubbles on an infinitesimal speck of dust, whirling about in an inconceivable universe, itself having no intelligible purpose, and presenting unfathomable mysteries." What then does he

---

[1] *The Positivist Review* for August 1895, p. 140.

and the Power of God

suggest?—" We utterly repudiate the dismal suggestion that the business of man is to contemplate this unfathomable universe, without pretence of sympathy, or hope of ever reaching to its realities."[1] He intimates that, without disputing the conclusions of science, he and his friends will disregard them. For, as he writes, "human reason has no preponderant part in a world which is to us pervaded with a sense of human love and human energy. The mysteries around us and within us do not paralyse men whose dominant desire is to achieve some practical result in the world of reality and to hand it on better to their successors." "We admit that, absolutely, in the nature of things, the earth is a bubble and man is a mite; but we insist that for purposes of human progress and happiness we must think and act as if the world revolved round our globe, and man was its master and its ruler."[2]

Such is the attitude of men who have been supposed to be devotees of science, who have emancipated themselves from Christian doctrines and have discarded the idea of a God, but who cling to morality and to human dignity with persistent loyalty. They cannot persuade themselves that a rational reconciliation between science and morality is attainable; they see that a choice must be made between the two, and they solemnly determine to choose morality, and therefore to think and act as if the world were the opposite of what science declares it to be. They are for human love and human energy against human reason. They say with Tennyson—

[1] *The Positivist Review* for August 1895, p. 141.
[2] *Ibid.* p. 142.

> For tho' the Giant Ages heave the hill
> And break the shore, and evermore
> Make and break, and work their will;
> Tho' world on world in myriad myriads roll
> Round us, each with different powers,
> And other forms of life than ours,
> What know we greater than the soul?

In refusing to know anything higher than the human soul, in declining to go on with the poet and say " On God and Godlike men we build our trust," the Positivists seem to us to deny some of the profoundest needs and instincts, and to crush down some of the finest developments, of the human soul itself. But in their resolve not to make-believe as to any harmony between science and morality, and in their defiant adhesion to morality, I think they set us Christians an example.

The persuasion entertained by many of our earnest believers that the Gospel of the Cross, rightly understood, can find a place in its large domain of truth for all the wisdom of men, including the latest science and criticism, may justly be traced to an ardent desire to do honour to Christianity and to Christ. We are saying with emulous confidence that all truth is one, that the one God is the Maker of all the worlds, that in Jesus who died and rose again the Eternal Word of the Creator took flesh; and we not unreasonably conclude that, if we Christians are conciliatory towards science, and look at both the doctrine of the Church and scientific truth with candour and reverence, we shall have the reward of seeing that science supports, whilst it enlarges, our Christianity. We have lecturers who undertake to justify the Christian Faith in the field of open discussion against all comers. In discourse upon discourse Evolution is welcomed as the true form of Divine creation. Especially is it insisted that what the discovery of the law of Evolution has done has been to compel us to think of God as *immanent*, and that thus to think of God is the true and orthodox theology. This term means that God abides in all things, is not a Power outside the world, but the Energy working in all existence and causing the universe to be at each moment what it is.

That certainly seems to be the theology which St. Paul teaches, as when he says of God, " From Him, and through Him, and unto Him, are all things." We cannot but rejoice in connecting the word "all" with our God. But those to whom the immanence of God solves a great problem, and makes theism scientific and science theistic, can hardly be facing the simple inference that if God be in all things He is in many things in which we shrink from seeing Him. He is in the rage of the tiger and in the subtlety of the serpent as well as in the innocence of the lamb ; in the wave that dashes the helpless crew against the rocks as well as in the lifeboat that goes out to rescue them,—nay, in the wickedness of men as well as in the grace that lifts them out of their natural sinfulness.

The law of Evolution is a developed form of the principle which science has always seen in the nature of things,—that each existing thing or relation is entirely caused by what has gone before it. If this is a true fact,—and it is at least very difficult to show that it is not true,—science seems to deny human free will and responsibility. But it is not only natural causation that contradicts free will. When we think of God as the First Cause of all things, and as a Being to whom the past, the present, and the future are all one, we cannot see how a man can change by his will the order which God has appointed; the predestination of God seems to make it impossible for things to be otherwise than as they are foreordained to be. Further, it is a doctrine of the New Testament that all that is good in man is from God, even the first stirrings of good desire. Following St. Paul, who says that God worketh in us both to will and to work for His good pleasure, we confess that all holy desires, all good counsels, and all just works, proceed from God. Yet St. Paul did not deny human responsibility and power of choice; he actually urges, "Work out your own salvation with fear and trembling, *for* it is God that worketh in you to will and to work." An exhortation more defiant of reasoning, or one spoken with more simple conviction, we cannot well imagine. And we all—even the most necessitarian philosophers and theologians and men of science—think and speak and act as if we were free and responsible. And we see that morality and hope and thankfulness and providence, and all that is best and highest in human life, would be blighted to death, if we assume that the future is already fixed by what has been and is. We do not know which of two contradictory principles we ought to hold the more earnestly, whether that all is of God, or that each of us is called upon to choose for himself between good and evil. Those who hold that they can bring the predestination of God, or a fixed chain of antecedents and consequents, or the Divine inspiration of all good desire and purpose, into rational coherence with individual responsibility, only delude themselves.

The effect of what I have been saying is to discourage the confident persuasion that what science discovers and reason infers must be in harmony with what the Gospel declares. That hereafter, when the reason has been made a match for the spirit, this persuasion will be justified, I cannot doubt; I can hardly imagine a Christian not cherishing it as a faith and hope for the future. But at present it seems to be appointed, for the sake of the supremacy of the spirit over the reason, that the reason should be baffled and put to confusion.

So St. Paul implies, in what he says to the Corinthians. At Corinth, where he was in contact with the Greek intellectual eagerness and love of reasoning, he found that his Gospel, announcing the love of God manifested in the crucified and risen Jesus, was foolishness to the philosophical mind. This experience evidently set him thinking. And he came to these deliberate conclusions—that the spirit in man was a higher and more trustworthy faculty than the reason; that his Gospel addressed itself to the spirit; and that in speaking to hearers given to intellectual speculation it was especially desirable to forego appeals to the reason. " I determined not to know anything among you, save Jesus Christ, and Him crucified. And my speech and my preaching [or, my word and proclamation] were not in persuasive words of wisdom, but in demonstration of the spirit and of power: that your faith should not stand in the wisdom of men, but in the power of God." He saw that it might have been really disadvantageous to the cause which he was serving if his Gospel had commended itself to the wisdom of men. He was sent to draw men into a spiritual kingdom; and with that view it was necessary to bring them into a dependence of thankfulness and trust upon the living God. Such dependence the wisdom of men would not tend to promote. It was good therefore that the wisdom of men should rather be set at naught than courted and satisfied.

To these convictions of his the Apostle returns from time to time in both the Epistles to the Corinthians. As he dwells on the glories of love, he is led to think how superior love is to intellectual conceptions. With love he joins faith and hope. These are the three chief faculties of the spirit; and these he perceives to have the great quality of permanence—they abide. Knowledge is partial, and "When that which is perfect is come, that which is in part shall be done away. When I was a child, I spoke as a child, I felt as a child, I thought as a child; now that I am become a man, I have put away childish things. For now we see in a mirror —as on a badly reflecting metallic surface—confusingly; but then face to face. Now I know in part, but then shall I know even as also I have been known." Thus subject to change are human intellectual conceptions; but this is not the character of the spiritual apprehensions—they are abiding, and do not change. Faith and hope and love are essentially the same in the child as in the old man, will be essentially the same in the life to come as in this life. But St. Paul was not therefore an obscurantist; he scorned the policy of getting hold of people by the use of mystery and by managing the emotions. He aimed at being perfectly open and straightforward; if his ministry was of the spirit, it was also a ministry of light. By manifestation of the truth he commended himself to every man's conscience in the sight of God. His Gospel was the shining of light; if men would open their eyes, they would see and welcome the light, and then they would walk by it. Men, he was convinced, were made to know and love the heavenly Father, and the heavenly Father was adequately manifested in Jesus Christ; through Christ men were invited to come to the Father who was seeking them, pardoning them, and reconciling them to Himself; and to come thus to the Father was the supreme interest of every man, the way of light and life. By trusting in God, by hoping for the Divine glory, by loving the gracious Father and the Father's children, men were planting their feet upon the eternal reality, were partakers of the Divine nature which endures.

Can we of to-day, my Christian brethren, improve upon this method and teaching of St. Paul? There is much, I cannot doubt, with which St. Paul would sympathise, in that yearning endeavour to effect a reconciliation between our faith and positive science which I have assumed to be characteristic of the Christian thinkers of our age. It is clear, for one thing, that St. Paul would have claimed no immunity from change and improvement for theological propositions. The definitions of theology are of the class of things which were specially in his mind when he spoke of the knowledge which is in part. Some of the doctrines which increased secular knowledge or a finer moral sensitiveness has compelled Christians in general to give up or to modify have a strong resemblance to the conceptions which childhood inevitably forms, but which the grown-up man puts away. It is not the part of the spiritual man to cling obstinately to early forms of thought. What he will be anxious about, when improvement is suggested to him, will be to see that faith and hope and love do not suffer in the change. We ought to welcome any modification of theological statements which will help us to trust in the living God more happily, to hope more joyfully for the Divine glory, to love God and men more fervently—in other words, to grow into a closer fellowship with the Son of God.

We are not so made that we can do without intellectual forms of feeling and thought. We cannot believe in Christ without having some notions of His mysterious incomprehensible Divine and human nature; we cannot cherish reverence and thankfulness and devotion towards the Eternal Father without putting His Divinity under some limitations; the Spirit, when we try to open and submit ourselves to it, will be known to us in some inadequate images of His action. We have to use our numbers—our Three and One—in guarding ourselves against the worship of separate Beings in the ultimate heaven. The heaven which is God's abode can hardly be thought of except as space over our heads. Just as, when we grow up, we are bound to welcome the best corrections of our childish ways of representing to ourselves things visible and invisible, so the Church should willingly grow out of any immature definitions into more rational thought. Christians should get all the profit they can out of the wisdom of men. But this should be on the stern condition that no wisdom of men, naturalist or metaphysical, be allowed to put a veil between us and Him who reveals Himself to our faith and hope and love. We are bound to care more for the heart and conscience which Christ quickens and feeds, than for the laws of thought and the demonstrations of science.

And this obligation will constrain us, for the present and whilst we are what we are, to be tolerant of much that baffles and confounds us, to assent to contradictory statements, and—whilst we use our reason as an instrument and subject—to deny its paramount authority over us. The ambition to justify Christianity at the bar of reason or science seems to be a mistaken and a hopeless one. Any sciolist can find out weak places in a Christianity which undertakes to prove itself rational. Better to let the sciolist have his way and prove what he pleases when he calls upon us to reconcile the Incarnation with the law of evolution, or to explain and defend the immortality of human beings,—and then to point out to him that his reasoning is equally destructive to morality and to all the higher functions by which man lives and the human race makes progress; and then, and always, to awaken the conscience into a longing for deliverance from sin, to give an anchor to hope, to bring sunlight into the soul, by affirming the grace of God in Christ.

The God in whom Christians are taught to believe, as the Source and the Lord of all things, as Light without any darkness in it, is one whose dwelling is in the future, rather than in the present and the past. It is our distinction to be forward-looking creatures; and the more we can throw ourselves into the future in our visions and aspirations, the truer we are to the Divine purpose and creation in us. The most real God to us is the God towards whom we are striving. That is one view in which we may find some satisfaction. Another, which I suggest in conclusion, is that action and life and progress, which are more real than speculation, and have the dominant authority for men, not only respond triumphantly to the revelation of God in Christ, but have some power in reconciling contradictories. Knowledge, says St. Paul, puffs up; the Positivists support us if we add that knowledge paralyses, kills. It is the Spirit that gives life, it is Love that builds. What is there that has proved so capable of inspiring men, of lifting them above nature, of building human society, of promoting and sustaining progress, as the grace of God manifested in Christ, the warmth of the Spirit of Christ, the promises which are to be read in Christ? The man who offers himself up to the righteous and loving God finds himself equally moved to refer all that is good in him to God, and constrained by a sense of obligation to put forth his own best efforts in the service of God. When we treat the world as the work of the God who has been revealed to us, and look for signs in it of His wisdom and love, and endeavour, as his fellow-workers, to subject it to

His good purposes, it shines more and more with a Divine glory. If we have grace to walk in the light of God, we are not only preserved from stumbling, but the goal before us is seen, and the things around us are illumined. If we walk in the light of heavenly righteousness and love, we have fellowship one with another, and all the relations in which our Maker has bound us together here on earth will be rich in life and joy.

II

THE TRINITY[1]

"The Spirit Himself beareth witness with our spirit, that we are children of God : and if children, then heirs ; heirs of God, and joint-heirs with Christ."—ROMANS viii. 16, 17.

THE Sunday which has now for a long time been named after the Trinity, follows close upon Whitsuntide ; and this place of Trinity Sunday in our Church year may be a hint to us to look at the incomprehensible nature of God, as indicated by the name of the Trinity, in the light of the Spirit. We are still retaining in our religious thoughts the vital truths associated with the great Day of Pentecost ; we are remembering the promise of the Lord Jesus which was fulfilled on that day—the promise that a Spirit or Divine Breath should come down with power upon His disciples, through which He and the Father would come to them and abide with them, and make a great house or home in which all believers in Him should find their proper places, a Spirit which would fill them with joy and lead them into all truth, and enable them to bear witness of Him ; we

[1] Preached in Sedbergh School Chapel on Trinity Sunday 1897.

are remembering how the Spirit, when thus sent by the Son of God from the Father, first gave to the humble company of Galileans confidence and courage to proclaim the rejected Jesus as Lord and Saviour, and then smote the multitudes with remorse for the national sin of crucifying the Divine Saviour, and then drew the old believers and the new into a wonderful fellowship, in which the tenacious instincts of self-importance and the love of possession were for the moment conquered and dispersed. In the events of that day we have heaven opened and the Eternal Glory revealed to us. Through this revelation we apprehend the essence of what we can know about the Trinity. We see Jesus, the Son of God, sending the Spirit, and Himself coming in and with the Spirit, into the hearts of those who acknowledged Him as Lord; we see Him in such a degree and in such a sense one with the Father, that where He comes the Father comes also; we see the powerful influence of the Spirit making men feel that Jesus, their Lord, is one with the Father, and that they themselves are brought into a blessed unity with the Son and the Father, and with each other. We Christians cannot think of our God without paying our homage to the Spirit, to the Son, to the Father—without recognising the unity of God.

Can we understand the nature thus brought within the apprehension of our hearts and lives? Assuredly not. All men, when they have tried to understand God, have found Him to be incomprehensible. We might very truly say that to us, and to every man, God is unknowable. We can frame no intellectual conception of God which will not in a moment seem to us inadequate and futile and self-contradictory. There is no attempt in the writings of the Apostles to give us definitions of the Divine nature like those of the Creed commonly but not rightly called the Creed of St. Athanasius. We stand helpless with our reasoning and unifying faculties, before the mystery of the Divine nature. This inability to understand God is fully recognised in the New Testament, and is admitted or insisted upon by our Lord and by the Apostles who were taught by His Spirit. And yet it is true that they speak with great earnestness about knowing God, and assume that Christians may make progress in the knowledge of God. It is the very announcement of the Gospel that God has not chosen to hide Himself from men. I have been speaking of the revelation which the Day of Pentecost gave to the believers in Jesus, and which we have under our eyes in the records of that day. We cling to the belief that that which Jesus and the Spirit reveal of God is true and real and trustworthy, and that we have a knowledge of God which does not mock us, and will not betray us. But God, as thus revealed, is made known to the heart and life rather than to the understanding; and when the understanding attempts to reduce to an intelligible form what we are thus led to believe about God, it fails, signally and hopelessly, in the attempt.

There is a kind of definition of the Christian's God in one passage of St. Paul. It is in 1st Corinthians viii. We know, he says, that there is no God but one. "For though there be that are called gods, whether in heaven or on earth; as there are gods many, and lords many; yet to us there is one God, the Father, of whom are all things, and we unto Him; and one Lord, Jesus Christ, through whom are all things, and we through Him." That is, I think, the nearest approach to a professed definition of the Christian God in the New Testament. And a very valuable passage it is. But the definition has not a Trinitarian appearance. There is no mention of the Spirit in it. The one God is said to be the Father, not the Father, the Son, and the Spirit. And by the side of the one God the Apostle places a single Lord, the one Lord Jesus Christ, whom he exalts far above any heathen god in saying that all things are through Him, and that we men who acknowledge Him and speak about Him are ourselves through Him. So any one, taking this passage by itself, might reasonably conclude that Christians acknowledge one Divine Being called the Father and the one God, and another Divine Being called Jesus Christ and the one Lord. But St. Paul had a very strong consciousness that the Eternal God, to whom Christians have been brought, could not be *defined*. He was speaking practically,—speaking, as I have said, to the heart and life,—not philosophically or theologically. He has plainly warned us of this in the immediately preceding words. Knowledge, he says, puffs up, but love edifies or builds up. "If any man thinks he knows anything, he knows not yet as he ought to know; but if any man loves God, he is known by God." The reader would expect St. Paul to say that the man who loves God, he it is that knows God. But he thinks it best not even to say this, not to give any excuse for assuming that God can be known by the understanding; and he changes the expression. Instead of saying he knows God, he says that God knows *him*. That is our better way of regarding our relation to God. St. Paul would rather have a Christian say "God knows me," than "I know God." We see that the Apostle was choosing his words deliberately, from what he says to the Galatians: "At that time, not knowing God, ye were in bondage to them which by nature are no gods: but now that ye have come to know God, *or rather* to be known by God, how turn ye back again to the weak and beggarly rudiments?" Elsewhere St. Paul speaks abundantly of knowing God and of the knowledge of God, but he was anxious that such language should not be misunderstood. If Christians were in danger of assuming that God could be known as the things of science are known, it was safer for them to say God knows me, than I know God.

St. Paul had made his own position with regard to this question quite clear to himself. He was well aware that men could not love God, or trust Him, or worship Him, without bringing Him before the mind, without having intellectual conceptions about Him. But he held that these conceptions were of necessity inadequate, were subject to change and enlargement, were secondary in importance. He makes this, as I said, quite clear in that priceless chapter about love. "We know in part, and we prophesy or preach in part: but when that which is perfect is come, that which is in part shall be done away. When I was a child, I spake as a child, I felt as a child, I thought as a child: now that I am become a man, I have put away childish things. For now we see in an imperfect mirror, perplexingly; but then face to face: now I know in part; but then shall I know even as also I have been known. But whilst knowledge is thus partial and transitory, there are faculties which abide, are not transitory; faith, hope, love, these three, abide."

The main thing, therefore, in St. Paul's view, was to look upon God as He appeals to our faith and hope and love, to our spiritual nature. There is much more that is trustworthy in our spiritual apprehensions than in any conceivable intellectual apprehensions. It is the will of God that our understandings should fail us in our relations to the high things of His nature and working. We must make the best use we can of our understandings, and we can do nothing, even as spiritual beings, without them; but we must not be surprised by their being incompetent, by their leaving us quite confused when we try with them to comprehend and define what God is.

It is to the heart and the life that God reveals Himself; and He has spoken to us as spiritual beings, as living and social persons, in His Son. The Gospel presents to us what it has pleased God to make known concerning Himself. We find that we are led and constrained to believe in a Divine Father, in a Divine Son who is one with the Father, in a Divine Spirit. The faith is in each case spiritual, it is vital and fruitful, and it expressly attaches itself to each of those three names. And our faith in each does not result in our setting before us three Beings separate from each other;

but the more thoroughly and vitally we believe in each name, the more are we drawn to recognise an ultimate unity. This, it is sufficiently evident, is the New Testament teaching about the Trinity. Explanations of the Trinity, and arguments in support of the doctrine of the Trinity, are apt to assume that the Divine nature can be understood by man, and it is not wonderful therefore if they are found unsatisfactory and inconclusive. The knowledge that feeds the heart and enlarges the mental conceptions is that personal knowledge which the written records and the uniting and animating Spirit join to impart to us.

Let me briefly illustrate this knowledge.

1. It is Christ, the Son of God, who gives a name to ourselves and our religion. We are Christians, adherents of Christ; and our creed and worship are called Christianity. The first account of Christianity which has come down to us in Roman literature describes the Christians as singing hymns to Christ as to a God. Our sacred volume, the New Testament, may be said to be all about Christ. But how does this volume present Him to us? Expressly as the Son of God. That was the character in which He Himself insisted upon being known. He was come from the Father, come to make the Father known and to execute the Father's will. His words were not His own, nor His works; the Father spoke, the Father wrought, in Him; the Father through Him was seeking men to be His children. We can know Jesus Christ, can have at least some knowledge of Him; but if we know Him at all truly and well, He constrains us to know the Father through Him.

The Trinity

"He that hath seen Me, hath seen the Father"; "I and My Father are one." Our knowledge of Christ, which is personal, which implies reverence and gratitude and love, which may be increased by meditation and study and by following Him, opens our eyes to the Fatherhood of God. The Son and the Father become really and livingly One to us.

2. Men who have not known Christ have been led to give the name of Father to God. They have felt after the invisible Father. But He whom we Christians call upon as Father is strictly the God whom His Son has made known to us. We do not derive our knowledge of the Eternal Father from His visible works or from our own instincts. We ascend to Him with Jesus Christ; He comes to us as the Father of Jesus Christ. Knowing the Father thus, we are able to put our trust in Him; for the Father of Jesus Christ has every quality which should induce sinful man to trust Him. As we cannot think of or know Jesus Christ without joining the Father with Him, so we cannot think of or know the Father without joining the Son with Him.

3. Whitsuntide has been reminding us what a great place is occupied by the Spirit in the faith and life of the Christian Church. On the Day of Pentecost, and afterwards, this power from God took possession of men and mastered them; and His presence and activity were shown by emotional disturbance in the bodily nature. The believers in Christ were so filled with ardour and enthusiasm that they burst forth into peculiar utterances of praise. Outsiders might wonder what this remarkable affection was, but to the Christians the Power

was the Breath of God, the Spirit of the Son and of the Father. It filled them with filial emotions towards God, it made them cry "Father" to Him; it drew them to Christ, enabled them to feel that He was with them and to rejoice in His nearness; created a society of persons bound to Christ, and calling on the Father. They knew it to be their duty to yield to this Spirit of the Son and of the Father, not to resist or quench or grieve Him, to allow Him to make them filial in Christ towards God.

Thus are Christians kept in personal allegiance to the Spirit, to Christ, to the Father, and may increase in the knowledge of what each of these names signifies. When we try to get beyond such knowledge, and ask questions about what lies outside of the sphere of our spiritual life, the idea of unity, of a one Divine Being, shines from afar upon our minds; but we cannot understand it, we find ourselves to be in the presence of a mystery which transcends our comprehension. We are still more uncomfortably baffled; we are confused with contradictions; what we say at one moment we seem to have to contradict in the next. No one can help us out of these difficulties; we can only dimly conjecture why they are allowed to trouble us. But all the experience of mankind, and all the efforts of thinkers, seem to prove that our Maker intends us, as reasoning creatures, to become conscious of being rebuffed and baffled. To the understanding, God chooses to be unknowable; to the spiritual affections which are expressed in emotion and act, to faith and hope and love, to the aspirations which build up society,

God has revealed Himself, and will continue to reveal Himself. That is the will of God ; and we are invited to bow ourselves humbly before it, and to prize and seek the gifts that are offered to us ; to pray that the eyes of our hearts may be enlightened, to hope that in another world our understandings may receive a satisfaction denied to them here, and to strive that as sinful imperfect human beings we may grow in that knowledge of the Father, of the Saviour, and of the Divine Spirit, which is the true Life Eternal for men.

III

THE PERMANENCE OF THE SPIRITUAL AFFECTIONS[1]

"Now abideth faith, hope, love."—I CORINTHIANS xiii. 13.

THE stress in this statement is on the word *abideth*. St. Paul affirms that faith and hope and love are not transitory in their nature, but permanent. He claims this great quality of essential permanence not only for love, but for faith and hope also.

It is curious that this meaning has been so generally missed by readers of the passage. Learned readers, as well as unlearned, have failed to observe it. You may frequently see it assumed, in hymns and other religious literature, that faith and hope, instead of being associated with love in this quality of permanence, as St. Paul declares them to be, are contrasted with it, in that they are transitory, whilst love is eternal. "Faith will vanish into sight; Hope be emptied in delight; Love in heaven will shine more bright." Such language is plausible enough to be generally accepted. But it is at variance with

[1] Preached at St. Peter's, Edinburgh, to University students, 11th December 1892.

St. Paul's view. The passage we are considering is not one of doubtful meaning; no competent interpreter could question that St. Paul's purpose is to say that faith, hope, love, all three abide; and that by "abide" he means that they have not the changing and transitory character which belongs to other things of which he has been speaking. It is true that he is asserting the supreme glory of love; it is greater, he says, than faith and hope. But these two sister graces share with it the significant distinction that they all abide.

And this is a very interesting light in which to regard them. We have great need in these days to recur frequently to the essential superiority of the spiritual as compared with the intellectual nature and apprehensions. We find that on this superiority will turn our belief in God and in Christ. The proof given to us in the region of our senses and of historical testimony, of the existence of the God revealed to us in Jesus Christ, is often felt to be inadequate to support satisfactorily so weighty a belief. But we are justified, we contend, in the deference which we and our fathers have paid to the instincts of our spiritual nature. When faith and hope and love point to certain objects, and persistently demand them, and cling to them with joyful and confident recognition, we have the deepest, the most real, of all possible reasons for believing in those objects. It is very desirable therefore that we should accustom ourselves to appreciate duly the authority of the great moral organs of our life. And it is a main element in the dignity of faith and hope and love that they are exempt from the dominion of that law of change and decay which is written on all the visible things around us, and on so large a part of our own being.

The lesson is one which commends itself especially to those who are immersed in intellectual study, waiting on the instructions of eminent living teachers, and mastering the greatest books and latest treatises in which the mind of man has expressed itself. For the things which St. Paul pronounces to be subject to change and dissolution are intellectual conceptions and modes of utterance. "Prophecies," he says, "will be done away, tongues will cease, knowledge will be done away. For we know in part, and we prophesy in part: but when that which is perfect is come, that which is in part shall be done away." St. Paul had in view, no doubt, that kind of knowledge—or of speculation believing itself to be knowledge—which concerned itself with spiritual and invisible things; and those kinds of utterance in which the prophets of the Church poured forth their convictions, and the more emotional members of it their feelings. But the knowledge and the utterances may stand, in St. Paul's argument, for forms of thought and modes of expression in general. We have now, he says, partial and imperfect knowledge, partial and imperfect modes of communicating thought or feeling. And that which is evidently partial cannot put forth the claim of being permanent. We expect it to give way to that which is complete. Now it is to be admitted that we cannot think of any exercise of faith or hope or love as entirely dissociated from the work of the understanding or from the faculties of expression. We must have some intellectual ideas about the objects of our faith and hope and love. And, further, it is to be admitted, as St. Paul would, of course, have been ready to allow, that there are degrees of faith and hope and love, there being more in one man than in another, more at one time than at another in the same man. But in themselves the faith and hope and love have a uniform and permanent nature. That is the purport of St. Paul's assertion, and I think we may see for ourselves that he is right.

He illustrates his meaning by the universal human experience about forms of thought and modes of utterance. "When I was a child, I spake as a child, I felt as a child, I thought as a child: now that I am become a man, I have put away childish things." Each of us is able to say the same thing of himself. You can all remember something of your childish conceptions of things. You are inclined to smile as you recall some of the notions of your childhood which now strike you as absurd. The mind was active, and had not the materials of knowledge, the correctives of error, which have since been acquired. Your childish notions were curiously marked by a disproportion, for example, which an enlarged experience has in some measure rectified. These imperfections of knowledge, St. Paul, you see, did not shrink from recalling; nor did he shrink from inferring from them, as many of us might not have the courage to do, the liability to improvement of all our human knowledge. By the side of the history of our personal growth from infancy to adult age we may place the history of mankind through a longer period. That which grown men have thought they knew in past ages does not seem equally true to the grown men of this age. There are stages of growth in the knowledge acquired by mankind as well as in that acquired by a man. And mankind, in the more advanced ages, has had to put away many of the conceptions of its childhood. The contemplation of this imperfection of knowledge did not, however, fill St. Paul with scepticism and despair. Being the Christian that he was, he was able to draw even occasion of joy from it. It set him thinking how much better the fuller knowledge of the future would be. "Yes," he says, "now we see in a mirror darkly, but then face to face: now I know in part, but then shall I know even as also I have been known." It should comfort us, and not make us miserable, that our recollection of our childish fancies about things suggests to us that our present conceptions also may be similarly imperfect—not entirely wrong, but limited, disproportionate, imperfect. We are encouraged to believe that we may look forward to progress and improvement in our knowledge. We shall not always be so baffled as we are now in our endeavours to grapple successfully with the problems of life and the world, and to see further into the mysteries of good and evil, of the Divine Nature, of the origin and the end of things, of the kingdom of heaven, of our own souls. The sense of perplexity by which we are troubled may be claimed as a witness of our higher destiny, a prophecy of more satisfying knowledge to be hereafter enjoyed.

St. Paul would have made his argument more complete if he had dwelt more fully upon the contrast between love and the forms of the understanding.

There is something of an ellipse in his reasoning, which we may supply in this way. If we fix our thoughts upon love, we do not perceive in it this same kind of growth, from imperfect forms which the full-grown man can see to be inadequate to forms which better satisfy him. The things of the spirit in a child never become the reasonable occasion of a smile to the spiritual adult. Love in a child does not differ essentially from love in a grown man. And so it is with faith and hope. These three functions or graces of the Spirit—are they not the same yesterday, and to-day, and for ever? And if so, what a glory they have as compared with logical acuteness, with learning, with religious eloquence, which bear upon them the signs of inevitable defect and change!

Faith and hope and love, these three represent the spiritual or Christian life, called also the eternal life, in the soul of man. It is this which has in its history and essential nature the witness of permanence. I have shown that St. Paul found comfort in the evident progress from the more imperfect to the less imperfect which is to be traced in a part of our human nature. But he also derived comfort, and the more indispensable comfort, from contemplating the signs and working in man of the perfect and eternal Divine nature. And in order to realise that this which seemed to him best in man was really unchanging, he must have looked at it, as he did at the changing forms of mental conception, in the stage of human childhood. In the child—he implies, if he does not fully affirm—he found the spiritual affections at least as admirable as in the man. These things, faith and hope and love, he perceived, manifest themselves with heavenly beauty in the young; they are also the signs of God's truest presence in the instructed and experienced man, and they will stand the shock of death, and remain with us, in virtue of their imperishable and eternal nature, in the dimly imagined world that lies on the other side of the grave.

St. Paul could not have said, "When I was a child, I trusted as a child, I hoped as a child, I loved as a child: since I have become a man, I have put away the things of the child." No: in these respects, on the contrary, he desired to put on the child more and more. For it is in the nature of the child to show faith and hope and love with more freshness and simplicity, less disguised and smothered by feelings learnt in the world, less fettered by the forms of the understanding and of education, than they are as we see them manifested in later life. Hence there is something in these qualities which we willingly describe as childlike. Indeed we might interpret our Lord's saying, "Except ye turn and become as little children, ye cannot enter into the kingdom of heaven," by substituting the words, "Except ye become trustful, hopeful, loving, ye cannot become my spiritual subjects."

The faith of the very young child is not in God distinctly realised as dwelling in the heaven above. His trust is rather in his parents, or in those who occupy towards him in any degree the place of a parent. But I think we ought to claim even this early trust as having in it the nature of the faith which abides. For it is trust in love and goodness, in wisdom and providence. And through these qualities in the parent the Eternal God is revealing Himself to the child. The trust of the child is repelled and discouraged when he finds hardness and carelessness and frivolity substituting themselves for the protecting kindness with which God endows a parent. As warmth answers to the rays of the sun in the object on which it shines, so is trust fostered in the child by the goodness and wisdom which he is so ready to recognise and assume in those above him. And it is the Creator's ordinance that human faith should be nourished in its beginnings by the parents who are seen, until it can discern through and above them the heavenly Father who is not seen. A child, therefore, trusting in one above himself presumed to be good and wise, is showing the same filial disposition as the grown man, who looks away from flesh and blood to put a calm and thankful trust in the Eternal Father of all.

Glance again at what hope is in the child. It may be a hope of selfish gratification, of dainties to please the palate, or amusements to excite and occupy the imagination; and then it is not hope in God. But there are similarly misplaced hopes in adult life, and the sentiment then differs in kind from that of which St. Paul is thinking. The hope that abides is the hope of the glory of God, and the glory of God is revealed in all diffusion of light, in all promotion of that which is good, in all triumphs of justice and humanity over disorder and wrong. A most blessed and Divine sentiment is the hope of such things, full of saving and creative force; and surely you may recognise it in a child, brightening the young face and sending thrills of wholesome life through the nature, more easily than in the grown man. It is characteristic of the young to be hopeful; their enthusiasm, we say, has not been quenched by the painful experience of the slowness and folly and wickedness of mankind. A boy or a girl looks yearningly for the success of the cause which has been identified with righteousness and nobleness. And this hope, instructed by experience but not changed or different in essential nature, is what seems so Divine and beneficent a gift in men and women, which produces the enthusiasts and the martyrs to whom the world owes so much, which cheers the dullest lot, and makes weariness and suffering supportable, which—in words which Plato quotes from Pindar—"more than ought else, steers the capricious will of mortal men." Certainly one part of becoming as a little child is to recover the hopefulness of youth.

It is still more obvious that love in a child does not differ in nature from love in the grown man. Love takes various forms, according to the relations which draw it out. It is conjugal, parental, filial; love of a friend, love of country, love of Christ, love of the Father. There are also corruptions or counterfeits of true love. But at the heart of the genuine affection, in all its forms, there is the same essential motive. It is the subordination or sacrifice of self for the sake of a worthy object. It is the drawing of the soul towards that which is properly attractive, truly desirable and precious. It may be true, as Henry Taylor has written, that "still the source, not object, gives The secret food whereon love lives."

The persons loved may be unworthy. But the true love does not delight in the evil in them; it has in view their good, their worth, their real happiness; and it grieves, in proportion to its warmth and keenness, over all that is contrary to good in them. And the love which clings to ideal worth grows abundantly in the virgin soil of youth. It has not in children the intensity or steadiness which it may have in older persons, but it has a touching tenderness and capacity of devotion. It is attracted at first by persons who are seen; but you know, I daresay, what a profound and reverent attachment the records of Jesus Christ are able to inspire in the hearts of children towards our blessed Lord. The experienced Christian may well envy the pure and fresh emotion with which the love of children goes forth towards the Saviour. This, surely, if anything does, flows from the infinite and eternal Fountain.

If we were to transfer our thoughts for a moment to the earlier and the more adult stages in the life of the human race, we should be equally ready to admit that the faith and hope and love of primitive generations could not differ substantially from the same qualities in the most advanced race. They may look different at first, through the great difference of the intellectual conceptions, of the religious and the social habits, with which they are complicated. But the trust in fatherhood, the hope of the glory of God, the love of God and man, have never been wholly wanting amongst men of whom we know anything; and these same affections are the chief constituents of Christian life in the apostolic age or in our own.

Having looked backward and seen these three graces to be thus identical and unchanging in stages of human growth which are in mental conditions so far separated from each other, we shall have confidence in them as we look forward even beyond the grave. Are we to part with faith hereafter? Only if we give to the name Faith some narrow interpretation. Not, surely, if it is filial trust in the Father. It cannot be part of the rewards of the future state that the children of God should cease to be filial, or to cherish that confiding trust in the Fatherly wisdom and goodness which was perfectly exhibited in the perfect Son of God. No; if childlike faith has continued from yesterday until to-day, we may know it to be of a nature to continue and abide for ever. But must not hope, as they say, be swallowed up in fruition? Not, it would seem, until the whole work of the Divine creation and government be brought to a standstill. Such an end is beyond the reach of our faculties to imagine. But the death of a Christian will not leave him without objects of hope. After each of us dies there will be plenty of evil still to be purged out of God's world; there will be endless evolutions of the Divine Purpose for the revealing of the Divine Glory. Those that have gone before us, we may well believe, instead of having ceased to hope, are now hoping more earnestly, more continuously, more joyfully, more calmly, than we are. Of the continuance of love in the life to come I need say nothing, as it has not been possible to fall into the mistake of supposing that love could be stopped by death unless all conscious existence be believed to be stopped by it also.

They abide then, these three. They have continued since God breathed into human nostrils the breath of life, and they will continue for ever. Through these we are related to God's own eternity; they live upon the eternal attributes which are their constant objects. It is the very excellence of the redemption wrought for us by Christ that it draws our faith and hope and love towards the true unseen God. Let us look with due reverence on these affections which are ours and yet not ours. It is more that we should be able to trust, to hope, and to love, than that we should have knowledge to unlock mysteries and should speak with the tongues of men and of angels. Let us cherish these functions of our spiritual nature as our human distinction, as our pledge of immortality.

There are some special reasons why these truths, which are truths for all, should be urged on the attention of an audience of University students. (1) In coming up to the University of this ancient capital you are introduced into a famous centre of intellectual movement, a renowned house of the most various kinds of knowledge. You are here expressly that you may acquire knowledge, and that your mental capacities—those of expression and influence, amongst others—may be cultivated. You can scarcely fail to be impressed, if not fascinated, as you have not been before, by intellectual power. The members of a University must always need to be reminded of what the clever and disputatious Corinthians required to be taught—that on all the functions of the mind there is a stamp of transitoriness, of manifest inadequacy; that the greatest learning, the keenest philosophical insight, all cleverness, and all eloquence, are in the sight of our God but poor things compared with those spiritual endowments which the child may share with the most learned. (2) Again, it is a part of your experience here that your own conceptions and opinions undergo change, and that you become acquainted with the general change which has been going on for some time in our ways of looking at the most important things. Religious traditions have no more succeeded in making themselves immutable than the other traditions which science and criticism have disturbed. St. Paul prepares you for this experience. The mental forms which men must use when they trust and hope and love are subject to change by the law of their nature. Opinions ought not to be changed lightly, but it is only by being altered that they can be improved ; and the greater and more interesting times of history are those in which the gravest changes have taken place. It is the truest mark of Divine development when the loosening of a traditional conception sets faith or hope or love free from some restriction which had confined and fretted it. (3) Once more, the time of entering upon manhood is a season in which there may be a dangerous hurry to put away the things of the child. I need not enlarge upon the familiar temptations through which the young man has to pass ; upon the risk of his being corrupted by worldliness, made a spoil of by false philosophy and vain deceit, taken captive by ambition, drowned in destruction by foolish and hurtful lusts. Ah ! let no voice of man or devil persuade you to look down on simplicity, reverence, goodness, as childish things, to be put away by the grown man. Beware of the vanity of knowingness. Believe St. Paul and St. Paul's Master, believe the experience of all the Christian generations, that faith and hope and love are the precious things, the enduring forces of human life. Through whatever stages and changes you may be destined to pass, pray that in you these eternal things may abide, for this life and for that which is to come.

IV

THE CONVICTING OF THE WORLD[1]

"He, when He is come, will convict the world in respect of sin, and of righteousness, and of judgment: of sin, because they believe not on Me; of righteousness, because I go to the Father, and ye behold Me no more; of judgment, because the prince of this world hath been judged."—St. John xvi. 8-11.

THE words "when He is come" draw our attention to a particular time. The time to which our Lord refers is the great Day of Pentecost. In the consolations and promises which He gave to His awe-struck disciples on the night before His crucifixion Jesus dwelt chiefly upon a double Coming—we might rather say a threefold Coming. He was Himself to come, and to rejoin His friends and envoys; the Spirit was to come, and to work through them and upon the world; Jesus and His Father were to come and to make their abode or mansion with them. Thus they would have mansions or abodes in a Father's house; they would be inmates, whilst yet living their mortal lives, of a spiritual home; brothers together of a divine Elder Brother; children of the Eternal Father,

[1] An Ordination Sermon preached in Ripon Cathedral, 31st May 1896.

animated and impelled by an immortal Spirit. The coming on which these results were to depend was to take place at a near and definite date. It was to be for a little while only that the sorrowing disciples were to be left in their desolation. And the promise was quickly fulfilled and the sorrow turned into joy. First came the Resurrection, raising the disciples from their prostration and filling them with wonder; then the transitional time of occasional appearances of their risen Master, closed with the sign of the Ascension; and then the mighty outpouring of the Breath of the Father and the Son, which moved the Apostles to bear witness to Christ, and brought the Church of Christ into existence.

The Spirit, then, that we are to think of as convicting the world was expressly the Pentecostal Spirit, known to us through what He wrought on that day. It was the Power that spoke through the Apostles and created the Church. Its first work was to bear witness to Christ. We see the Apostles, on and after the Day of Pentecost, fired with an extraordinary zeal for Christ. They saw Jesus the Crucified, their Galilean Master, at the Father's right hand, and felt Him to be none the less present with them upon the earth. They were encouraged to proclaim Him Saviour and Lord. The seeing of Jesus Christ and the impulse to proclaim Him were from the Spirit. Then their hearers, those who believed, were drawn to Christ in reverence and gratitude and devotion. They were thus drawn, out of the world, from under the power of darkness and the tyranny of their own desires and wilfulness, into a new life of partnership and self-mastery. And this influence was from the Spirit. It is the Spirit of the Apostles of Christ and of the Church of Christ that we see manifesting Himself when the promised Coming took place.

That same Spirit has never deserted the Church from the Day of Pentecost to this our time. And the acknowledgment of this living and active Spirit makes us think very seriously of the Church and of its ministers. The Church, we are bound to confess, is inspired, and its ministers are inspired. All the faith and hope and love of Christendom are from the one Spirit, are the Spirit itself stirring in the body of Christ. Those who are called to bear witness to Christ have Christ revealed to them by the Spirit, and all the force of the testimony that comes through their faltering lips is of the Spirit. There are persons to whom it seems evident that, if this is a true belief, then there must be an infallible Church, and its duly authorised ministers must be armed with some exclusive supernatural prerogatives. But that is a perfectly gratuitous inference. An infallible Spirit breathing into fallible men does not necessarily construct them into an infallible society; an infallible Shepherd does not confer a necessary infallibility upon His flock. It is easy to understand the importunate craving with which men ask for an authority to tell them with the voice of God what creed they are to profess and how they are to act; and the disappointment, if not anger, which they feel when they are referred to the heavenly Lord and the invisible Spirit is also intelligible enough. It is from these feelings that the doctrines of an infallible Church and a magical priesthood have their origin, and not from the infallibility of the Head of the Church and of the inworking Spirit. Human beings, however they may be organised, remain helpless in themselves and dependent on Christ and the Spirit. But that we have a Christ to depend upon, a Spirit to work in us, this should fill us with awe as well as thankful joy. It made the Apostles rejoice, but it made them fear also. "Work out your own salvation with fear and trembling," said St. Paul, "*for* it is God which worketh in you both to will and to work." Let those who are called to the ministries of the Church of England not shrink from believing that they are organs of the Spirit of Christ. But let the effect of this faith be to make them anxiously docile and submissive towards the infallible Guide, fearful lest vanities of their own and inconsistencies of their lives should mar the work they are appointed to do as witnesses and as teachers. It should be one of their constant studies to consider how the Spirit of Christ has wrought in the history of the Church, and how He is therefore sure to work when He is using us as His instruments.

On this day, so sacred to those who are being sent forth with holy commissions, so full of interest to the assisting congregation, let us listen to our Lord predicting what His Spirit was to do to the world. By the world we are evidently to understand the population surrounding the believers—the unbelieving world as affected by the Church with its new faith and its new life.

1. The Spirit "will convict the world in respect of sin, because they believe not on Me." To convict

the world in respect of sin is to make it conscious of sin, to bring home to the world the reality of sin and the blameworthiness of it.

The consciousness of sin has never been entirely absent from mankind. It has been the main cause of the fears with which men have regarded the powers of the supernatural world. The heathen religions have been for the most part religions of fear; and "'tis conscience that makes cowards of us all." In all times and places men have been constrained to accuse themselves—that is, they have been conscious of sin. But it has also been natural to them to *ex*cuse themselves. When men know nothing but this earth, there is no room for the conception of sin in their thoughts. In this our day there are persons who profess to be guided by science only; and the observations and conclusions of science will not teach a man to blame himself, or justify him in blaming others. These scientific persons reply to the questions, "Why is a man what he is? Why does he act as he does?" by showing that he has inherited a certain nature from his parents and forefathers, and that he has been subject during his life to certain influences; and they maintain that the inherited nature and the influences brought to bear upon it from without fully account for what the man is and for what he does. Do not suppose that it is easy to refute this theory of human conduct; I should not be surprised if you never found a way of refuting it that satisfied you. But we can see that it leaves no room for sin—that is, for blameworthiness. If a plant flourishes, you do not praise it; if it withers, you do not blame it;

and if a man is as absolutely a result of his antecedents as a plant is, you can hardly praise him when he acts for the advantage of his neighbours, or blame him because he injures his neighbours. The naturalistic theory of life knows nothing of sin. The consciousness of sin has existed in the world because men have believed in a supernatural law having authority over them.

Christ told His Apostles that, when the Spirit should come, the surrounding world would become conscious of sin through not believing in Him. And that has been so.

Nature does not explain sin; but Christ and the Church do. Imagine yourselves to be in the first days hearing an Apostle and looking upon a society of believers. Jesus Christ is proclaimed. You are told of the Son sent by the Father to save men by bringing them to Him. You learn something about the character, the acts, the teaching, of Jesus the Son of God; you are assured that He gave Himself up to death and was raised again; you are invited to come to the Father through Him, to the loving Father through the loving Son; you are asked to join others who have been induced to attach themselves to Christ. What hinders or delays you? You are obliged to say within yourself, " This Son of God condemns me; I am such a one as to be repelled by the Father, not approved by Him; if this Gospel is true, if these Christians with their repentance and new life are in the right, I am terribly in the wrong. If I believe, I shall have to confess and ask for forgiveness, and consent and desire to be delivered from the things in me and in my habits of life which I see to be displeasing to God." I was asking you to put yourselves in the place of the world when the Spirit was first moving in the Church. But you may perceive that in our own day the same Spirit forces the same conviction of sin upon the conscience. From various causes the sense of sin is not strong or acute in these days. What is it that avails to quicken it, that has power to make sin felt as a reality, and as a painful reality? Is it not still Christ and believers in Christ? To perceive Christ as He was and is, is the gift of the Spirit; and that men should live as members of Christ is also the gift of the Spirit. And it is the vision of Jesus the Crucified, sustained by the assurrance of reality derived from the faith and lives of true Christians, that makes us feel what sin is. A notion used to prevail that conviction of sin was wrought by threats of punishment; it is indispensable, it was said, that men should be convinced of sin, and to convince them of sin you want terrible punishments to alarm them, and therefore the salvation of mankind requires that all the horrors of the future state that have ever been imagined should be kept alive. But the fear caused by dreadful threatenings, whilst it may possibly have some good effects, is not the sense of sin. That, I insist, is shame, the feeling of being in the wrong without excuse; and we recognise the truth of our Lord's statement when He says, "The Spirit"—not the tortures of the future state—"will convict the world in respect of sin, because they believe not on me." Sin is estrangement from God; Jesus Christ and Christians show us the wickedness, the needlessness, of sin; the one escape from the burden and the power of sin is in that which makes it most deeply felt, in being freely forgiven, in accepting with wondering thankfulness the reconciliation offered through the Spirit.

2. Again, "He will convict the world in respect of righteousness, because I go to the Father, and ye behold Me no more."

Righteousness or justice is, as regards most of its ordinary external features, understood with sufficient agreement in each country and generation; but as regards its essence, what it is and how it is to be explained, it is mysteriously difficult to understand. We know it best, as I think, when we take it to be the moral order of the human world, the fulfilment of those relations which the Creator is developing between Himself and men, and between human beings among themselves. Law is an interpreter of justice, though a very inadequate and imperfect one; and law says with authority, backing up its injunctions with force and penalties, "You shall render this and that to your neighbour, and your neighbour shall render this and that to you; you shall do to each other, so far as you can be compelled, what the experience of mankind has found it proper to do if harmony and progress are to be realised." Righteousness is the fulfilling of the Divine order, the carrying out in human life of the Divine will.

Now those who know this earth only, can make nothing of righteousness. They try various definitions of it, such as equality of exchange or of condition and what is good for the greater number;

but these accounts, besides failing to satisfy the idea of justice, carry no constraining authority to the individual conscience. In the New Testament age, whilst there was a strong tradition amongst the Romans in favour of orderly administration, thinking men were at a loss how to understand justice or righteousness in itself, and the general mind was not dominated by any clear conception of its nature or its authority. What was justice? What was a just man? Why was any one bound to be just?—to such questions no answer was found. Our Lord says, "The Spirit will bring the world to the knowledge of righteousness, because I go to the Father, and ye behold Me no more." Righteousness was indeed set plainly, by Christ and the Church, before the world's mind. The Son of man, the perfect man, was at the Father's right hand; no longer a good and righteous man, but *the* Man, owned as His Son by the Father. The invisible God had revealed Himself; His will for men had been seen in Jesus Christ. The inner mind of the Maker and Ruler of the world was to be known henceforth through Jesus Christ. Therefore the purpose of the Eternal was seen giving birth to and sustaining all that was good in man and for man. Towards God the right relation of every man was seen to be that of grateful and reverent dependence, of spiritual sonship. Jesus was the Just One, and He depended on the Father, and yielded Himself to the Father, without reserve. And Jesus lived and died for men, gave Himself up for men's sake; and all things were now known to be just, that were good for mankind, that tended to keep human society in peace and harmony, in health and happiness and growth. Seeing Jesus, not now with the bodily eye at their head or by their side, but with the spiritual eye at the Father's right hand, the disciples knew that there was a blessed beneficent order proceeding from the Eternal Throne, an order of which all human duties were parts and fulfilments. And as the Spirit in the Church testified to the world around concerning such a one as Jesus revealing the invisible God and ruling from the Father's right hand, the world became aware of a righteousness fulfilled in all good human relations, and commended to men's observance by the authority of the Supreme. This is the one satisfying idea of righteousness, combining the elements of immutability and progress,— man to man what God his Maker would have him be, and because his Maker wills it.

3. Once more: the Spirit was to convict the world in respect of judgment, because the prince of this world had been judged.

To judge is to distinguish, for approval and for condemnation. One who judges says, "This is right and that is wrong; this man is to be approved, that man is to be condemned." There must be something to go by in judging, and that measure or standard is justice, by which we have understood that arrangement or order of mutual acts and affections which the Eternal God designs.

The world in our Lord's day was by no means sure to judge according to the Divine standard. A spirit was in the world's air which defied God's estimate of things. Money, success, power, were held to be the substantial things, the things to be lived for, to the gaining of which truth and justice and mercy, if they stood in the way, were to be sacrificed. That was the worldly view, and it had a great deal of experience to support it. Common sense seemed to many to teach them that money, success, power, pleasure, were the primary objects of life; that truth, consideration, humility, self-restraint, were secondary. A different doctrine was taught by one Jesus of Nazareth; but what came of it? A good many of the common people were attracted to Him, and regarded Him for a time as a prophet sent from God; but what was His end? The rulers of the Jewish people were provoked by Him, and this poor Prophet, pursued by their enmity, after going though a trial which was a mockery of justice, was nailed to a cross and made a spectacle. The rulers of this world seemed triumphant; they did not know that it was the Lord of Glory whom they were crucifying. Shortly before that humiliating crucifixion Jesus said, "The hour is come that the Son of man should be glorified." And again, "Now is the judgment of this world: now shall the prince of this world be cast out." So different a thing was the Crucifixion in the eye of the invisible God and in reality from what it was in the view of the world and in appearance. When the humble followers of the Lord were moved to proclaim Him they defied the judgment of the world. The world said, "Your Master perished ignominiously on the Cross." "Yes," they replied, "that is why we worship and proclaim Him." To the Jews a crucified Messiah was a stumbling-block, to the Greeks foolishness; but to those who believed in Him Jesus the crucified was the power of God and the wisdom of God.

The Cross of Christ was the judgment, the condemnation, of the prince of this world. The world had not known how to judge rightly, had imagined that all was gold that glittered. The Eternal God, the Maker of those very things which the world prized, was the Father of the poor man who hung upon the Cross, was glorifying Him, was actually glorified in Him. In order to judge profitably, we have to take the invisible world into account.

Wherever Christ crucified has been preached and followed, there the world has been challenged to recognise the true principles of judgment. The world, it is true, is very hard to put right. It has found it possible to make Christ Himself a sort of Prince of this world. All kinds of pride and fashion have managed to make alliance with the religion of Jesus of Nazareth. A jewelled crucifix may minister to vanity as really as a jewelled sword or sceptre. But where the Son of man is glorified in the spirit, there false judgment is arraigned, the worldly spirit is condemned, and the Divine—that is the true—estimate of things is asserted and vindicated. What are the high things, the things to be honoured and chiefly cared for, in the light of the Cross? They are humility, self-suppression, fearlessness, patience, brotherly kindness, love, the things which Christianity has taught us at least to profess to honour, which we do all honour in our hearts, even if we allow them to be pushed aside by the baser things of human desire in our practical judgment and efforts.

In the profound words of which I have been endeavouring to develop the meaning, may not you, my brethren of the Christian ministry, see your functions and your hopes defined as in letters of light? You, as I have said, are organs of that Spirit of which Christ speaks. One of His great purposes in using you as His organs is to convict the world. By your witnessing to Christ, and by the stirring up of Christian life in yourselves and in others, you are to serve the convicting and convincing Spirit. There is some danger in these days lest that grand aim should be superseded in your minds by endeavours to *defend* Christianity and the Church. In speaking thus I may not be quite in agreement with some of the advisers whom you are bound to respect. But when you discover how hard a task it is to defend Christianity or the Church, and are led to doubt the wisdom of challenging opponents and critics to find out and assail whatever is most assailable and least easy to defend in the traditions and system which we have inherited, it may be a relief to you to remind yourselves that you are called not to defend but to attack. The Apostles have not taught us to regard ourselves, priests or people, as shut up in a fortress which we are to defend. Let us think of ourselves rather as organs of the inspiring Breath of Christ and of God. The title of the Apostles means that they were sent forth; they were sent forth as witnesses and heralds of Christ, the conquering King. They were emissaries of light and warmth, carrying home conviction to the consciences and taking captive the hearts of men. Christ and the Spirit were the real Powers of which the Apostles were the instruments; they *are*, my brethren, let us believe, the real Powers that will work through our poor agency. It is our commission to constrain men to know sin through the reconciliation, righteousness through the exalted Son of man, judgment through the Divine condemnation of the worldly spirit. May the conviction be first wrought in ourselves, that the Spirit may work it through us in others with the more power.

And let us all, my Christian brethren, ask for grace to submit our hearts and our lives to that triple action of the Spirit of Christ. By looking on Christ as the Spirit reveals and commends Him to us, let us be ready to learn what sin is, and righteousness, and judgment. May we grow more and more heartily ashamed of all estrangement from the gracious God, of the setting of the perverse human will against the will of the Father of Jesus Christ. Whilst we try to be just and fair in ordinary matters of human dealing let us see behind this external justice the righteousness which is the fulfilling of all divinely appointed relations, which is put on in being conformed to the image of the Son of God. And let us seek for that judgment which is a true estimate of all things, which discerns what is really dross and refuse and pays homage to that which is precious in God's sight, which declines to accept unsuccess and the world's low opinion as condemning deeds or causes, but asks what sort of sentence will be passed upon them at the judgment-seat of Christ. Let us not doubt that the promise of Christ holds good still for the humble and teachable, and that the Spirit of truth, the infallible Spirit, will in His own time guide them into all the truth.

V

THE CHRISTIAN INTERPRETATION OF THE TEN COMMANDMENTS

I

"Thou shalt love the Lord thy God with all thy heart, and with all thy soul, and with all thy mind. This is the great and first commandment."—ST. MATTHEW xxii. 37, 38.

A CONSIDERABLE part of the language which we use in our forms of worship might, with some reason, be said to be antiquated. It is not such as would issue naturally from our lips. It implies circumstances quite different from ours; it cannot be accommodated to our circumstances without undergoing a process of translation. The old Jewish writings have first to be translated from Hebrew into English, and then again the terms of the ancient Jewish life need to be —mentally at least—translated into terms of our modern Christian life. Some difficulties would be removed if this necessary process were borne in mind. We of this age find ourselves using compositions—histories, prayers, confessions, songs of praise—which embodied the faith and experience of men of other times. Now, in proportion as the feeling of those men was deep and genuine, so it was sure to express itself in allusions and imagery and modes of thought which were peculiar to their age and circumstances. It is better to keep such words, wise men have thought, in their original freshness, and not to try by alterations and omissions to bring all the language of religion into external agreement with the circumstances of each new age. But how can we make such utterances of old times true and living for ourselves? We may do so by accepting them according to the spirit, when we cannot accept them according to the letter. We are to penetrate to the spiritual substance, which was always the real life, of each ancient record, and to try to appropriate *that*. We ought to go through a double process of ascending and descending, as if we were going up a mountain from one country and going down it on the opposite side into another country. We ought to mount up with the speaker or writer from the original region of facts and circumstances in which he dwelt, till we reach what is spiritual in his thought, and then to come down to the modern region of facts and circumstances in which we ourselves dwell. This is most obviously necessary in our use of the Psalms. It is plain even to a child that much of what we say in reciting the Psalms is not literally true of ourselves. The history, the geography, the religious ceremonial, the civil customs, are those of another world. It is hoped that through recalling in our devotions the living piety of the godly men of old we may ourselves be touched and drawn into similar affections with reference to our own duties. For this purpose we take into our mouths the words, as of the Psalms so of other parts of Scripture and of later hymns and prayers, without pledging ourselves to a literal appropriation of them. We must go through, as I said, some process of translation.

To do this perfectly would require more knowledge and thought than most of us can bring to bear on our services. But we all do it imperfectly. And sometimes a little increase of knowledge through explanation and attention will enable us to do it with more consciousness and more spiritual benefit.

I propose to consider the Ten Commandments from the point of view thus indicated. We make them our own by teaching them to our children and praying every Sunday that God will incline our hearts to keep them; but in their external features, as you will see easily enough, they are Jewish, and such as could not be observed in the letter by us modern Christians.

They begin thus: " I am the Lord thy God, who brought thee out of the land of Egypt, out of the house of bondage. Thou shalt have none other gods but Me." " The Lord " here, as very commonly in the Old Testament, stands for Jehovah. " I am Jehovah thy God." This beginning of the Commandments manifestly suits the circumstances of the children of Israel, to whom the Commandments were given. They had come out of Egypt, in which country they had been serfs or bondsmen. They were now independent, about to occupy a land of their own, and to be governed by their own laws. Other nations had their respective gods, always more than one, each with his or her name. The children of Israel had their God, one only, whose name was Jehovah. He said to them, "Thou, Israel, shalt have no other gods but Me, Jehovah thy God, who have delivered thee from thy bondage in Egypt."

It was the universal practice amongst surrounding nations, at the time when the children of Israel received the Commandments, to worship their gods by means of images. These images had various forms. Sometimes they were shapeless masses, sometimes they were figures of men or women, sometimes of beasts, sometimes they combined together incongruous parts in a symbolical monster. In primitive times sculpture and painting were mainly religious; probably in Egypt and the countries with which the children of Israel were connected these arts were almost exclusively associated with the worship of the gods. This was, no doubt, the reason of the severe restriction enjoined in the Second Commandment. "Thou shalt not make to thyself any graven image, nor the likeness of anything that is in heaven above, or in the earth beneath, or in the water under the earth." The arts of sculpture and painting were thus absolutely prohibited amongst the Israelites. No likeness or representation was to be found in their tents or houses. If any images had been allowed, they would have been sure to be the objects of the perverse veneration which idolatry engendered. And Jehovah, the God of Israel, was declared to be a jealous God. He claimed the whole veneration of His people for Himself alone. They were not to know Him by any image or symbol, and He would not tolerate that the worship due to Him should be alienated to the symbols of other gods. He would punish those who defrauded Him of the honour He claimed, whilst He would reward those who loved Him. Divine punishments and rewards, the Israelites were told, would not expend their whole force on those who had personally deserved them, but would be felt to the third and the fourth generation.

The God of the Hebrews, who refused to be represented by images, had a name to be known by. To this name the Israelites were called upon to pay the homage which it was then more natural to pay to visible symbols. This name, Jehovah, is incessantly invoked and presented throughout the Law and the Prophets, as the English reader would perceive more clearly if it were not disguised in the rendering "the Lord." Pains were taken by legislators and prophets to associate historical actions and moral attributes with the name of Jehovah. This name was to be regarded with solemn reverence. The Third Commandment enjoins, " Thou shalt not take the name of Jehovah thy God in vain, for Jehovah will not hold him guiltless—Jehovah will condemn the man — who takes His name in vain."

When a name is chiefly known as a spoken name, uttered by the lips and heard by the ear, it has naturally perhaps more of a *living* character than when it is chiefly known by the eye as a written word. At first it would seem as if this Third Commandment was hardly capable of being perverted. Nothing but good could come of cherishing seriousness and reverence whenever Jehovah, the God of Israel, was

of the Ten Commandments

named by an Israelite. But it shows the ingenuity, as well as the tenacity, of superstition that in later times when the Jews were completely weaned from any craving for images to venerate, so that they might have broken without inward guilt the letter of the Second Commandment, they took to worshipping the mere letters of the name Jehovah. And they worshipped the name in a curious way—by never using it. They substituted for it some expression by which the name was understood to be indicated. They thought the safest way not to take the name of Jehovah in vain was not to take it at all. So possible was it for men to make the Commandments of God of no effect by their tradition. But when this Commandment was first given, and for ages after, the name of their God was continually on the lips of the people. One of their dangers, a snare into which the example of the idolatrous nations round about was likely to lead them, was that of treating their God too familiarly and regarding Him as a being of like passions with themselves. They were bidden, therefore, never to name Him without seriousness, so that thus the feeling of inward reverence towards Jehovah their God, their Ruler and Benefactor, the Righteous Being, might be made habitual to them.

These Commandments, then, which we accept as binding upon ourselves and pray that our hearts may be inclined to keep, appear to be strictly adapted to the Jews of a remotely distant age. We are not Jews, nor are we in the circumstances assumed in these Commandments. We have not, nor have our fathers, been bondmen in Egypt. We do not call the God whom we worship by the name of Jehovah.

We are in the habit of freely making to ourselves graven images and likenesses of all things real and imagined in heaven above, and in the earth beneath, and in the water under the earth. How can we be sincere in praying that our hearts may be inclined to keep these Commandments?

We must apply the principle which I began by laying down. We must look to the inward spirit of these laws, and translate their outward expression into the language of our own calling and condition.

The Jews were bidden to worship a Being who had called out and instructed their fathers, who had brought them by a great deliverance out of a state of slavery, a Being who was distinct from and superior to all visible things, who was the dispenser of punishments and rewards, whom every Israelite was bound to regard with unqualified reverence and love. This is the substance of the Commandments we have been considering. They turn, as you perceive, on the nature and character and claims of the God from whom they profess to come. He is the God of the seed of Abraham, who has bound that people to Himself in peculiar relations; but He is not a mere national God, the rival of other national gods. All other gods are either imaginary or feeble beside Him. He dwells in a heaven above their spheres. This God has delivered the nation whose allegiance He demands, and He bases His requirements and commandments on what He has done for them, especially on the great act of forming an independent nation out of a multitude of serfs. He is the God of freemen, and will not consent that His subjects should be slaves even though they should wish it. He trains them to the difficult and responsible duties of freedom. He frames an orderly constitution and manner of life for them. He desires to be known by them as a Protector and Lord, ruling them in righteousness and goodwill.

We Christians may place ourselves in thought before the God whom we worship, and may ask ourselves what is suggested to us by each clause of the Jewish decalogue. We remember, to begin with, that our God is the same Being as He who redeemed and governed and instructed the Jewish people. He who sent His Son into the world was always declared to be the same as He who had given promises to the Jewish fathers; the kingdom of Christ was always declared to be the fulfilment of those promises. What is the name of our God? Not, properly speaking, Jehovah. That name is not used in the New Testament. Rather it is Our Father, or the Father of our Lord Jesus Christ. How do we know Him? Upon what ground does He claim our obedience and worship? We know Him through His Son, Jesus Christ, who came that He might redeem us from slavery to sin and death, and make us into a society of free children and servants of His Father. Our God says to *us*, therefore, " I am the Father of Jesus Christ, who have redeemed you out of darkness and bondage and have brought you into the light of freedom, and have shown you the true relationship by which you are connected together as children of God and brethren: you shall have no other gods but me. I, the Father, am the only God; I bear no rivals. Worship Him only, from whom all good things come, Him who would have men be freemen and not slaves, Him who is light and in whom is no darkness at all." Should we keep the Second Commandment any better by making all images and visible representations unlawful? Surely not. To keep it thus in the letter would not in the least degree help us Christians of the present day to keep it in the spirit. We therefore break the letter of the Second Commandment without scruple. What we have to remember is that our God, the Father of our Lord Jesus Christ, is a jealous God. He is distinct from and above all visible things whatever; and any tendency to give to visible things the homage which is due to Him, any tendency to let the affections end in visible things, is as wrong as ever, and as sure to draw down punishments from heaven. Put all things most beautiful, most precious, most artistic, the works of nature or of man's device, in competition with the heavenly Father, as claiming our reverence and love: the Second Commandment bids us beware how we give away any of our filial love of the Father to the most attractive of visible things. He willingly permits, nay, He encourages and teaches us, to admire and care for all beautiful and precious things; but He would have us think of them as His gifts, and use or contemplate them with thankfulness as well as pleasure. It is a mistaken interpretation of the Second Commandment to understand it as forbidding art in churches only, and allowing it in other places. There is no such distinction in the Commandment, nor was there anything answering to it in the mind of the ancient Jew. If we are to keep the Commandment in the letter, we must have no images, no statues or paintings, in our houses or public places any more than in our churches. If we are to keep it in the spirit, we must strive that no images in churches or in houses, no visible things whatsoever, shall steal our affections from our Father in heaven; we must strive so to regard visible things of nature and art that they may help us in knowing God and being grateful to Him. The Second Commandment does not legislate specially about art in churches, but it bids us bear in mind that art everywhere ought to be subservient to our higher duties and functions.

The Third Commandment, as we have seen, taught the Jews to cultivate a habit of reverence towards the person and nature of their God. This, then, is what it equally prescribes to us. We are not in precisely the same kind of danger in which the Jews were to whom the Commandments were given. The familiarity in which the worshippers of false and local gods indulge towards those whom they believe to be divine but yet capricious or in other ways morally weak is not a snare into which we are likely to fall. But there is too much irreverence amongst Christians; too much of inward irreverence towards the Father of our spirits, which shows itself in various outward symptoms. In judging of reverence and irreverence we need discrimination. We cannot estimate them safely by conventional rules. Our blessed Lord was thought irreverent by those who prided themselves on outdoing the reverence enjoined by the Third Commandment. Whenever reverence for outward sacred things has been corrupted into superstition, then it is not irreverence, but rather a profounder reverence, that prompts a true servant of God to outrage and break through the superstition, as Hezekiah broke in pieces the brazen serpent, calling it Nehushtan. This necessity has arisen over and over again in the history of religion, so that we evidently need to distinguish between things that differ in denouncing irreverence. Let us take as our guide this Third Commandment. It demands especially reverence for the name of our God—that is, for the name of our Father in heaven, and therefore also for the name of His Son, Jesus Christ, through whom we know and come to the Father. To speak always with seriousness of our Father and of our Lord Jesus Christ is a kind of guide and key to all true reverence. In naming our Father we think of all that is highest and yet most condescending, of all that is perfect in love and providence and goodness. In naming Jesus Christ we think of Him who gave Himself up for us, of Him who was compassionate, kind, fearless, true, sinless, of Him who was the Son of man. The man who inwardly reverences the Father and Christ, knowing of them what no one who reverences them can fail to know, cannot be really irreverent. He may possibly infringe some conventional regulations of sacredness, but he will do so either from want of knowledge, or from a belief that he is usefully protesting against a superstition; he will not be reckless or scornful towards the religious feelings of others. There is nothing, perhaps, towards which the really reverent man will be more careful to be tenderly respectful than towards the higher emotions and prepossessions of the human heart, such as we instinctively call sacred. Delicacy is a form of reverence. Those who are governed by the Third Commandment will be reverent towards human beings, made in the image of God; and, in human beings, not towards rank or wealth, but towards weakness, simplicity, purity, modesty; towards childhood and old age, towards womanly refinement, towards poverty and sorrow, towards the piety of God's little ones, towards the memory of the departed. Reverence, in other words, will tend to produce habitual gentleness and consideration; to bring out into flower and sweetness what is most beautiful in a human character. And if you exercise yourselves in being respectful to what is most divine upon the earth, you will find your reverence become deeper towards the Father in heaven. His name, the name of the Maker and Giver, will be hallowed in your hearts when you daily learn and feel how much of His own nature He has inscribed upon His works.

We have often joined in the prayer that God would make us to have a perpetual fear and love of His holy name. And we have felt, I doubt not, how much need we have so to pray. What is the fear, what is the love, which we may have in our hearts towards God, compared with those profound and penetrating affections which *should* rightly respond to the grace and the holiness of God? We are wanting in the just sentiments towards God because we really know so little of Him. We need that God should reveal His own name to us in all its living power. We cannot love God, or fear Him, or combine the love and the fear into filial reverence towards Him, until we see Him to be indeed worthy of our love and our fear and our reverence. Let us bear in mind the warnings of the Commandments—not to forget the great work of redemption on which the Father's appeal to us is grounded, not to let visible things distract us from inwardly acknowledging the spiritual distinctness and superiority of God, not to allow ourselves in habits of levity. Remember that we must look up to God if we are to see Him. We must look up to Him as the high and lofty One who inhabiteth Eternity whilst He dwells also with him that is of a contrite and humble spirit. We must look up to Him from the acknowledged lowness of our own sin and unworthiness. We must confess our natural incompetence, and ask that God Himself will give us a child's heart, and eyes of enlightenment and understanding, that we may not be blind to Him who is very near to us. These great Commandments, speaking to us in the Spirit, will often convict us of our shortcomings. What can we do but ask for that gift of love which is God's most excellent gift, that in keeping His Commandments from the heart we may please Him both in will and deed? By sincerely trying to please Him, we shall learn to know Him better. We shall find Him to be in truth what Jesus Christ declared Him to be. We shall not cease to fear God, but the fear will be of the kind which blends with and does not neutralise love. Our knowledge will not be that of a proud wisdom, which flatters itself that it can fathom the mysteries of the Divine Nature, but that of a humble faith, which can trust where it does not understand. We shall be ready to say with the devout son of

Israel, " Lord, whom have I in heaven but Thee? and there is none upon earth that I desire in comparison of Thee. My flesh and my heart faileth: but God is the strength of my heart, and my portion for ever."

VI

THE CHRISTIAN INTERPRETATION OF THE TEN COMMANDMENTS

II

"Remember the Sabbath day, to keep it holy."—Exodus xx. 8.

THE Fourth Commandment has often been pronounced to be properly a Jewish ordinance. It is so. But it is not in this respect unlike the others. The Commandments bid us have no other God but Jehovah, who brought us out of the land of Egypt. They prohibit the arts of sculpture and painting. They require us to pay especial honour to the name of Jehovah. Yet neither we nor our fathers were ever bondmen in Egypt; we make images and likenesses with the utmost freedom; the name of Jehovah is not so sacred to us as that of Jesus or the heavenly Father. The preceding Commandments prepare us therefore to find the Fourth wearing at least a Jewish form. It is, in fact, just like them—a Jewish ordinance, capable of a Christian application.

The children of Israel were bidden by the Fourth

Commandment to keep a day of rest. For the word Sabbath means "rest." " Remember the Sabbath day" means "Remember the rest day." Rest on one day out of seven suggests labour on the other days. Accordingly, labour is plainly enjoined in the Commandment as well as rest. Six days thou (the people) shalt labour ; on the seventh day thou shalt rest. The rest, it is emphatically declared, shall be for servants and cattle and strangers, as well as for those who can do what they please with their time. Jehovah, the Jews are told, wrought six days in the making of the world, and rested on the seventh. Therefore the people governed by Jehovah are to have six days of labour and one day of rest.

In the version of the Commandments contained in the book of Deuteronomy the allusion to the creation of the world is omitted, and another reason for the observance of the Sabbath is put in its place. After employers have been forbidden to require work on this day from any persons whatever, "that thy man-servant and maid-servant may rest as well as thou," it is added, "and remember that thou wast a servant in the land of Egypt, and that the Lord thy God brought thee out thence through a mighty hand and by a stretched-out arm: therefore the Lord thy God commanded thee to keep the Sabbath day."

Amongst the Jews, then, no work was to be done on the seventh day. The Commandment sounds precise and emphatic, but when you consider it you will see that the word "work" might occasion much doubt and questioning. Who can say what is *work*, and what is not? Endless controversies about this might be raised amongst ourselves, and so they might, no doubt, amongst the ancient Jews. The Fourth Commandment gives no explanations of what is to be regarded as work unsuited for the Day of Rest; but such details are partly supplied in other places of the Books of the Law. We see that the Commandment was to be carried out with a good deal of strictness. Primitive legislation was apt to be absolute and peremptory. Two orders are given, one of which must have occasioned some inconvenience if it was scrupulously observed. No fire was to be kindled upon the Sabbath day. Gathering sticks was to be reckoned a thing prohibited. On the other hand, we are not told how the people were to pass their time on the Day of Rest. They could not go to church, for there were no churches to go to. They could not read good books at home, for there were no books for them to read. Apparently they were intended to pass their time in quiet social intercourse, and in such recreation as did not compel the man-servant and the maid-servant to go through hard work.

So much is what we know of the external ordinance. The best way to arrive at its spirit or principle is to ask what was its purpose. And this —its purpose—is declared with sufficient plainness in the Commandment itself, and illustrated by many references in the Prophets. The main object of the institution of the Sabbath day was that the common people might have a breathing-time from work. "That thy man-servant and thy maid-servant may rest as well as thou." Nor are the dumb cattle forgotten. The following is one of the repetitions of this Commandment in the book of Exodus. "Six days thou shalt do thy work, and on the seventh day thou shalt rest; that thine ox and thine ass may rest, and the son of thy handmaid and the stranger may be refreshed." The breaches of this Commandment which called forth rebukes from Jewish reformers consisted in carrying on work for the sake of gain. Thus we read in Nehemiah (xiii. 15), "In those days saw I in Judah some treading wine-presses on the Sabbath, and bringing in sheaves, and lading asses; as also wine, grapes, and figs, and all manner of burdens, which they brought into Jerusalem on the Sabbath day." These practices Nehemiah as a Reformer succeeded in putting down. When we bear in mind that a great part of the work in ancient times was done by slaves, who worked by compulsion and not by contract, we understand better how the Fourth Commandment was addressed with peculiar urgency to the well-to-do and employers, in the interest of those who were in danger of being oppressed. "Remember that thou wast a servant or a slave in the land of Egypt." Those who were now in the enjoyment of fields and vineyards owed their prosperity to the act of redemption by which Jehovah had rescued their fathers from bondage. They were bound, therefore, to show sympathy towards those who were still bondsmen. But it was, no doubt, believed also amongst the Jews that men needed to be protected against themselves as well as against masters. The desire of gain may tempt men to a drudgery which is a real bondage when they are free to rest if they choose. The law of the Day of Rest was therefrom a general security against the oppression of overwork, a general provision for all those benefits which come from a regular breathing-time in the midst of labour. The principle of the Fourth Commandment is, let labour and rest alternate duly in the life of man.

The succession of day and night is one great witness of the necessity of rest. "Man goeth forth to his work and to his labour until the evening." But night is the time for sleep. It cannot play the part of a Sabbath day. A day of rest is not merely for the restoration of the exhausted energies; it is a pause in the routine of common occupations; it sets the mind free as well as the body. If it were capable of being maintained that in any given condition of society the benefits aimed at by a seventh day of rest would be better secured by shorter hours of work on every day without a whole day of rest, then, I think, we should be keeping the Fourth Commandment in spirit by observing such an arrangement. I mention this not because I suppose it likely that any one would support such a theory, but in order to illustrate the reason of this Commandment. Labour and rest in turn, each aiding and balancing the other,—labour that men may earn rest, rest that men may be the better able to labour, —are declared to form part of the essential constitution or order of human life.

This principle is supported by an appeal to the Divine work in Creation. Jehovah wrought for six days and rested on the seventh. This is an attempt to express a mystery. The mystery is that in the Divine nature, as exhibited in the created universe, we see activity and repose in harmony. God works,

God rests. The Divine work and the Divine rest are not in reality separated by intervals of time. Time-language applied to God is rarely more than symbolical or illustrative. But men see a Divine energy operating, they think also they can apprehend a joy and satisfaction, a Divine repose, balancing and sustaining the energy. I do not ask you to try to understand more of this than may come home to your minds in seasons of contemplation. But believing as we do that man is made in the image of God, we shall not be unwilling to believe that everything permanent in human nature is a witness or shadow of something in the Divine nature.

The appeal in the book of Deuteronomy is a simpler one. Men are to remember with gratitude what God has done for them, so that they may be more considerate towards those who do not possess their advantages. The Commandment, speaking to thoughtful religious and well-to-do men, says, Be careful for the liberty of those who seem to be in the bonds of necessity, remembering that you have received your comparative freedom as a gift from God. If you have been placed in comfortable circumstances, take care that you are not indifferent to the comfort of the less fortunate.

You see that I have not been speaking of religious observances as appointed by the Commandment for the Sabbath day. This is because neither the Commandment nor the Old Testament so speaks of them. The Mosaic legislation about the Sabbath is perfectly plain; it has reference only to work, and the kind of work it means is chiefly that by which gain is made. Nothing is said about devoting the day to religious observances. The distinction between religious and secular, between things proper for Sundays and things proper to week-days, does not present itself anywhere in the Old Testament, and there is nothing in the Fourth Commandment that implies it.

And now, having considered what the Fourth Commandment was in the letter for those to whom it was first given, and also what the spiritual law was to which this Commandment was intended to bring the Jews into obedience, we have to ask how we Christians are to keep it with reference to our own times and circumstances.

If the Fourth Commandment had said to the Jewish people, Thou shalt give up the seventh day to religious assemblies and studies, and shalt not allow the thoughts and interests of common life to encroach upon it, we might have said, This is precisely what *we* must do, the only change being the substitution of the Resurrection Day, the first of the week, for the Jewish seventh day. But, as I have pointed out to you, that is not at all what the Fourth Commandment says, nor is it so interpreted in the Hebrew Scriptures. It enjoins an alternation of labour and rest, and prescribes that the seventh day shall be kept sacredly free from work, in the interest of the humbler classes especially, and as a boon of the God who desires that His people should be free. The obligation which the Commandment imposes upon us, therefore, must be of this purport—to see that we respect the ordinance by which God assigns to men regular periods of rest from work, and to aim at carrying out, in the best possible manner for all classes, the Divine alternation of labour and rest. This Commandment condemns idleness; it condemns also a never-intermitted round of work. Against idleness we ought to hear the warning, "Six days thou shalt labour"; against oppressive and unbroken work we ought to hear the warning, "On the Sabbath day thou shalt rest."

But, so understood, the Commandment remains somewhat vague and indefinite. We need not leave it so, for we naturally associate it with an institution which flourishes amongst ourselves, an institution which, to say the least, corresponds very closely to the Jewish Sabbath. We have our Christian Lord's Day, kept more or less strictly as a Day of Rest. What can be more obvious than to interpret the Commandment as binding us to keep this Lord's Day as it bound the Jew to keep his Sabbath?

This is a most reasonable application of the Commandment. The Sunday, we may rightly say, should be to a Christian people what the Sabbath was to the Jews. What then should it be?

It should be, as a Day of Rest, a witness in favour of those who are in danger of being oppressed by drudgery or incessant toil. The aim and purpose of our Sunday, regarded in the light of the Fourth Commandment, and kept in the spirit of that Commandment, should be the most effectual refreshment of the whole population of the land. We should say to ourselves, "God, in His providence, has given us this day in order that due rest may be secured to the toiling people. Whatever tends to secure that rest is in harmony with the Commandment; whatever tends to impair it is against the Commandment."

It belongs to practical wisdom and Christian experience to determine what usages are on the whole favourable and what are unfavourable to the desired end. The Church of Christ has from the beginning followed *one* custom. And what application of the day can be imagined more suitable to the idea of the Day of Rest than that on it Christians should meet together for common recollections and common fellowship, "to render thanks for the great benefits which we have received at God's hands, to set forth His most worthy praise, to hear His most holy word, and to ask those things which are requisite and necessary as well for the body as the soul"? So long as Christian services have anything of the elevating and restorative character which ought to belong to them, there cannot be conceivably any truer or better occupation on a Christian Sabbath than to join in those services.

At the same time, it is quite possible for religious observances and restrictions to be so multiplied and enforced, and to be so inflicted like penalties upon the human conscience, that they should become a burden and not a refreshment. As soon as they assume this character they offend against the idea of the Sabbath day and the principle of the Fourth Commandment. There is perhaps no more remarkable feature of our Lord's teaching than the steadiness with which He refused to keep the Sabbath as the Pharisees thought it pious to keep it. When the Day of Rest has become a day of religious bondage, it is not enough to protest against an excess of religious observance as being more than what God requires of us; we ought not to think that there is merely too much of a good thing; we ought to understand that God's ordinance of the Sabbath is actually thus violated, inasmuch as what He gave in order to promote man's freedom has been perverted so as to crush his freedom. The Pharisees, with all their zeal for the Sabbath, were in God's eyes the true Sabbath *breakers*. They were not keeping the commandment of God; they were making it of no effect by their tradition. And there is another remark of practical importance with regard to rules of religious observance on Sundays. Christians who feel the duty and advantage of going to church at all, are sure to think it desirable and becoming to go to church on Sundays. Religious persons will desire to keep the Day of Rest religiously. But a difficulty arises when we have to consider the case of those who do not admit the obligations of Christian fellowship, and to whom churchgoing is neither a duty nor a pleasure. We none of us at the present day would force our neighbours to go to church. But something more is necessary than this abstinence from compulsion with regard to the class of which I have just spoken. When we are laying down laws for the community, whether in placing enactments on the statute-book or in applying social pressure, we are bound by the Fourth Commandment to consider how on the whole we may best promote the refreshment of the entire population. On this point honest differences of opinion would arise. The prevailing feeling of serious persons in this country has been for centuries in favour of a very quiet as well as religious observance of the Sunday, of abstinence from ordinary pleasures as well as from painful labour. Great offence was given to this feeling by an unwise act of King James I., who, advised by a bishop, put out a proclamation signifying his pleasure that after divine service on the Lord's Day people should indulge themselves in all kinds of sports. The clergy were required to read this proclamation in the churches, and one clergyman, after doing so, remarked, " Now you have heard on the one hand the commandment of God, and on the other hand the commandment of man." But there was no such plain contradiction as he implied between the Fourth Commandment and the King's proclamation. What the Fourth Commandment forbids is work, not play. Whether play of any kind, and what kind of play, should be encouraged on the Christian Sabbath must be determined, not by the Commandment, but by the general feeling as to what is desirable. And many and various considerations will go to the making of this feeling. To wish that picture galleries and museums may be opened on Sundays is compatible with the utmost reverence for the Fourth Commandment. But we most of us feel a reasonable unwillingness to break with the strong tradition which has come down to us from our Puritan forefathers, and there is unquestionably much to be said in favour of general quiet rather than exciting pleasures on our Sabbath day.

In dealing with the question of the observance of the Sunday there is one aspect of it which I would ask you to bear continually in mind. This Commandment is a public one, intended for a community first, and for individuals as members of a community. If it is clear that some must work on the day of rest in order that the general population may rest, the interest of the community must prevail. The most conspicuous example of this law is in the case of those who serve sacred things. " The priests in the temple profane the Sabbath, and are blameless." These are our Lord's memorable words. Nothing could be more religious than the work of the priests in the temple, but it was work, and therefore it was a violation of the letter of the Commandment. The priests profaned the Sabbath, but they were blameless. Therefore we must not let our consciences be troubled by work done on Sunday, if it is work without which the general rest would be seriously impaired. The interest of the community must prevail. On the other hand, we must consider the question how we individually are to spend the Sunday, not only with reference to our own feelings, but with an eye also to the general good. A Christian should ask himself, not whether he may himself do this or that without injury to his spiritual life, but whether it would be for the general good that all should do it. He will feel it a duty to conform to what he sees to be on the whole a good public custom, whether he would think it necessary for himself as a separate individual to observe it or not.

Let me add one more remark. The Fourth Commandment gives no countenance to the theory that the serving of God belongs any more to the one day of rest than to the six days of labour. Such a notion is one of our chief dangers. All days, of labour and of rest, belong to God alike. We must not so call the Sunday God's day as to imply that the six days are ours or the world's. The rule—no public worship except on Sundays, nothing but worship or religious work on Sundays—is one which tempts us to keep secular things separate from religion. This is an unnatural and unscriptural divorce. God claims the six days as well as the seventh, our work as well as our rest. We are to serve Him in our labours, to be thankful to Him in our repose. There is no exception to this absolute law. God, our Maker, has made us for work and for rest. We can only work rightly, we can only rest rightly, by remembering that whether we work or rest we are the Lord's.

VII

THE CHRISTIAN INTERPRETATION OF THE TEN COMMANDMENTS

III

"Thou shalt love thy neighbour as thyself."—ST. MATTHEW xxiii. 39.

I HAVE made a great point, in two former sermons, of our bearing in mind that all these Ten Commandments, being originally given to the children of Israel, were adapted to their peculiar circumstances. For this reason it is necessary to ascend to the higher or spiritual significance of each Commandment, and so to ascertain what is the essence of it, and then to consider how such a spiritual or moral principle as is expressed in the Commandment would find its proper applications in our modern life. In the latter six Commandments we are not so forcibly reminded that the Law was given by Jehovah to the children of Israel. With the exception of the Fifth, they might have been given to Greeks or to Hindoos as well as to Jews. The Fifth, however, it is important to read in the light of the Jewish history. It is a Commandment, as St. Paul mentions, with a promise. "Honour thy father and thy mother, that thy days may be long in the land which Jehovah thy God giveth thee." The true meaning of this promise is not always understood. It does not engage that each individual who honours his parents shall have a long life. "Thou" in the promise stands for the nation or people. It is true that in the first clause of the Commandment, "Honour thy father and thy mother," we are obliged to think of individual sons and daughters. But this Commandment, to honour parents, was regarded as given, like the rest, to the whole people, and it is to the people as a whole that the latter clause refers. "Let parents be duly honoured amongst you, that you may have a long and prosperous existence in the land which Jehovah your God is giving to you." In other words, national permanence and prosperity are made the reward of a habit of paying honour to parents.

Having translated the Fifth Commandment into this more general form, we have all the six Commandments in language which is as intelligible in one age or country as in any other. But it is as impossible to be content with the letter, and as necessary to find out and be governed by the spirit of them, in the case of these as in that of the preceding Commandments. Take the Commandment, "Thou shalt do no murder," or, more simply, "Thou shalt not kill." It requires but little thought to perceive that all putting to death cannot be forbidden by the Commandment. Our legislators, like those of other civilised nations, have taken great pains to define what acts of killing are lawful, what are more or less excusable, and what are to be visited with the utmost condemnation of the law. But as students of the Commandments, our business is to consider what is probably the mind of God in forbidding men to kill, what is the principle which He desires to condemn, and what the disposition which He desires to encourage. In the eye of God the outward act is only significant as expressing the inner mind. Now every child can understand that killing is the act of an enemy, that it naturally represents hatred or ill-will. Therefore if the Sixth Commandment has any spiritual significance, it must forbid hatred and all kindred emotions—"envy, hatred, and malice, and all uncharitableness." But when once we have realised that ill-will is forbidden by this Commandment, how universal and far-reaching the Commandment has become. The act of killing is not regarded with the same abhorrence in all stages of civilisation. In modern times, and especially in this country, human life is guarded with such extreme caution and tenderness, that no crime seems so heinous as that worst kind of killing which the law defines as murder. In rougher times and societies, to kill another man has not been thought to imply of necessity the deepest guilt. And even amongst ourselves what the law calls murder is sometimes palliated by circumstances which tend greatly to excuse it. But the hatred which God looks at and forbids is independent of the act of killing. We are most of us in extremely little danger of committing actual murder. The vast majority of human beings go to their graves without killing a fellow-creature. But many a man now living is more guilty in the sight of God of breaking the Sixth Commandment than may a homicide of less civilised days. We are all of us guilty ; we have all broken in some degree the spirit of the Commandment ; we all have need to pray that our hearts may be inclined to keep it.

One effect of reading the Commandments in the spirit is that they thus rise above the want of completeness and of systematic arrangement which may be easily observed in them. These six Commandments do not fill the place of a modern code. When we think of the vices which afflict our own country, drunkenness is sure to occur to our thoughts as one of the most injurious and obstinate. But there is no Commandment against getting drunk, nor against other faults which some moralists would place with this in a third section, under the heading " My duty towards myself." And we may fail to discover any rule of order according to which the Commandments are arranged. But we may see that they express in a very simple and unartificial manner great principles of human conduct, which are so fundamental and reach so far to the innermost qualities of the character, that you could not in fact name any vice which would not be exterminated, or any virtue which would not be guaranteed, by a perfect spiritual observance of the Ten Commandments.

The Church Catechism, which illustrates admirably the wide practical applications which may be given to the Commandments, follows the ancient language of the Commandments themselves, and of the Old and New Testaments generally, in speaking of our fellow-man by the name of " our neighbour."

"My duty towards God, and my duty towards my neighbour." There is something simple and homely in this term, although it may not at once occur to our children or to ourselves to think of father and mother as neighbours. But we may take the word as suggesting an instructive principle of all duty. My duty is towards him who stands near to me, towards each person with whom I am brought into contact. My first duties, we may go on to say, are towards those whom God has placed nearest to me. Here is some guidance as to the duties to be preferred whenever there is a conflict of obligations. If I can only see clearly which relation is the closest, then the duties, which are the fulfilment of the relation, will take rank and place corresponding to the nearness of the relation.

Let me illustrate this from the Commandments. If we suppose young children to be learning their duty, who are the persons nearest to them? Obviously father and mother. Then it follows that the first duty of children is that towards their parents. Many reasons might be given why the honouring of parents should always hold a foremost place; but if we regard duty as the fulfilment of relations or connections which God has created, then it is evident that the persons the child finds placed nearest to him are his parents, and to be a true good child towards father and mother is his primary duty.

But if we are dealing with grown persons, the relation between parents and children may be left behind by one yet closer. Nature and the Bible both teach us that the relation of husband and wife is, according to God's ordinance, the closest possible.

Therefore the conjugal tie takes precedence of that which binds parents and children together. To fulfil worthily the conjugal relation becomes the primary duty of married persons. A man is to leave his father and mother, and cleave to his wife.

These are the two primary and fundamental relations of human life, those of parents and children, of husband and wife. The duties arising out of these are of supreme authority and can never be superseded. Persons well grounded in these are not likely to be regardless of other Divinely-ordained obligations. To be perfect in these would imply a never-ending advance in the highest moral qualities. Other relations add themselves variously to these primary ones. A child who has parents has also, very probably, brothers and sisters. These are very near to him, and his obligations or duties to them correspond to that nearness. There are the relations of the household, of business, of citizenship, of churchmanship, of the simple brotherhood of humanity. " I am a man," says a well-known line of an ancient poet; " I am a man, and nothing that is human is strange or indifferent to me." Obligations, revealed and defined for the most part by actual life and experience, rise out of all these relations, and stand to one another in the proportion in which the relations are closer or less close.

In the Commandments, though probably without any intended system or method, those nearest neighbours of whom I have spoken have the most conspicuous place. "Honour thy father and thy mother"; " Thou shalt not commit adultery." Let us notice, by way of example, how the principles which are involved in these laws are seized and traced out in our Catechism. It is possible that it may have escaped your observation how the Fifth Commandment is there interpreted. My duty is "to love, honour, and succour my father and mother; to honour and obey the King, and all that are put in authority under him; to submit myself to all my governors, teachers, spiritual pastors and masters; to order myself lowly and reverently to all my betters." All this is drawn out of the command, "Honour thy father and thy mother." And it is so most reasonably. This interpretation is justified by experience. Imagine a child well grounded in filial respect towards his parents. It will be natural for him to feel a proportionate respect towards those other persons named in the Catechism. A dutiful and respectful son will naturally go on to be an orderly and loyal citizen; he cannot be impudent, or rude, or irreverent. By the very fact of having reverence made a part of his character through the inward performance of duty to his parents, he will instinctively behave with reverence towards all who have any claim upon him, similar in kind, though less in degree, to that which his parents have had. The *teacher* is *in loco parentis*, in the place of the parent. The authorities of the land, temporal and spiritual, have their Divinely-ordained rights of government. Those who are older and wiser and better have the rights of their relative superiority. Let me give one caution here by the way. Let no one imagine that by "my betters" are meant merely those who are *richer* than I am. I am not bound to order myself lowly and reverently to all who are richer than I am. To be the richest person in the land does not of itself constitute any claim upon the reverence of others. My betters are those who are really *better* than I am—better in experience and knowledge and wisdom, better in self-restraint, better in virtue and piety. Education and manners do make a kind of superiority, though not the highest kind. But riches do not. And we need rather to be on our guard against reverencing them. Indeed, the habit of cherishing reverence towards father and mother, and towards those who are wiser and really better, and towards all in authority, whether richer or poorer, will of itself be some security against paying reverence to what is intrinsically so worthless, and so apt to injure and lower the character, as riches. There is no more gracious and beautiful quality than that of reverence towards goodness when found in a humble station and allied with poverty. That is the kind of reverence which the Fifth Commandment would teach us to cultivate.

Now let us look in the Catechism for what corresponds to the Seventh Commandment. We find the following words: "To keep my body in temperance, soberness, and chastity." These must be intended as an interpretation of that Commandment. They show us how the Commandments are naturally and reasonably brought to bear against drunkenness and other misdoings which are not directly prohibited by them. The duty of conjugal fidelity involves, amongst other qualities, a control of the desires, an habitual self-government, a subordination of the lower impulses of the nature to the rule of reason and to the higher enjoyments. Well, but any one who is trained in these is brought to a state of mind to which insobriety is repugnant and impossible. I do not deny that there are cases in which a man is temperate in some things and intemperate in others, but I say that the partial temperance which does not struggle at least, and with some success, against the partial intemperance, has not got a thorough hold of the character. Any sincere endeavour to be faithful and pure and refined will tell upon the whole character.

Thus we might say, if we pleased, that in hunting after one virtue we catch other virtues also. Certainly, to those who desire to hear and obey in the spirit, one Commandment stands in the place of several. And however few Commandments there be, when regarded spiritually, they run into and overlap each other. It is impossible to steal without coveting, not easy to steal without hurting. You can hardly lie without defrauding, without hurting. To commit adultery is to injure and to defraud. Still, there are great departments of life to which each of the Commandments most properly belongs. To refrain from ill-will, from licentiousness, from fraud, from falsehood, is to beware of the great temptations which meet a man in the common universal human life. The Tenth and last Commandment seems of a somewhat different character from the rest. It might be thought to be included sufficiently in the Seventh and the Eighth. It hinders us from thinking of the Ten Commandments as a systematic code. But it has been of great value as a distinct and separate warning against the covetousness which is so ingrained in human nature. St. Paul in one place treats this

Commandment as a kind of summing up of the law. "I had not known sin, but by the law: for I had not known lust or desire, except the law had said, Thou shalt not covet." This Commandment speaks strongly in favour of contentment and a peaceable and unselfish life. As the Catechism puts it, my duty according to the Tenth Commandment is, "not to covet nor desire other men's goods, but to learn and labour truly to get mine own living, and to do my duty in that state of life unto which it shall please God to call me." An important lesson to learn! Worthy of a special Commandment to impress it distinctly upon the conscience!

The most properly Christian view of the Commandments is that suggested by the words of our text, Thou shalt love thy neighbour as thyself. It is true that these words do not appear in the New Testament for the first time, but are quoted by our Lord from the book of Leviticus. But this principle is more distinctly brought out by our Lord and His Apostles than it had been before—that by love the whole law is fulfilled. St. Paul points out how the fact of a man's loving his neighbour would of itself prevent him from doing any of the forbidden acts by which his neighbour is wronged.

My purpose in these sermons has been to explain and illustrate the method in which we Christians may still intelligently receive the Ten Commandments and endeavour, with God's help, to keep them. It is true, as St. Paul teaches us, that Christians are no longer under law, but under grace. It ought not to be our first conception of ourselves in relation to God that we have certain injunctions to obey. We are called to a life of privilege, of freedom, of happiness. But it remains true that the Commandments set forth the principles to which the life of the redeemed of God will conform itself. They who love God and their fellow-men will keep the Commandments. And these ancient ordinances serve as sign-posts and warnings which may have their use in helping us to walk in the right path. They still threaten us beneficently when we are tempted to go astray. The two great requisites for the right use of the Ten Commandments and of all similar precepts are spiritual insight to understand their true meaning, and practical wisdom to apply that meaning to circumstances. If these are granted to us, it is impossible that the Commandments should bring us into bondage; but if we blindly read and apply them in the letter, the best commandments may lead us into confusion and moral servitude.

Let us use, then, these ancient Commandments thankfully and wisely, remembering always that a spirit of life has been offered to us which will move us to keep them in freedom and with joy. The law of the spirit of life in Christ Jesus makes us free by making obedience natural and happy to us. The image of a body, consisting of a head and members, suggests to us the ultimate principles of our Christian duty. Let each Christian regard Christ as his Head, and every man as a fellow-member, submitting himself loyally to Christ and honouring his fellow-members for Christ's sake, and he will naturally fulfil all his obligations. Love, supported by a study of the relations which God has ordained, will compass all duty. Study, then, the relations in which God has placed you, beginning with those of home life, and seek the Divine gift of love, in which alone you can fulfil those relations, and God Himself will guide you in the ways in which He would have you walk.

VIII

MORALITY PROGRESSIVE[1]

"This I pray, that your love may abound yet more and more in knowledge and all discernment."—PHILIPPIANS i. 9.

IF we have occasion to look back to what was taught in former generations concerning the principles of morality, we find that the moralists who took what was considered the higher ground affirmed strongly that morality was immutable. They had in view the opposite doctrine of those who maintained that moral laws were derived only from the experience of what had been found to be generally advantageous; and it seemed to them that if it were believed that duty was nothing more than what men in general had perceived to be for their advantage, individual men were not likely to regard it with any profound reverence. True enough, it was instructive to a man to know what had been found by the mass of his fellow-men for an indefinite number of generations advisable to do, and there was a reasonable presumption that conduct which had been ascertained to be prudent for the many would be equally

[1] Preached in Lincoln's Inn Chapel, 30th January 1898.

prudent for the one. But it was also quite possible that the interest of the one might in particular circumstances not be coincident with the interest of the many; and it was more than possible, it was probable, that under the pressure of strong temptation a man might say to himself that the knowledge of what was generally expedient should not hinder him from seizing upon an immediate pleasure. To guard against this danger, those who were concerned for the authority of moral laws denied vehemently that duty was nothing but what common experience had proved to be advantageous. They maintained that there were eternal laws of human action which men were bound to obey, and they made themselves champions of an immutable and independent morality.

But I think it must be admitted that these moralists were not felicitous in the position which they thus took up. They had great, if not insuperable, difficulty in accounting for the historical variations of morality. It was obvious that in different ages and different lands men had different notions of what it was their duty to do. If conscience was an infallible interpreter of an immutable law, how did it happen that one man's conscience could bid him act in one way, and another man's conscience could bid him act in a dissimilar and even opposite way? The advocates of immutable morality had to give such answers as they could, better or worse, to this question; but their systems seemed to their opponents, and perhaps to many who sympathised with them, to be in the air, supported by energy of assertion, rather than built upon the solid ground of fact and reason.

The mistake of these moralists, who were so right in insisting that the laws of duty must have authority over men, lay in their preliminary assumption that they had to separate morality from religion. They were in general Christians, by personal profession and belief; but they wanted to enter the field as pure moralists against rival speculators who did not share their Christianity. They persuaded themselves that it would be irregular and unscientific, and even a hindrance to the cause of morality, if they introduced the name of God, not to say that of Christ, into their ethical systems.

But a Christian cannot possibly for himself separate the acknowledgment of Christ and of God from his conceptions of duty. Duty is simply and adequately explained to him by his faith. What he is bound to do is what he believes to be the will of God; and the will of God, as he believes, has been effectively manifested in Christ. No variety of Christian creed can reject these fundamental truths. Let a Christian be what he may—Anglican, Roman Catholic, Methodist, Unitarian—there is no higher law for him than to find out and do the will of God, and he knows of no other revelation of the will of God which can transcend what has been given in Christ. And therefore a Christian moralist is engaged in a very artificial process of construction when he tries to abstract from the accepted morality certain principles of conduct or propositions of duty, and then gives to these an independent existence over men's heads, and declares them to be independent and immutable. It is a different thing to say that whatever we perceive to be right for us to feel and to do has the authority to us of the absolute and immutable God Himself.

No doubt a man may tell us that for his part he knows no God ; and if such a man so far contradicts himself as to acknowledge any binding law of duty, we may be glad to meet him on that ground of morality which we have in common with him. But duty is to us the will of God, whatever may be the philosophy of those who speak of duty without being willing to name God.

And when we believe and affirm that morality is the will of God, we are under no necessity to make right conduct immutable or independent, and to involve ourselves in the difficulties with which such language would embarrass us. On the contrary, we are led to repudiate respectfully those terms. Human morality is not independent ; it is dependent on what is made known to us of the will of God. It is not immutable, but progressive. It is one of the great tasks of Christians to set before themselves and others a dependent and progressive morality. Now more than ever we perceive the need of an authority prescribing conduct which appeals from above to the conscience. We have to stand out, not only against the utilitarian but also against the evolutionary explanation of what is right. When our minds are bent upon the process of development, we see how apparently reasonable and unavoidable it is to regard all action as the necessary result of what preceded it, and yet how destructive such a view is to a belief in right and wrong. And human life cries out for an ethical doctrine which, whilst it allows for development and progress, at the same time bears witness to a more real and substantial authority than that of abstract terms or principles.

According to our Christian faith, the God whom we know as the Father of our Lord Jesus Christ is leading His human world onwards. In accordance with this action of His, morality, by which we mean men's conceptions of what they ought to do, will advance by degrees from the less perfect to the more perfect. We frankly admit the difficulty,— the impossibility, perhaps,—of reconciling progress, improvement, change for the better, with the idea of a perfect unchangeable Creator. But in the teeth of this difficulty, or impossibility, we see that movement manifestly going on before our eyes, and we refer it with confidence to the incomprehensible Power in whose perfectness we cannot but believe. It is a practical faith, amply commended to us in the New Testament, that we are bidden to grow in knowledge and discernment by attending to the lessons which are given to us, and that as our knowledge grows our action is bound to keep pace with it. When we look at the Apostolic writings to see what they teach us about duty—say especially at those of St. Paul—we find that Christian conduct is to be such as suits and is required by the Christian calling. It is not laid down for us in precepts ; it is to be learnt freshly from the considering of what children of God in Christ ought to do in the circumstances in which they find themselves. The Christian is to study the will of his God in what we of these days call his environment. He is to look reverently at the relations in which his personal history has placed him, and then to ask, What would the heavenly Father have me do in this and this relation? By what conduct will these relations be best fulfilled according to the design of their Maker? Duties will become more clearly defined, through devout and disinterested attention and study; they will vary also, as the environment varies. When the Christian does not see his way distinctly, he is to go on in hope, trying the most likely directions, resolving always to be faithful to what he sees. "If in anything ye are otherwise minded, God will reveal even this unto you; only, whereunto we have already attained, by that same rule let us walk." Loyal obedience to what is believed to be right is the condition of further enlightenment. We are to advance in morality by feeling our way courageously. We are to prove—that is to say, to ascertain by testing and verification—what is the good and acceptable and perfect will of God. The attitude of the Christian towards duty or morality, therefore, ought never to cease to be that of an inquirer. Let us not fancy that we put a stumbling-block in our way by recognising progress in the morality of the past; let us look for similar progress in the present and in the future. And let our morality not be essentially a code of rules, but modes of action commended to us in the spirit. When any new question as to conduct arises, the inquiry of the Christian should be, What would the Father of Jesus Christ approve, for the building up of the society which is to be the body of His Son?

But as we consider this society itself, we can hardly help being discomposed by a characteristic feature of our age—I mean, the breaking down of enclosures which have separated Christians from the rest of the world. In the Apostolic age the Christians had to live as little companies of people who had come out from the world, who shrank from the religion and the morals of their neighbours, and who were in their turn an offence to those about them. Now there are no social barriers between those who profess and desire to be Christians and the rest of mankind. It is an age of the breaking down of enclosures, of the *grading* of convictions, of a desire for largeness of apprehension and comprehensiveness of union. Many good Christians view this feature of our time with dread and disapproval; to all it may reasonably be a source of some disquietude. It presents new difficulties; it brings, must we not believe? new duties. It is not wonderful that such a movement should set many upon saying, "We *must* enclose ourselves; we must have distinctions between the Church and the world; we must have distinctions of social life between believers and the unconverted; we must have distinctions of dogma between the Church and Nonconformists; we must revive discipline and tests, and show to the world what a properly fenced-off and self-respecting Church is. We who are religious must take care of our religion, and let those who are secular go their own way, in an age which seems given over to forgetfulness of the world to come." Christians may speak thus; but the great influences of the time continue to prevail, and those desired barriers are found to be hard to set up. Christians of the school of St. Paul will therefore be earnestly asking themselves what their duties are in an age of fusion, of permeation;

and will they not see, as they do so, that while trying responsibilities and perplexities are laid upon them, inspiring opportunities are likewise offered to them?

We are called upon to entertain seriously the question, what the world would be if it were subjected to Christ. This is a different inquiry from that of considering how the believers of a limited society should conduct themselves. And our first impulse may well be to refuse to entertain the question. What! the world, with its wars, with its political parties struggling for the spoils, with its competitive trade, with its absorbing pursuit of wealth, with its questionable pleasures, with its arrogant determination to impose a worldly standard upon common opinion? No wonder that it seems the easier, even the more practical, course for the religious to let the world alone and to see to their religion. But I think that the providence of God is calling Christians to the more arduous duty, and will keep them to it—the duty, I mean, of applying the Christian standard with grave insistency to all secular action. See how we are forbidden to call anything common or unclean; how the sincerest Christians cannot help taking a part in all that is going on; how they seem compelled to acquiesce in a compromise, in a second best, when this is evidently better than what went before it and they cannot secure the best; how impossible it is to keep the words right and wrong out of politics, out of international affairs, out of the competitions of trade and industry. And, as I have said, the Christian knows no right but the will of his God, no wrong but that which is contrary to His will. A Christian of our day can hardly escape from the conviction that he must be genuinely *in* the world, though he is not *of* it; he proves his loyalty to his Master by bearing witness that there is a right and a wrong in all human relations, and that the whole world must by that gradual process which everywhere characterises the Divine government, be made more and more the kingdom of our Lord and of his Christ.

It is manifest that old traditions will not be enough for guidance in new circumstances. The character of God stands firm, independent, immutable, in heaven; and the spiritual activities with which we apprehend and respond to the Eternal Nature, those which St. Paul has summed up under the names faith and hope and love, partake of the abidingness of that nature. But when things are changing and developing around us, we may have to walk in untried paths. What hopeful docility is required of us, when, for example, we realise that the ways of industry and trade must not be allowed to defy and outrage the Christian law of fellowship! Consider this one great economical change—the substitution of combinations for individual employers and individual workers. It is idle to denounce combinations as such; they cannot be said to have anything in them directly opposed to Christian morality. It follows that we have to inquire what the duties of combinations and of their members are. There is an old saying—whose I do not remember—that a company has neither a soul to be lost nor a body to be kicked; but we could not seriously hold that in becoming members of a combination we put ourselves quite outside the pale of moral Christian obligations. Yet we cannot say that the member of a company, a trust, a federation, a union, has exactly the same duties as an individual. The necessary growth of law, in having to deal with such developments as these, is a familiar fact. And law is an expression of the received morality, subject to the two well-known limitations: (1) that law deals with outward acts, and with motives only as they qualify acts; and (2) that law for the most part declines to give any commands which it cannot enforce with adequate penalties. The conventions of International Law have the strict name of law sometimes denied to them, because they have no defined penalties to threaten for the breach of them. But it may be said that these conventions are feeling after a force which might give them legal sanction, and that already they can inflict some indefinite penalties.

As belonging to that great union, our country, now our vast empire, we are confronted with problems which we may not be able to solve, but which we ought not to give up as hopeless. What are the claims which other countries have on us? Within what limits is a country justified in considering its own interests only? When is it permissible to go to war? How far are dissimulation and simulation excusable in war, how far in diplomacy? To what length should the obligations of a treaty be held binding? I do not think we can expect a conscientious Christian, or the cleverest of Christians, or a Christian saturated with Holy Scripture, to answer these questions at once and definitely for us. If what a St. Paul would say may be inferred from what St. Paul has said, his advice would be something to this effect—Go into these practical problems with the fear of God upon your consciences, but with faithful hope in your hearts, and in time God will show you what you prove yourselves to be earnestly seeking; do not shrink from any personal sacrifices which may be demanded of you, but beware of supposing that you divest yourselves of responsibility by going away and leaving things to themselves; and where you can see that you are helping on progress, that you are doing some good, though you may be apparently tolerating much evil, be encouraged by the belief that in doing the best you know and can, you will have the approval for which alone you care—that with which God rewards the good and faithful servant.

True Christians will not allow themselves to despair of guidance in any matter. They know how to breathe up to heaven the old aspiration, "O send out Thy light and Thy truth, that they may lead me!" Let us be sure that our faith can only be real for ourselves by being ambitious for the world. We cannot have a Divine Spirit which is not the one Spirit of the whole family of God; we cannot have a Saviour who does not will that all men should be saved and should come to the knowledge of the truth; we cannot have a Father in heaven who is not the God of heaven and earth, "greatly providing for" the creatures whom He has made for earth and for heaven.

IX

LAW AND REVELATION

"Ye are not under law, but under grace."—ROMANS vi. 14.

THE word Law is one which St. Paul is continually using. His ideas concerning the place and function of law enter largely into his theological teaching. When he speaks of "the law" he may be supposed to have in his mind the law of Moses, by which Jewish life was governed; but he often names law without the article, meaning law as such, law in its generic or ideal character.

In modern science the word law is of still greater importance than in Pauline theology. The laws of which science speaks are the laws of nature; but science also abstracts law from particular laws. Science magnifies law, and has its being in the discovery and ordering of laws.

It would be an error to confound the law of St. Paul's Epistles with the law of modern science; but I propose to put the one by the side of the other, and to consider what instruction we may derive from the comparison of them.

To St. Paul, law was the voice which said to

men, "Thou shalt do this, thou shalt not do that." The form which law naturally took for him and his Jewish readers was the law accepted by all Jews as having been delivered to their fathers through Moses. It was a law of commandments contained in ordinances ; moral and ritual directions were mingled in it. Some of St. Paul's language concerning the law, language apparently of repudiation and hostility, might suggest the notion that he had been converted from Judaism to Christianity, and was denouncing the faith of his fathers with the characteristic zeal of a convert. But that would be a mistake ; St. Paul never abandoned the faith of his fathers, he never repudiated the authority of the law of Moses. He might never have departed from the traditional language of respectful submission to that law but for a movement which opened his eyes and led him to a new and firm apprehension of the nature and function of law. This movement was the attempt to Judaise the Gentile believers in Christ. The Judaisers held that the Gentiles in coming to Christ were accepting the Jewish law, St. Paul held that they were accepting the grace and redemption given in Christ. The question came to be, which of the two was supreme and to be made most of—the law which commanded men, or the Divine grace which invited and claimed them. When this question was put to him and to the Church, St. Paul was moved to answer with ever-increasing energy that he was on the side of grace against law ; that whatever law might have to say for itself, it must be thrust aside, rather than that it should be allowed to usurp dominion over grace.

We may sum up under two heads the weaknesses of law as they presented themselves to the mind of St. Paul. (1) Law could not give life. He appealed to facts; he made himself the mouthpiece of the universal human experience. But he was speaking especially to fellow-believers, who had received the Gospel with joy; and he knew that their inward history must have in some degree corresponded to his own. They had known what it was to disobey the law, though they recognised it as Divine; not only had they been weak for obedience and righteousness, they had found in themselves a rebellious nature which was even irritated by commands into resistance. Their outward conformity, whatever it might have been, had not necessarily implied inward happy service. The Gospel, or God declaring His love towards men and inviting them to peace and sonship, had done what the law was powerless to do. Hope had been kindled in the breasts of those who believed, and hope had exerted in them its magic influence. " By hope," St. Paul says, "we were saved." The law was from God; it was holy and just and good; but it could not give life; the Gospel had proved that it could give life; and life was what men wanted. What a folly it was, what treason against the highest interests of men, to exalt a law which killed over the Gospel which gave life, and so practically to make void the Gospel, and to destroy its power! (2) A kindred weakness of law was that it did not represent the best relations between God and man. St. Paul was ready to admit that the law was a voice of God; but it was the voice of God as a Ruler. "Well," a legalist might say, "and in what other character can man know his God? Is not the true God the Ruler both of the armies of heaven and of men upon this earth which He has made? It is through the law, the voice of God the Ruler, that our God has manifested Himself to us. Our place and duty are to know ourselves as His subjects, and to render obedience to His commands." "Say not this," St. Paul would have replied, "to men who have heard of Jesus Christ. The envoys of Christ are sent into the world to report to men the voice of a Father in heaven. The characteristic utterances of the Lord Jesus were such as these— 'Thy sins are forgiven thee!' 'Come unto Me, all ye that labour and are heavy laden, and I will give you rest.' 'Be not anxious, saying, What shall we eat? or, What shall we drink? or, Wherewithal shall we be clothed? For your heavenly Father knoweth that ye have need of all these things. But seek ye first His kingdom, and His righteousness; and all these things shall be added unto you.' In preaching Jesus Christ, the Son of God, we are declaring the Father, and inviting men into the confidence and rest and hope of sonship. And we bear witness that a Spirit has been given, which moves mysteriously in the heart of each believer, and sighs out yearning appeals to God as to a Father." To St. Paul the relation of men to God as of subjects to a ruler was a secondary and subordinate relation, and to choose this as superior to the relation of spiritual children in Christ to a heavenly Father was to do dishonour to God and injury to men. Law was the note of the inferior relation, Promise of the superior.

That laws and commandments, when they are

kept subordinate to the dispensation of grace and promise and sonship, have even under this dispensation their appointed use and value, St. Paul would not have us doubt. In religion as well as in morals he himself set an example of law-abiding habits. He must have held that, even for a righteous man, the observance of regulations was helpful. Imperative rules of conduct may serve as witnesses and warnings, and to some extent as guides, for weak mortals, even when they are striving to surrender themselves to the motions of the Spirit of the Father and the Son. But the chief function of law and the penalties associated with law is, according to St. Paul, to restrain transgressions. We may wisely make much of law; we are bound to honour and enforce it, provided always that we do not exalt it above grace.

There is a tendency, however, in human nature, which St. Paul was led to combat for the benefit of all generations of Christians, to choose the lower relation of man to God, and to regard God by preference as a Ruler who imposes ordinances upon men, and demands from men the observance of them. That was the habit of mind of the Pharisees, and we see what aversion and anger it excited in the Lord Jesus. It is associated with ceremonialism in religion, with outwardness in morality, with dependence on legal machinery and penalties for the raising and purifying of national life. Against this tendency it is necessary for those who would take high views of human well-being to be continually on their guard. The Gospel, which we as Christians have received, seeks to bring men into close spiritual relations with God. In it God reveals Himself; and man's part is to respond to the revelation. The revelation is given to us in Christ living, teaching, dying, rising again, sending His Spirit. Through Him, received and believed in as the Son of God, we see and know the Eternal Father claiming men as His children. To be at peace with the Father is our happiness; to know more and more of our God is our progress; to be conformed to the Divine will is our duty and our safety. Yes, and to reject the Fatherly grace of God is our danger. We cannot with impunity follow the devices and desires of our own hearts and set God's will at naught. If we think we can put God off with certain outward conformities and observances and keep our hearts to ourselves, we shall find that we are the victims of a ruinous deception. Not in any attempt to obey regulations, however good and Divine, but in responding with heart and mind and will to what can be seen of God, will man find his highest life.

Thus far we have been considering law in the Pauline sense—as the voice of the heavenly Ruler giving commands supported by threats, a voice exemplified to the Jews in the ordinances which they traced up to their law-giver Moses. We Christians, if we receive St. Paul's teaching, are to reckon ourselves not under law, in this sense, but under grace. Let us now bring before our minds the law of which modern science is the exponent and advocate.

It has been doubted whether the word "law" is a happily chosen term for the relations or connections which science seeks after and verifies. There is nothing imperative in the laws of nature. I am not sure whether there is any definition of a law of nature accepted by men of science as entirely free from objection; but it is not necessary for our purpose to seek anything more accurate than the ordinary impression conveyed by the term. We mean by a law of nature an observed succession of phenomena, some relation of antecedents and consequents which may be relied upon as sure to recur. The unscientific man, looking around him, sees phenomena and occurrences as a mere aggregate; the scientific man sees them connected together in various relations, and what he contemplates is not an aggregate but an order. It has not, indeed, been reserved for modern science to behold order in the world of nature; even upon the primitive mind the world made some irresistible impression as an orderly structure, and it was the order in it that touched men in the earliest ages, and drew forth their admiration and delight. The Old Testament begins by presenting the creation as the product of an arranging purpose, and its poets and prophets are moved to rapture by the mutual interdependence and regular successions of natural phenomena, such as awaken in us the idea of order. But a man may be said to be scientific, just in so far as he can penetrate more deeply than others into the secret relations which bind the parts and processes of nature together into orderly coherence and unity.

To the primitive mind the order of nature seemed to imply design and a Maker. And from the most advanced mind it is surely difficult to eradicate the instinct which traces arrangement to an Arranger, structure to a Builder, functions to a Purpose, a vast work to a Creative Mind. But it is pointed out that, if we are inferring from nature only, we have no right to infer—if so much—anything more than a Power capable of giving existence to what we behold. The ordinary action of the human mind contemplating nature has gone beyond this. Men have imagined a Maker like themselves. They themselves design and shape, and, regarding the world as a product, they have jumped to a belief in One who designs and shapes as they do, and they have represented to themselves a magnified Man as the Creator of the universe. The tendency to place a magnified Man in the invisible heaven has received the technical name of anthropomorphism, and has been used to explain away all religious belief. We might put the case rather differently. We may say that the God who has spoken to men by divers portions and in divers manners, and has constrained them to believe in Him, has been naturally assumed to be the Creator of the world, and that all the beauty and order of nature and all the adjustments of things to uses and ends bear witness of the Being thus revealed. But we must accept the caution, and take care not to affirm that nature by itself can make known to us the God whom we worship. We must not wonder that science, investigating nature, should report that it finds no just and merciful God, but only a suggestion of some originating Power or Cause, such as the unity of the world seems to demand.

That is enough, let Christians say confidently, to

prove to us that the knowledge of natural things and processes is not intended to suffice for us or to dominate our minds and lives. For us, as creatures with spiritual affections and members of society, this kind of knowledge—whatever its present prestige—has defects which sentence it to take a lower place. The same terms in which the defects of imperative law were declared by St. Paul will serve to express the defects of natural law.

In the first place, law does not give life. Some of the most famous exponents of science have found pleasure in dwelling upon the inexorableness of natural law. They tell us that we are placed in the midst of a world which moves on by absolutely regular and unvaried processes, and that—do what we will, or pray as urgently as we may—nothing will persuade a law of nature not to execute itself. A hand put in the fire is sure to be burnt; a cottage standing in the path of a devastating torrent is sure to be swept away. We are entitled to point out that in the midst of these encompassing invariable laws there is a mystery of human will which seems to have power to vary the course of nature, a power which every scientific man is irresistibly compelled to assume to be real, though no man, scientific or other, can explain it or show at what points or in what manner it touches the natural order. But, putting this mystery aside, let us suppose that we know nothing of any Power with which we have to do except that it manifests itself in laws of nature, and that in the presence of these we are powerless; could there be any condition less likely to give us life? Natural law, dominant over us, may fill us with wonder; it may greatly interest our intellectual faculties; it may put us on our guard, so that we may avoid, till our time comes, being crushed by it. But what is there in it to encourage us, to put hope into us, to stir us into effort? Its moral influence can scarcely be other than to daunt and depress us, or to chill us into an attitude of apprehensive caution. But if the acknowledgment of law, necessary and unvarying, were to advance upon us and embrace ourselves,—and it is difficult to see how, in a world known only as one of natural law, man is to be made an exception to its universal range,—there is worse than depression from without, death strikes us at the heart of our moral being. To be convinced that we are automata, mere machines, going, in all our thought and will and action, just as we have been made to go, is surely to give ourselves up, and to consent to drift as lifeless creatures upon the stream of time. If St. Paul could say "the letter kills," we are still more clearly warranted in saying nature kills—nature, that is, recognised as exclusively supreme over us.

May we not go on to say that our relation to the natural order is a manifestly inferior one for a creature organised as man is, and living as man has lived? When we can believe that God has revealed and is revealing Himself to us as the Father of our spirits, our spiritual faculties and affections leap up to the recognition of Him. All that we think of, and cannot help thinking of, as noblest in man, all that is associated with the best progress of our race, is justified and explained. Conscience becomes the spiritual ear, by which we listen to the voice of our

Maker and Spiritual Father saying to us, "This is the way, walk ye in it." Duty becomes the claim of this heavenly authority over us, a claim which speaks for itself and needs no external argument or enforcement to one who in any way acknowledges that authority. Those beautiful and gracious emotions, reverence and gratitude, the entire absence of which makes a man repellent to his fellows, have their inspiring object and receive their daily nourishment. Humane behaviour is a self-commending obligation to those who know themselves and their fellow-men to constitute a spiritual family of God. The sense of sin—that is, of being blameworthy—is accounted for, as nothing but the consciousness of having a Father whom we may love and obey or offend by alienation and rebellion is able to account for it. And hope, the bright nurse of patience, the stimulant of endeavour, the worker of salvation, which makes all present difficulties and troubles inconsiderable, which brings sunlight from heaven into human life, offers itself as the natural heritage of those who can say, "If God be for us, who is against us? He that spared not His own Son, but delivered Him up for us all, how shall He not also with Him freely give us all things?" When such things as these, my Christian brethren, are in question, it is not wonderful if we have hardly patience to consider whether it would be wise and rational to throw them all away as empty idols, that we may know ourselves according to the latest lights to be nothing but involuntary instruments of nature.

Our faith is, that God makes some revelation of Himself in nature, and puts us in a certain relation to Himself through our being parts of "that stupendous whole," but that He gives the higher revelations in history, in moral discipline, in inspiration, in Christ. Through these we apprehend the righteousness and the love of God, the attributes by which He is our Father. These ought we to care for; but we may add—and not to leave the other uncared for. Just like St. Paul with the law, the Christian of to-day, fighting for what he knows to be most precious to man, may be led in appearance or in temporary expression to depreciate the natural order, and that knowledge of it which is the special pride of our age. But our docile reverence is due to all that men find out in the visible creation, and especially to the order and unity which bear witness so powerfully of God, and make deliberate choice and forethought possible to us; and Christians should be amongst the readiest to pay grateful honour to all who help to make the world better known.

Believing that we are under a Divine education, and that God plants us, His spiritual children, for instruction and discipline in this world of nature, our relation to the natural laws and processes to which we are subject must be a matter of abiding interest to us. And it forms a problem of curious and baffling difficulty. The study of nature invites and occupies and rewards our intelligence. We see plainly enough that, by a part at least of our constitution, we ourselves belong to the nature which we study. Students of nature are drawn, let it be admitted, towards the acknowledgment of nature as supreme.

> Earth fills her lap with pleasures of her own;
> Yearnings she hath in her own natural kind,
> And, even with something of a mother's mind,
>   And no unworthy aim,
>   The homely nurse doth all she can
> To make her foster-child, her inmate man,
>   Forget the glories he hath known,
> And that imperial palace whence he came.

But this forgetfulness our heavenly Father will not suffer; and he breathes into us higher beliefs with which the supremacy of nature is incompatible, and gives a summary rebuff to our understandings. We are made to feel that our observing and deducing intelligence is a key which fits some locks exactly, but that there are other locks opening other doors to us which it does not fit. We are bidden to believe that this universe, which seems to go on with a regularity impressed upon it from the beginning, is, by some method which evades our understanding, plastic in the hands of the Providence which watches over the most insignificant of God's creatures. And the final lesson seems to be that we are to hold down our self-confident understandings and to make them know their own place; that our reasonings and our expositions, whilst they should be as good as we can make them, are, after all, those of children, compared with what they may hope to be in some future stage; and that the supreme calling of man is to know his Father in heaven, to worship Love and Righteousness as dominant over Law, imperative or natural, and to go out with the dutiful response of his whole being towards every revelation which it pleases the Father to give us of Himself. And let us not doubt that, as he who casts away his life for Christ's sake will find the life which he has seemed to lose, and as love is the fulfilment of the commandments which it overrides, so the pious devotion to the Father which puts nature in the lower place will involve in the long-run the most appreciative admiration and the richest knowledge of nature and its laws.

X

BROAD CHURCH TEACHING[1]

THE influence of Broad Church teaching during the Victorian era is to be chiefly traced in the modification of general religious belief which has been effected within that period. Let those whose age enables them to look back for a good many years recall what was commonly believed around them in their early days. They will remember that the Bible was then regarded as the one foundation of the faith—that is to say, it was held that everything in the Bible was true, and that Christians were to believe as their necessary creed all that was stated in the Bible. Concerning the future state, the commonly received tradition was that all human beings after death went into one of two conditions: either into endless unchangeable happiness and goodness, or into endless unchangeable misery and wickedness. It was a widespread belief, held with most decision by those who had received the Evangelical doctrines, that those who were to escape the future misery must undergo a change in this life,

[1] Read at the Church Congress at Nottingham, September 1897.

a change which separated the converted by a deep chasm from the unconverted, so that the one serious division of mankind was into the two classes of the converted and the unconverted. The chief characteristic of the converted was that they had accepted the Atonement, or believed that Jesus Christ had died for them; in other words, that Jesus Christ had borne upon the Cross the punishment due to their sins, and had thus made it possible for God to forgive them. These doctrines may still be held and professed with their old vigour by some English Christians, perhaps by some clergymen of the Church of England; but I think it will be admitted that throughout English Christendom in general, they are either openly repudiated, or tacitly ignored, or avowed with bated breath. The late Mr. Spurgeon used to denounce the "down grade" which had proved tempting to many Baptists: if those doctrines are to be figured as the high level, the majority of English Christians must be conscious of having moved down to varying distances from them.

And when those doctrines—concerning the Bible, the future state, the separation of the converted from the rest of the world, the Atonement—began to need defence, it was Broad Church teaching that was denounced by their defenders as doing the mischief. It would be easy to illustrate this statement from the controversial literature, and especially the religious newspapers, of fifty years ago, but I do not think it will be called in question. My older hearers will remember the anger and alarm excited by the volume of *Essays and Reviews*, which was regarded as especially assailing the infallible truth of the Bible;

and it is matter of history that Maurice, who took the lead in rejecting the prevalent doctrines of the future state and the Atonement, was dismissed from a Professor's chair at King's College for heterodoxy on the former of these subjects. And the authors of *Essays and Reviews*, with Dean Stanley, who might have been expected to be one of them, and Maurice, though he protested against being identified with the Broad Church party, have been universally looked upon as the prominent Broad Churchmen of the earlier years of the Queen.

There is a word which has often been applied as an epithet of reproach to the Broad or Latitudinarian or Liberal school in the Church—the word *negative*. To a considerable extent the arguments which have been brought against the doctrines which I have specified may be rightly so described. The greatest name of the Broad Church party, considered as a critical and dissolving agency, is that of one whose work and influence have lately been brought before the public by his biography, Professor Jowett. Many years ago I happened to meet my friend Mr. Huxley when he had just returned from paying a visit to the Master of Balliol at Oxford. He was much interested by Jowett, and, like many other persons, could not make out distinctly what his beliefs were; and he wound up his talk about him by exclaiming, "I call him a disintegrator!" Huxley, I need not say, thought that there was nothing more desirable than that the traditions of the time should be disintegrated; and I do not suppose that Jowett would have felt hurt by the description. But to Maurice the title could not have been given without extreme injustice, and he himself would have been painfully wounded by it. Maurice's true influence has been that of a most positive and constructive theologian. Not only, however, does the word Broad apply well enough to his views, but he undoubtedly was often by the side of the advocates of liberalism and working with them. For erroneous beliefs may be dissolved in two ways : either by being simply shown to be untenable, or by the announcement and recognition of the true views on the same matters. Maurice hardly cared to expose any error except by showing the truth which turned it into falsehood. He had the consciousness of being a witness in many things to the real nature and action of the living God ; and it is through this testimony of his that he has exerted a precious reforming influence upon the thought and life of the time. With Maurice as a positive teacher may be associated the two chief poets of the Victorian age. For there is a great deal of theology in both Tennyson and Browning, and what there is would be described as Broad Church, of the Maurician type ; and if we could weigh and measure influences, we should perhaps find that their poems, with the subtle and penetrative power of poetry, have done as much as any other writings to give to the general Christian belief its existing character and tone.

The volume of essays entitled *Lux Mundi* represents the views of a school which is well known to be carrying with it in a forward movement a large proportion of the younger clergy. The writers, under their able and courageous leader, Canon Gore, regard themselves as adjusting the High Church theology of Dr. Pusey and his generation to the new knowledge of our day ; and their innovations caused great distress not only to the stalwart veteran, Archdeacon Denison, but to a student of modern thought like Canon Liddon. There is no mention of Maurice's name from the beginning to the end of the volume, but a reader who is familiar with Maurice's writings will trace what will seem to him the lead of Maurice in every one of the essays. Whatever in *Lux Mundi* has been welcomed as advocating a wise and necessary modification of traditional doctrines is included in more positive and profound statements of Maurice. It is not to be supposed that so-called Maurician views all originated with Maurice ; he himself freely confessed his obligations to Coleridge, and also to the remarkable Scottish lay theologian, Thomas Erskine of Linlathen ; but he thought and saw for himself, if any thinker or seer ever did ; and his doctrines have a large comprehensiveness, due to their unity and depth, which keeps them still in the forefront of the whole theological advance of our time.

Maurice came, it has been said, like John the Baptist, to bear witness of the Light. His mind was set on the gracious will of the perfect God, as revealed in Jesus Christ ; and he brought all doctrines to the test of that living Will. If he could not accept the tradition that the mass of men were consigned to hopeless rebellion after death, or assent to the theory that the justice of God was satisfied by the infliction of the pains due to the guilty upon His innocent Son, it was because he held that the grace and righteousness of God absolutely and necessarily repudiated and condemned such doctrines. If he declined to build a system of Christian *credenda* out of the sentences of the Bible, it was because such treatment of the letter of the sacred records was essentially unspiritual. It was his belief in God as the Father of Jesus Christ that obliged him to regard all men as God's children, and that led him to look confidently for signs of Divine revelation and of human feeling after God in all the religions of the world. And believing as he did in the Father of all men, and in the Spirit of the Father and the Son as working in all human life, he could not regard any of the institutes of human society as outside the Divine kingdom. Human duty meant to Maurice surrender to the good Will of God ; the principle of sacrifice was at the root of right human action, and the particulars of ethics were to be found by a teachable consideration of what God's will might be at each time and for each society and person. It was obvious to him that Christ claimed industry and trade, politics and recreation and art, no less than religion, for things of His kingdom ; that the mind and the body belonged as well as the soul to the dominion of Christ and the sphere of the Spirit's operation ; that the progress of true civilisation was part of the growth of the Body of Christ.

To the religious world Maurice was the theologian who, refusing to be bound by traditions, bore too audacious a witness to the righteousness and love of God ; but his countrymen in general, so far as he was known to them, knew him chiefly through his Christian Socialism. The movement thus named was with him a natural inference from his belief in Christ and in the kingdom of heaven. That any province of human life should be placed by Christians outside the domain of the law of Christ, and that men should have mutual dealings as employers and workers, buyers and sellers, makers and spenders of money, on principles with which Christ was not to interfere, was in his eyes an intolerable denial of Christ. Human society he held to be a Divine creation; and it belonged to his theology or his faith to make a distinction, of which some of those who worked with him were a little impatient as a mystical or fanciful one—to insist, I mean, that men were not to construct an improved society according to their imaginations of what was best, but should rather assume that the society into which they were born would be right if only the members of it would live and act according to the real and ascertainable designs of its Maker. The bold assertion of self-interest as the one or supreme principle of industry and trade roused Maurice into his most vehement protests. Instead of teaching that society *ought not to be* built up on self-interest, he declared that it *was not*. In his Christian Socialism he was not merely preferring one economical method to another, he was a witness for Christ and His social constructions against a power of this world which set Christ at defiance; he was maintaining the absolute supremacy over human life of the laws of the Body of Christ.

Those who were Maurice's disciples in Christian Socialism were as a rule his disciples in other religious beliefs also; and what we are now calling Broad Church views owed much to the zealous propaganda of the men who fifty years ago stood by

Maurice's side—Kingsley, Hughes, Ludlow, Hort, and their comrades. It is difficult now to think of these men as having been regarded with suspicion and disapproval by most of the religious persons of their day, and of young people being warned against reading anything that they wrote. But so it was; and their leader and they had the inspiring consciousness that they were a minority fighting for what they believed to be the Gospel of the kingdom against the Pharisees and the Sadducees of the age. In these latter days of the Victorian era we may enlarge Sir William Harcourt's famous *dictum* and say for the religious world, "We are all Christian Socialists now!" For we are all confessing that the well-being of the weakest classes should be the special care of a community which calls itself Christian, and that all economic relations should be strictly subjected to fairness and the common interest. In advocating on high grounds and promoting to the utmost of their power the extension of educational advantages and of the privileges and duties of citizenship to the working classes and to women, Maurice and his followers were in the front of a double movement which has become eminently characteristic of our epoch.

The subject with regard to which the high spiritual teaching of Maurice has made least way is the nature of the Body of Christ or the Church. I feel sure, indeed, that the divines of the *Lux Mundi* school, to whom I refer as marking the general theological progress of the time, would shrink from using such language as that of a couplet in *Hymns Ancient and Modern*, "And still the holy Church is here,

Although her Lord is gone" (Hymn 352). The conception of the Church as consisting of a certain number of organised persons to whom a Divine authority of direction has been delegated in the absence of Christ, and who have had a certain store of spiritual force put in their sole charge, is one which has found a natural expression in the constitution of the Church of Rome, with its supreme Vicar of Christ; but when Anglicans try to hold it they are confronted with overwhelming difficulties. This view is the Pauline idea of the Church carnalised. Let me not be supposed to speak of belief in a living and present and active Christ, giving direction and communicating life, as an easy faith to hold; God knows how difficult it is. But that was St. Paul's faith; and it delivers the Christian who can hold it from the confusion in which those are involved who think themselves bound to recognise some corporation set up on earth with exclusive authority to act for Christ. If it is a carnal Church of so many mortal men that is to be reverenced as holy and catholic, the spotless bride of Christ, where is this separate organism to be found? But the body of a living and present Christ has a perfection which depends on *Him*, an ideal spiritual perfection which is independent of the miserable shortcomings of the persons and communities holding on to Christ and drawing life from Him. We can speak freely of the Church as holy and catholic if we mean a holiness and catholicity subsisting in Christ, if we are thinking of the Divine pattern made in heaven for the societies of earth, the ideal which they should assume to be their true nature, and up to which they ought to be always striving. As in each Christian there is the true Son of God, defined and claimed in His baptism, of whom it has been said by St. John that He cannot sin because He is begotten of God,—so there is in the actual Church the true body of Christ, the holy Catholic Church, seeking continually to realise itself in all the unsatisfactory communions which confess Christ as Lord.

The chief work which remains to be done by that high Broad Church teaching which bears witness to the living God and the living Christ is to help the present generation of English Churchmen to attain more thoroughly to this Apostolic view of the Church.

XI

THE HIGHER LIFE: HOW IS IT TO BE SUSTAINED?[1]

IN a recent article[2] on "Science and the Bishops," Professor Huxley writes thus: "That this Christianity is doomed to fall is, to my mind, beyond a doubt." The Christianity of which he predicts the fall is defined to be "that varying compound of some of the best and some of the worst elements of Paganism and Judaism, moulded in practice by the innate character of certain people of the Western World, which since the second century has assumed to itself the title of orthodox Christianity." "The fall," he says, "will be neither sudden nor speedy"; because enlightenment has always been slow in dispersing darkness. But this Christianity, he holds, will disappear just as rapidly as men in general come to the knowledge of the truth. Now that definition might suggest the inquiry, What is Professor Huxley's view about the Christianity of the first century? How is that to be distinguished from the singular

[1] From the *Fortnightly Review* for January 1888.
[2] *Nineteenth Century*, November 1887.

compound which dates from the second century? Can "orthodox Christianity" fall without involving in its fate the Christianity of the Apostles? To such an inquiry Professor Huxley himself gives a partial answer. He affirms that a faith which is in any way bound up with "the miraculous" will be rejected by all enlightened persons, not because a "miracle" is *a priori* impossible, but because no miracle is supported by evidence which can satisfy those who understand the nature of proof.

Professor Huxley shows his characteristic lucidity, both of thought and statement, in what he is accustomed to lay down concerning miracles and the laws of nature. He points out that a law of nature, which is a generalisation from our experience of the past, whilst it has no authority to pronounce any alleged fact whatsoever to be impossible, makes anything reported as a violation of it extremely improbable; that we reasonably require the stronger evidence of that which is the more improbable; and that writings of unknown date, by unknown authors, do not supply the kind of evidence which scientific training allows men to regard as incontrovertible. He says, with M. Renan, not that miracles could not occur, but that as a matter of history they have not occurred. I believe that it will be entirely to the advantage of Christianity that we should cease to build our religion upon "the miraculous." We are all familiar with the logical argument :—our Lord and His Apostles wrought miracles; miracles could only be wrought by supernatural power; it is at our peril if we refuse to accept the statements of those who had supernatural power at their back. Such an argument obviously challenges the keenest criticism of the evidence in favour of the alleged miracles; the kind of criticism with which we sift reports of modern miracles, if indeed we think it worth while to criticise them at all. It suggests to us to refuse belief to the Christian creed until we are satisfied that the evidence for the miracles is such as could prove the most improbable things to the most scientifically sceptical mind. If it is said that we are warranted by the goodness of the Gospel in being content with inferior evidence of the miracles, we are so far abandoning the argument from the miraculous. But in adopting this argument at all, we are departing from our Lord's method and incurring His reproach; and, as a natural consequence, we are so far spoiling our Christianity. It was His custom to make light of wonders, that is, of miracles; to assume that they might be shown by false prophets, to repel with aversion the support which His hearers were ready to give Him on the ground of wonders; to grieve with indignant disappointment over the demand for wonders. When He said, "Except ye see signs and wonders, ye will not believe!" was He praising the disposition which He notes? Is it not certain that He was deploring it? If critics will not allow us to take for granted that these words from the "Fourth Gospel" were spoken by Jesus, we can show that they express what is indicated by sayings and actions recorded in the Synoptic Gospels; and we must observe that it is very remarkable if this was the view of our Lord's mind which commended itself to Professor Huxley's second century. When it is urged that in those ages the demand for miracles was universal, and had the natural effect of calling forth the supply, we answer that the repudiation in the New Testament of the method of believing because of miracles is by so much the more striking.

Is it open to the bishops, then, to shake hands with Professor Huxley on the terms which he seems to have some hope that they will accept—that they will give up miracles, and he will "estimate as highly as they do the purely spiritual elements of the Christian faith"? That question raises another, How are we to conceive of these purely spiritual elements of the Christian faith? Recognising as I do to the full "the supreme importance of the purely spiritual in our faith," on which the Bishop of Manchester has insisted, and the admission of which Professor Huxley so courteously welcomes, I think it may be especially advantageous at the present moment to consider what this phrase means and involves. In the competition between the various creeds which are soliciting general acceptance and endeavouring to commend themselves to open minds, we can desire no better test to be applied to them than this, What support does each provide for the spiritual interests of mankind? If the question which I have put at the head of this article, "The Higher Life: how is it to be sustained?" be regarded as a kind of challenge addressed to these creeds, I believe that the most legitimate and the most effective defence of Christianity, and that which will best bring out its proper character and authority, will consist in answering the challenge.

The "purely spiritual elements of the Christian

faith" might include both the truest Christian dispositions and the spiritual objects of Christian belief. What are the dispositions which make up or minister to the higher life of mankind? We say that they are such as these—reverence, trust, self-condemnation, self-mastery, courage, self-devotion, regard for fellow-men, indignation against wrong, peace, joy, patience, hope, love. I do not give these as an exhaustive catalogue, but as indicating the qualities which men agree to admire as the noblest and deepest of which their nature is capable. I assume that, if any of these are to wither, the life of our race will be by so much the poorer; and it seems to me reasonable to contend that whatever beliefs these demand for their sustenance have an extremely powerful force in their favour.

It is Professor Huxley's point to lay stress upon the need and the nature of proof. Scientific men are trained to look for evidence and to demand it and to be governed by it. He holds that there is demonstrative evidence in support of the principle of evolution as explaining nature and man. He looks back, and sees everything growing out of its antecedents. When he can see antecedents no longer behind the molecules of the cosmic nebula, what he has to say is simply that he does not see them; he affirms nothing and accepts no affirmation about what is beyond his intellectual vision. He recognises the method of evolution in man as well as in the inferior animals and in the inanimate world; in the mind and thoughts of man as well as in his body. He admits the mysteriousness of human nature, and, as he cannot trace thought and matter to their junction, he professes himself an agnostic with reference to the questions which divide the spiritualist and the materialist. But he finds evolution to be as much the law of the mental world as of the physical. "The fundamental proposition of evolution is, that the whole world, living and not living, is the result of the mutual interaction, according to definite laws, of the forces possessed by the molecules of which the primitive nebulosity of the universe was composed." Mr. Huxley regards the antecedent causes, within the world of our knowledge, as adequately explaining effects within the same world; everything, to him, is what it is on account of the things that went before it, and it could not be otherwise than as it is. He finds no reason for excepting men's states of consciousness from this general order; what any one feels at any moment is the result of his organisation and the forces brought to bear upon it. He does not affirm it to be impossible that an unseen Being should—say in answer to human prayer—interfere with the course of nature; but he finds no necessity for resorting to such an explanation of anything which has actually occurred. So far as he can see, things have always gone as it was inevitable that they should go. Morality, like everything else, has grown out of the interaction of the primary forces. The interest or the desire of the strongest has prevailed. Experience soon taught men that union creates strength, and they were thus induced to join themselves together; and the united group, stronger than the strongest single person, has been able to impose its common interest upon the action of individuals. In this way the social instincts have been cultivated, and consideration for others has been bred as a persistent element in human nature. What a man feels and what he does, at any moment, are the results of his inherited nature and the forces from without that have acted upon it. He could not do otherwise than as he does, or feel otherwise than as he feels. Man is an automaton. That is a conclusion which seems to Professor Huxley, as a scientific observer, to be irresistible and incontrovertible.

I do not know that Professor Huxley has allowed the argument to lead him to the confident assurance as to the future which Mr. Herbert Spencer entertains and expresses. The same forces which have thus far socialised mankind must necessarily, in Mr. Spencer's view, go on to make the world a happier and a better one. We may trust to nature for that result. Any one who understands the working of the natural forces will see that no other result is possible.

Let us suppose these to be ultimate truths concerning man and his destiny, brought to light by scientific investigation and demonstrated by scientific evidence—the propositions, I mean, that man is an automaton, and that the forces which act within him and upon him can only work together for good. It will then be rational for us all to contemplate these truths, and to adjust ourselves to them. Even in so speaking we seem to give way to the inveterate delusion of supposing ourselves to have a choice as to what we shall do. According to the theory of naturalism, we shall all of us—the wisest and the most foolish alike, the Spencer and the Darwin as well as the idiot and the lunatic—feel and judge and act precisely as the primary molecular forces originally determined that we should. I observe that so-called "determinists" are accustomed to say, in self-defence, "Of course we shall speak as our fellow-men do. We are not going to let our determinism reduce us to silence and inaction. If you theologians taunt us with being by our own account nothing more than automata addressing other automata, we can meet you with an *argumentum ad hominem;* your own idea of a God implies that all things are determined beforehand by His will." It is true that we theists are in this difficulty. But our agnostic opponents are persons who make it their profession to be guided and governed by science, and it is a boast made on behalf of science that its truths never conflict with one another. Mr. Cotter Morison, who professes to be, as an agnostic and determinist, a devotee of science, writes as follows: "Not less marked in another respect is the difference between the truths derived from religion and the truths derived from science. The truths of science are found to be in complete harmony with one another. Where this harmony is wanting, it is at once felt that error has crept in unawares. We never give a thought to the alternative hypothesis, that truths in different sciences or departments of knowledge may be inconsistent and mutually hostile, and yet remain truths. On the contrary, we find that the discovery of new truth has invariably among its results the additional effect of corroborating other and older truths, instead of conflicting with them" (*The Service of Man*, p. 6). Mr. Morison, as I said, professes to be a determinist. "The doctrine of determinism," he says, "is now so generally accepted, that it will not be needful to dwell upon it at any length here" (*Ibid.* p. 284). He puts, however, a strangely superficial and, as I should have thought, unscientific interpretation upon determinism. He seems to take it as meaning nothing more than that human nature inherits much and is capable of being modified by training for better and for worse. "It will perhaps be said that this view does away with moral responsibility; that those who hold it cannot consistently blame any crime or resent any injury; that we should not on this hypothesis reproach a garotter who half murders us; he is a machine, not a man with free will, capable of doing and forbearing according to the moral law." Yes, that is what it seems reasonable to say. "To which the answer is, that the sooner the idea of moral responsibility is got rid of, the better it will be for society and moral education. The sooner it is perceived that bad men will be bad, do what we will, though, of course, they may be made less bad, the sooner shall we come to the conclusion that the welfare of society demands the suppression or elimination of bad men, and the careful cultivation of the good only" (*Ibid.* p. 293). "Though, of course, they may be made less bad!" May, or may not, according to the virtue and effort of those who choose to make them less bad or to let them alone! Why, Mr. Morison talks as if he and the philosophers and educators stood outside the course of nature and were not subject to the law of necessary evolution, whilst the rest of mankind form a part of nature ; as if mankind in general were the field, and the few who understand science were the cultivator, who may do as he pleases about cultivating the field. No wonder that, after abolishing moral responsibility as an unscientific absurdity, and therefore with it both merit and blame, he goes on, in the same paragraph, to use language which is nonsensical unless it implies it. " The soldier who deserts in presence of the enemy is deservedly shot. In civil life there are forms of criminality which are worse than desertions ; they are open hostilities to the best interests of humanity" (*Ibid.* p. 295). And he goes on to discuss the nature of duty, which he justly interprets as what is owed. " The sense of duty," he says, "is the recognition of claims ; and the altruistic man is one who is prompt in acknowledging claims." But what is this but a sense of " moral responsibility," which has just been repudiated as unscientific? And who or what can have "claims" on us, if we are merely products of a necessary evolution? Duty and claims are, on that hypothesis, quite as unmeaning as moral responsibility. Is not this doctrine of determinism, if it be held with the rigour which alone is scientific, absolutely irreconcilable with the universal and persistent conditions of human life? Can any one man live for a day, for an hour, upon the assumption that he and other men are automatic machines? But, "of course" (as Mr. Morison says), when the devotees of science come to deal with moral questions, they put their determinism on the shelf, and talk like their neighbours, praising, blaming, exhorting, warning, measuring out just rewards and just punishments, as if men were not automata but could go this way or that.

Let us suppose, then, that we are disciples of Mr. Herbert Spencer, speaking, because we cannot help it, as if we had some kind of freedom of action, but bending our minds upon the action of the forces inherent in humanity which have gradually and necessarily improved mankind, and which cannot possibly fail to bring about a perfect society. It is through the contemplation of these forces that our morality will be formed and nourished. Mr. Spencer gives a reasonable account of what it will be. It will be a nicely-adjusted combination of care for ourselves and consideration for others. We shall make it our aim to be at ease and agreeable. We shall cherish our bodily health, not only for the most obvious reason, but also because those who are in good health are in good spirits, and those who are in good spirits can make themselves agreeable to their neighbours, and their neighbours will in return make themselves agreeable to them. So, with the innocent illusion that we are by our own endeavours doing something which might have been left undone to forward it, we shall be consciously yielding to the movement which carries us on to the paradise of universal ease. That is the morality, I think, which conforms itself as closely as human nature will allow to the conclusions of natural science.

Mr. Spencer himself follows his argument with a more *doctrinaire* fidelity than seems possible to others of his school. Mr. Cotter Morison, who seems to have little taste for scientific consistency, calls out loudly for rigorous methods of suppression, without which he sees our modern society threatened with ruin. " The welfare of society demands the suppression or elimination of bad men" (*The Service of Man*, p. 293). "What shall be done with those who cannot learn belongs to another branch of inquiry, and concerns politics rather than morals" (*Ibid.* p. 298). "Society has a right to suppress the bad man in some effectual way, and, above all, prevent his leaving a posterity as wicked as himself" (*Ibid.* p. 294). It would be interesting to learn what practical measures Mr. Morison would recommend for the carrying out of his views—how he would have "the bad" first discriminated and ticketed, and then, if not put to death or mutilated, restricted to the company of their own sex. On the other hand, Mr. Morison gives high praise to saintly enthusiasms which Mr. Spencer would condemn as irrational and mischievous, and devotes several pages to the glorification of Sister Agnes Jones, Mother Margaret Hallahan, and Sister Dora Pattison. "Such flowers of exquisite perfume and beauty, grown in the garden of the soul, still arrest the attention of a rationalistic age" (*Ibid.* p. 218). And he has a notion that flowers like these may be "cultivated" by the approbation of society. His concluding words are: "An ideal society would be one in which an ideal education habitually stimulated and inflamed the good passions, while it starved and discouraged the bad" (*Ibid.* p. 318). The philosopher Hume was a more consistent advocate of the comfortable virtue of which Mr. Spencer proclaims the certain triumph. "What philosophical truths can be more advantageous to society than these here delivered, which represent virtue in all her genuine and most engaging charms; and make us approach her with ease, familiarity, and affection? The dismal dress falls off, with which many divines and some philosophers have covered her, and nothing appears but gentleness, humanity, beneficence, affability—nay, even at proper intervals, play, frolic, and gaiety. She talks not of useless austerities and rigours, suffering and self-denial. She declares that her sole purpose is to make her votaries, and all mankind, during every period of their existence, if possible, cheerful and happy. . . . The sole trouble which she demands is that of just calculation and a steady preference of the greater happiness" (Huxley's *Hume*, p. 204). But Mr. Huxley has too vivid a perception of the conditions of human life to be taken captive by this picture; he has too much—may we not say?—of the Christian in him to contemplate it with much pleasure. The passage calls up to his mind the pilgrims who toil painfully, not without many a stumble and many a bruise, along the rough and steep roads which lead to the higher life; "the hour of temptation in which the question will crop up whether, as something has to be sacrificed, a bird in the hand is not worth two in the bush"; the image of virtue as "an awful goddess, whose ministers are the furies, and whose highest reward is peace" (*Ibid.* pp. 205, 206). His own final deliverance about morality is a singular one for this rigorous and exacting preacher of a scientific rationalism. "In whichever way we look at the matter, morality is based on feeling, not on reason" (*Ibid.* p. 207). "As there are Pascals and Mozarts, Newtons and Raffaelles, in whom the innate faculty for science or art seems to need but a touch to spring into full vigour, and through whom the human race obtains new possibilities of knowledge and new conceptions of beauty : so there have been men of moral genius, to whom we owe ideals of duty and visions of moral perfection, which ordinary mankind could never have attained " (*Ibid.* p. 208). Mr. Huxley would hardly, with Mr. Morison, regard these exceptional apprehensions of moral beauty as products which ordinary mankind may hope to raise by assiduous cultivation ; but he seems to deny himself, as Mr. Morison does, the right of blaming treachery and foulness and cruelty more than he would blame the want of an ear for music or of an eye for form.

On the whole, how is the scientific view of things related to those dispositions which I have enumerated, or to what we may call the higher life in general? The following are effects which seem attributable to it. It assures men that they will add to their happiness by considering the feelings of others, and in that way promotes " altruism." It trains men in the habit of trying to understand things as they are and to represent them as they are, and is thus favourable to truthfulness. It brings men face to face with inviolable laws, to which every man must adjust himself; and it thus deepens and strengthens the sense of order. It brings them face to face also with the Unknowable, and contributes to form such religion as the Unknowable can inspire, that is, chiefly, a sentiment of awe and a sense of inadequacy. It seems to have nothing to do with reverence, self-reproach, self-respect, self-devotion, hope, aspiration, or with the higher flights of love and joy. It offers no explanation of duty, unless by suggesting that it is a disguise of compulsion or interest. What it has professed is that it can let these sentiments alone, leaving them outside the sphere of knowledge and reason, to assert their existence as they may, and to be cherished by those who like them.

Mr. Cotter Morison frankly admits that "a belief in the Unknowable kindles no enthusiasm." "Science," he says, "wins a verdict in its favour before any competent intellectual tribunal, but numbers of men, and the vast majority of women, ignore the finding of the jury of experts. They cling passionately to the belief in the supernatural. . . . Above all, they will believe, in spite of science and the laws of their own consciousness, in a good God who loves them and cares for them" (*The Service of Man*, p. 52). Mr. Darwin, with his perfect simplicity, records, in his Autobiography, how the more exalted feelings wither under the influence of agnosticism. "In my journal I wrote that, whilst standing in the midst of the grandeur of a Brazilian forest, 'It is not possible to give an adequate idea of the higher feelings of wonder, admiration, and devotion which fill and elevate the mind.' I well remember my conviction that there is more in man than the mere breath of his body. But now the grandest scenes would not cause any such convictions and feelings to reach my mind." In contrast with this action of scientific agnosticism on the higher nature, it may be shown that the Christian theory accounts for duty, calls out trust and worship and devotion, feeds a self-respect which involves shame and repentance, animates to the most beneficial exertion, justifies love, joy, self-renouncement, enthusiasm. These sentiments, we say, are the best and highest part of human nature, and have more right to rule our minds than the conclusions of science and logic.

Is that so, or not? Let it be assumed that there is a rivalry, at least, if not an absolute antagonism, between science and what, to use a single word, we may call the soul. Which of the two authorities has the primary claim on our loyalty? We might be glad if we could say that we can pay equal deference to both. I do not think we can. But in any case that question may be asked; and it is evident that the agnostics take for granted that it is science that has the primary claim. And their science, as we have seen, knows nothing of the convictions and sentiments of the higher life. What it knows is evolution, transformation of energy, order of nature, determinism. I say their science; they themselves, for the most part, profess admiration of these affections. They will regard them as beautiful things which they do not understand. They will even set to work to cultivate them by encouragement. We Christians welcome such personal acknowledgments as in all respects a valuable tribute; but, being confronted with the science of the agnostics, we deny its primary claim on our loyalty, and we hold that we are bound to place the soul, for the purposes of allegiance and surrender, above the scientific faculty. The most important question put to men has always been whether they would follow the light from heaven.

For the intelligent part of this generation the question appears to have taken this form, Which of the two will you follow, science or the soul? Science, which looks backwards and downwards; or the soul, which looks upwards and forwards? Science, which investigates phenomena, and takes things to pieces to see how they have grown; or the soul, which drinks in spiritual life, and so gains power to create poetry and art and the social affections and religion?

The Christianity of the New Testament appealed, in the most emphatic and almost exclusive manner, to the spiritual consciousness in men. I admit that historic Christianity has been very far from contenting itself with this appeal. It has sought to impose its creed upon men's minds instead of offering it to them as an awakening and inspiring Gospel. It has presented a Church, a Book, miracles, to coerce them into accepting its doctrines, instead of conveying a voice from heaven to their souls, and trusting to the self-commending power of that voice. Those whose object it is to overthrow and extirpate the religion of Christendom will bring against it all that they can find to its disadvantage. Those, on the other hand, who undertake to defend the traditional Christianity against attack are in some degree responsible for evoking unpleasant assaults like that of Mr. Cotter Morison, and will meet them as best they can. What I desire to do in this paper is to claim attention for what is primary and essential in Christianity, as compared with what rival systems have to offer, and to follow the order which Christians are bound to regard as having the highest sanction. If we are to judge by the methods set before us in the New Testament, it belongs to Christianity to assume spiritual needs, to appeal to the spiritual consciousness, and to seek confirmation in spiritual evidence.

I must briefly remind my readers of what is patent in the Gospels, and what will scarcely be questioned by any reasonable freedom of criticism. Christ came proclaiming the kingdom of heaven; He did this with authority in the Father's name; His chief pretension was to forgive sins. It was *not* His plan to announce Himself as a supernatural being, and to perform miracles as His credentials; on the contrary, He was deeply displeased by the demand for miracles, and repelled the support which men were ready to give to a miracle-worker. But from the beginning to the end He assumed authority as having come from the Father; He taught, and gave commands, and organised His followers, and made plans for the future, as one having authority. The adherents He desired, and whom alone He expected to win, were those who were childlike, and ready to believe in a heavenly Father. To them He offered pardon, guidance, grace, and help of all kinds. The Galileans whom He selected and appointed as His envoys were simple, trustful men, who believed in Him because they could not doubt His assurance. And when these envoys went forth after His death to proclaim Him as Lord, they still made the same remarkable offer—that of forgiveness and reconciliation to the Father. He was exalted, they said, to give repentance to Israel and remission of sins. The word committed to them was, "God forgives mankind, be ye reconciled to God." And St. Paul, the chief founder of the Church, was accustomed to protest that he stood on the self-commending power of this message, which was as light to those of his hearers who had eyes to see.

So far, then, as the Christianity of to-day is true to its origin, that is what it must primarily be saying to this generation. It cannot abandon the office of reporting a voice from heaven, without renouncing the proclamation and the power which brought Christendom into existence. It still offers forgiveness of sins in the name of Christ and of the Father; it is still careless of arguments and arts to win the support of those to whom reconciliation to God is unmeaning or unattractive. That offer, I say, is both the beginning and the heart of Christianity: it made the first Christians, and no man ever became a Christian such as St. Peter and St. Paul would have acknowledged as a fellow-believer, without accepting it. It is futile, I would urge, to enter into controversy about the Trinity, or miracles, or the efficacy of prayer, or the relation of science to religion, with those to whom there is no Father in heaven, and to whom Christ is a well-meaning enthusiast. And schemes of Christianity which leave out what it mainly was in the first century, representing it as a form which was taken, in accordance with the laws of thought of the period, by exceptionally pure and fervid aspirations after moral excellence, though they may seek to enable men who cannot believe in a genuine voice from heaven to acquiesce in the name of Christians, do not differ in kind from the ethics of an agnostic. They obviously retain no power to call out and sustain those qualities which I have spoken of as constituting by general admission the higher life of men.

The primary question at issue, I repeat, is whether the authority which Christ claimed was real or imaginary. That He professed to have a commission from the Father to introduce the kingdom of heaven and to draw men into it, that He invited His hearers to come to Him that He might give them rest, and that He assured men of the forgiveness of their sins, I assume to be a matter of history. I know how much there is to be said about the natural impulse which prompted men in the old times who were bent on improving their fellows to claim a direct commission from heaven, and I can quite understand how easy it is to speak of Gautama Buddha and Jesus and Mohammed as similarly remarkable persons. Unbelievers pronounce with confidence that the authority was imaginary. I wish to fix attention upon the opposite belief, that the authority was real, as being the primary and life-giving affirmation of Christianity.

Agnostics will smile at the simplicity of those who can imagine that the power giving existence to this universe can have anything special to do with the poor human creatures dwelling on this speck of a globe. "The miraculous," it may be said, "is the old stumbling-block; and what can be so great a miracle as a man charged with a communication from the incomprehensible Creative Power to this human race? Can it be supposed that the appearing of such a man is to be accounted for by the evolution which, according to science, explains everything?" Let it be frankly admitted that a strain hardly to be borne is put upon our spiritual faith by this initial Christian acknowledgment. We must be able to say to ourselves with a resolution not to be shaken by infinities of space or time or quantity, "Though worlds on worlds in myriad myriads roll, What know we greater than the soul?" But if we bring ourselves to pay such deference to the soul and its demands and confessions and interests as to refuse to surrender the belief that a God speaks to us from heaven, the greater and more incredible this wonder, the more reasonable is it that we should face without quailing any difficulties which it involves, and accept any conclusions to which it irresistibly leads. The agnostic position may claim to relieve us of many perplexities; if it did not involve the sacrifice of all that is best and most indispensable in life, it would be the simplest of creeds to adopt. But one who believes Jesus Christ to have been charged with a commission from heaven will not think it incredible —can hardly regard it as improbable—that a person so exceptional should go through exceptional experiences and do exceptional acts. If we are to believe that the man Jesus of Nazareth had a special commission to reveal the heavenly Father, we are admitting what every agnostic would repudiate as a stupendous miracle, and I cannot imagine that if an agnostic were persuaded to believe this, he would obstinately stumble at smaller miracles as incredible.

The belief that Christ was authorised to open the kingdom of heaven and to declare the forgiveness of sins will, it is obvious, carry many presumptions with it. It would not be strange if it should hurry believers into a positiveness of statement on many points which might need to be afterwards modified. So it has been seen that students of science, when they were under the first impressions made on their minds by the regularity of the order of nature, hurriedly affirmed that any variation of the general order was impossible; and that now the protagonist of science modifies that affirmation into the statement that any event for which the recognised laws of nature cannot account is so improbable as to require exceptional proof of its occurrence.

It was inevitable that those who were induced by Christ's envoys to believe in Him as having come from the Father and gone to the Father, should regard with reverence the institutions and the society which He founded. The Apostles reported that He had spoken much of a Spirit or Breath of God, best to be understood through thinking of the air which moves around the earth and men; and that He had promised that those who should form a society looking up to Him and bound together by their allegiance to Him should have this Spirit given to them as the power of their common life. This promise seemed to the first Christians to have been fulfilled. The Church of Christ came into existence, an imperfect and growing realisation of a living ideal; having for its chief institutions a washing of forgiveness and adoption, and a common partaking of bread and wine as representing the person of the Lord. This society has come down to our own day, but in a most broken and divided condition; and the nature of it has been very much confused by claims made on behalf of the whole body and of particular sections of it. The authoritative view of the Church appears to be that it is an ideal system, having its truest existence in the living divine purpose, and realising itself in features and fragments which yet "ask to be united in the wondrous whole" of a perfected humanity. But the believers in Christ also looked back from Him; and the history of the Jews was seen culminating in their Messiah, and the "Old Covenant" received a glory from Him to whom it led up. When they came into contact with the external world, the acknowledgment of a Son of Man as revealing the Father seemed to them to throw light on all the goodness and all the hopes of the heathen nations. "Of a truth I perceive," said the Apostle of the Jews, "that God is no respecter of persons,"—that is, of nationality or professed creed, —" but in every nation he that feareth Him and worketh righteousness is acceptable to Him." The Apostle of the Gentiles proclaimed everywhere that the God whom he preached was the God of mankind, who had been revealing Himself in less complete ways to all nations. We follow the original Christian teaching, when we recognise most reverently all that is true and good in the beliefs and practices of non-Christians, as having the same origin as the revelation given in Christ.

It was equally inevitable that they should contemplate Christ Himself with a peculiar reverence, and should wonder at His nature. They would naturally recall with especial interest what Christ had said about Himself. It was evident that He had been slow to put forward definite pretensions; He did not even announce Himself as the Messiah, but contented Himself at first with proclaiming the kingdom of heaven, and speaking with authority in the name of the heavenly Father. But His way of speaking of "My Father" implied that He was the Son of God; and His disciples came by degrees to the conclusion that He was the Messiah. All that they saw of Him helped them to believe that He was of a perfection above their imaginations. They called Him the Messiah, the Son of God; and when they found themselves constrained to believe that He had risen from the dead they saw, in this triumph over death, their faith confirmed and enlarged. His divine nature grew as they contemplated Him; and visions of what He must have been to the Jewish fathers, and to the creation, and of what He was to the spiritual life of every man and to that of the whole Church, gradually steadied themselves into positive assurance, and took shape in words which endeavoured to express those relations. It was a matter of course that the Christians should worship their Lord as a God, but they seem to have escaped for some time being troubled with the problem of His relation to the One God. But the problem could not fail to demand solution; and such solution as they could arrive at came through the name of the Son. The union between the perfect Son and the supreme Father seemed to them to be so close as not to break or infringe upon the unity of God.

Christ was preached at first without the help of books, just as He might now be preached to a heathen race by a missionary who had left his Bible behind him. But in the course of time the oral statements of the companions and witnesses of Jesus began to be written down; and letters of instruction were written by Apostles, which were treasured up by those who received them. The documents which were most valued by Christians came together, apparently, by some natural process of selection and collection. A concealing cloud rests upon the history of the early Church for a singularly important period of some three-quarters of a century; and when that is lifted the volume of the "New Covenant" is seen already existing and closed against additions. When we look at it we cannot wonder at the authority it acquired. To those who are worshipping Jesus Christ, and finding Him to be the way to the Father, this volume offers itself as containing all that can be known about Him, and all that can be known about the early years and original beliefs of the society which owes its foundation to Him. It cannot be thought surprising that the reasonable reverence for such a volume should have degenerated into an assertion of its infallible truth. All spiritual conceptions which have become popular have suffered some kind of degradation into carnal forms. Criticism has shown that the New Testament is not to be regarded as a mechanically accurate book; that we have scarcely any solid confirmation from without of its own statements as to authorship; that the history of which it is a record is curiously separate from the contemporary history of which we possess other records. Its authority depends primarily upon its reception by the Church, but much more substantially upon its own character. To those who see nothing supernatural in Christ it will be full of problems at once fascinating and irritating; whilst those who believe in Him will find it difficult not to read it as true from beginning to end. But modern Christians will do well to bear in mind that, whilst the Church was being founded in Asia and Greece and Italy, and throughout the period covered by the New Testament itself, the Church had no sacred book of its own; and that the Apostles, though they claimed disciplinary authority, had evidently no thought of claiming infallibility for any utterances of theirs. The destruction of the theory of the infallibility of the Bible has been one of the means by which we have been prevented from resting in the external and mechanical, and driven to what terrifies us at first as the intangibility and vagueness of the Spirit.

And what as to the future of mankind and of individual men? The belief in Christ could not fail to generate expectations of its own. We learn from the New Testament that the first Christians had their thoughts turned steadily with keen interest towards a crisis which was to occur at the close of their age. This is the feature of the New Testament which creates, perhaps, our chief difficulty in reading it as we do for our instruction. The word crisis means judgment, and it was a judgment that was looked for, but it was called by various names: it was a day of the Lord, a presence or an unveiling of the Son of Man, a coming of Christ, a reconstitution of all things, a conclusion of the ages. For the Christians of the New Testament age, this manifestation filled the horizon of their hopes and fears. It was to be in the main a heavenly event, but it was to have its earthly effects and signs, and the chief amongst these was to be the destruction of the Holy City of the Old Covenant. Those who look back on the close of that age with the spiritual insight of Christian faith can see that the epoch proved itself a momentous one in the divine government of the world, and that it was not unfitly described by the prophetical imagery under which it was foretold. But the anticipations of what then came to pass, which have so large a record in the New Testament writings, have not been exactly suited to the spiritual condition of those who have lived in the subsequent ages, and the devout use of the Scriptural language of expectation has given birth to some difficulties of belief. We have little direct guidance of any kind in forming ideas as to what will happen to the world in future ages or to human beings when they die. It is impossible for those who believe that Jesus Christ revealed the Eternal Father to look forward without hope; it is impossible to contemplate Christ as risen from the dead without taking for granted that there is a future life for men; it is impossible, we must add, to think of the Christ of the Gospels as ruling the world without associating the thought of judgment and punishment with the triumph of His power. But it is left to the faith and hope and fear of the believers in Christ to create for the most part their own imagery of what the world of the future and the life beyond the grave will be. And many Christians of our day find the traditional imagery of the Church failing them, as not suited to modern knowledge, without being moved by a common imaginative impulse vigorous enough to clothe the spiritual substance of their expectations in acceptable forms.

Most important of all the inferences which must in the nature of things be drawn from the acknowledgment of Christ's mission, are those which bear upon the spiritual relations of men with God. No single term sums up more adequately the purpose of Christ's coming than that which declares Him to be the way to the Father. If anything will be admitted to be certain as to the purport of His teaching, it is that He invited men to trust in God by assuring them that He was a Being in whom they might reasonably trust, that He encouraged them to pray to Him, and that He declared the will of the Father to be the ground and rule of all duty. His disciples repeated this teaching, and reinforced it by their proclamation of their Master as a Son of God who had gone down into human death and been raised to the Father's right hand. The old agnostic contention that prayer is made irrational by the fixed order of the universe has been modified by Professor Huxley into the admission that prayer may be rational if there is a Being who can hear it and who cares for those who offer it, together with a challenge to believers to show that prayer has in any instance been demonstrably efficacious. Christians may be preserved from giving unwise answers to this challenge by remembering two principles which have authority to dominate any theory of prayer. In one of the Prayer-Book Collects we are taught to address God thus: "Almighty God, the fountain of all wisdom, who knowest our necessities before we ask, and our ignorance in asking." And this acknowledgment rests upon what was laid down by Jesus when He was teaching His followers how to pray: "Your Father knoweth what things ye have need of before ye ask Him." The other principle is stated in words dear to all English Christians: "Prayer is the soul's sincere desire, Uttered or unexpressed; The motion of a hidden fire, Which trembles in the breast." The two principles are combined by St. Paul when he says that we know not what to pray for as we ought, but that the Spirit in our hearts intercedes for us in unspoken sighs. Surely the contention that, if a Christian would like something, the act of putting it into the words of a petition and addressing the petition to the Almighty will be a means of obtaining it, is alien to these principles and is forbidden by them. The logical comment on them might be that prayer is made irrational by Christ's teaching, more decidedly than by the fixed order of the universe. If desire unexpressed is prayer, and if we have a Father who knows better than we do what we want, why, it may be asked, should we do anything so futile as to put our desires into words, and address them to God? Yet Christ and His Apostles taught men to pray. They taught men to place themselves as dependent, desiring creatures at the feet of a perfect heavenly Father, and to utter in simple human language the aspirations which the belief in such a Father might stir in a childlike nature. Prayer is for those who have become as little children, not for philosophers engaged in estimating mechanical forces. We shall continue to pray trustfully and devoutly, so long as we believe through Jesus that we have access to the

how is it to be sustained? 157

Father, and shall decline controversy about the mechanical efficacy of calculated requests. "To labour is to pray," said the ancient Christian maxim, and it is certainly truer to regard prayer as the spiritual breath of labour, of voluntary effort, than to imagine that it can be utilised as a mechanical substitute for labour. Work or action, also, according to the Christian revelation, must look to God, and make His will its law and end: He has an absolute claim on all that we can do; there can be nothing better for us than to please God. "Under its theological aspect," as Mr. Huxley says, "morality is obedience to the will of God" (*Hume*, p. 207). Duty means what the heavenly Father can claim from His creatures and children. That is a reasonable and satisfying explanation of the word; no other does justice to its power over the universal mind. We speak, it is true, of duty towards God and duty towards our neighbour; but duty to man is included in and sustained by duty to the Father and Maker of men. "Morality is obedience to the will of God," and the will of God is to be learned from any modes in which it has pleased or shall please Him to make it known. To one who believes in a Divine Ruler of the world, no knowledge or criterion of duty is more valid than that which is obtained from the testimony of general experience, pointing out by what affections and acts the well-being of mankind is promoted.

I have distinguished between the conclusions of agnosticism and those of agnostics. In no one's case is it more necessary to do this than in that of Mr. Darwin. He has little of the Christian in him who can read without an emotion of reverence that statement of his: " The safest conclusion seems to me that the whole subject is beyond the scope of man's intellect; but man can do his duty." Duty is a word without meaning, or rather implying a delusion, to pure scientific agnosticism; but Mr. Darwin's attitude was that of a man humbly veiling his face, in conscious ignorance, and yet in recognition and trust, before a Power of righteousness and love to which he felt himself bound. No one speaks sincerely of duty without implying such a Power and a relation binding man to it. And to recognise the imperative authority of righteousness and love is to believe in God. A Christian who professes that he knows God with his intellect, knows nothing yet as he ought to know. The only promise of knowing God which we can claim is that which is made to faith and hope and love.

It is a mysterious condition of our human existence—a manifest part of the discipline, as Christians would say, by which we are trained—that our understanding is brought up against insuperable difficulties, like the invisible wall which stopped Balaam's ass. Any scheme of philosophy which professes to evade contradictions or to solve them convicts itself of superficiality. Our intellect gets unceremoniously buffeted by contradictions whenever it makes excursions into the world behind the senses. If, for example, there is one thing which the principle of evolution seems to make evident, it is that there is no beginning of things: it is, indeed, impossible for us to conceive an absolute beginning. But it is equally, or almost equally, impossible to us to imagine an absence of beginning. And evolutionists, quite naturally, however unscientifically, talk of the primordial atoms of the universe. It is not merely that we are made aware of things lying beyond our knowledge, but that contradictory conclusions seem forced upon our understandings. Space and time ought, one might have imagined, to be simple things, but the consideration of them leads us into insoluble problems. So we have to confess ourselves to be helpless before the problems of predestination and choice of action, of the existence of evil in the universe, of a good Power from whom all things proceed, of the nature of spirit, of the clothing of infinity with the finite, and the like. St. Paul held that human conceptions of things beyond the sense-world are no better than the mental attempts of young children, and may hereafter similarly make us smile. The frank apprehension of the inadequacy of our conceptions and of their transitional character will render it easier to us to acquiesce in traditional religious terms or statements which may not be quite to our mind, as well as in formally contradictory propositions. When we try to discover a purpose in this perplexing discipline, we are led to the conclusion that we are intended to learn a distrust of our reasoning faculties, as of instruments, useful and necessary indeed, but stamped with inferiority and inadequacy. We follow our best Christian teachers in holding that, with regard to the greater things of life, the mind or spirit which trusts and hopes and loves is the superior organ of knowledge, and that human beings are put to the test whether they will be guided by the superior organ or the inferior.

It is to these affections, of faith and hope and love, that the revelation of God given in Christ appeals. It assumes that in each man there is a spiritual need, of which it seeks to awaken a disturbing consciousness. This communication has the power—and no theory of life which does not profess to come from God can claim a like power—to move human nature to its depths and to raise it to its proper worth. What gracious or animating sentiment is there which it does not call forth? By its declaration of the good purposes of God it creates hope, and nurses its vivifying warmth under any depressing discouragements. By its display of condescending divine tenderness it softens the heart, and opens its pores to the best influences. By its assurance of a fatherly mind in God it constrains men to have confidence in the Supreme Power. It teaches them to blame themselves, as they look upon the goodness against which they have sinned and the standard of purity and love exhibited in the Son of Man. By presenting the Son of Man as divine, it makes every man sacred and dear to his fellow-men. It gives an entirely satisfying law of life, a sure basis of duty, a universal and progressive morality. It so far explains the sufferings and trials of life as to induce men to bear them with a refining patience. It holds out a light from beyond the grave which dispels the gloom of death. It opens a fount of joy too deep to be exhausted. If by the decay of Christian faith all these stimulants of the higher life should lose their power upon human souls, what could compensate to mankind for the loss?

XII

"THE ETHICS OF EVOLUTION"[1]

"The creation was subjected to vanity . . . in hope."—
ROMANS viii. 20, 21.

A DISCOURSE of singular interest was delivered some weeks ago at Oxford by Mr. Huxley, in which that accomplished man of science, repudiating the ethics of Evolution, declared his adherence to the old-fashioned morality, with its exaltation of duty, its condemnation of moral evil, its recognition of a paramount authority superior to the impulses of nature. The account of moral conduct given by those who derive their ethics from Evolution alone, if I rightly understand it, may be put into a few sentences, and is of an enviable simplicity. According to this view, the one essential motive of action in the animal world is desire. Each sentient being naturally desires pleasure and shuns pain. It does its best to crush or hustle out of its way whatever interferes with its own enjoyment of life. It lays hold of all that it can grasp; it keeps hold of whatever it has got. Man has this lust, in common with

[1] Preached in Westminster Abbey, 23rd July 1893.

his fellow-animals, for the core of his nature. But at an early stage of their separate existence, men came to see that by acting together in concert individuals might gain more of what they desired than by acting independently. What we call morality has all grown out of this increasing perception. More and more it has been proved and seen that life is bettered through the association of human beings: is bettered, that is, for each associated person, for the worst lot in society is better than that of a man living solitarily as a wild animal. But in order to make combination possible, men have to restrain themselves and to regard others. Self-restraint, and consideration for fellow-members of a partnership, thus imposed, are the beginning and end of morality. Human life, in the strict process of natural evolution, undergoes a kind of inversion. The self-regarding desire of the individual, operating amidst the conditions surrounding him, evolves the self-denial of the individual, and creates laws of society to which it is itself constrained to submit—an authority which not only bends the acts of the associated partners into obedience, but also captures their imagination and their reason. This account of the growth and meaning of morality, however little it may satisfy us, has a certain historical truth which must in candour be admitted by those whom it does not satisfy.

But where does it leave a thinking man? Desire remains the one law which he rationally knows as supreme. The principles of the highest morality are reduced to expedients which desire has found useful. Evil means nothing but what causes pain, or obstructs the gratification of desire. To be good is to choose what on the whole and in the long-run will best gratify desire. Duty is not paramount, but has a subordinate executive authority, under the paramount lordship of natural desire. A bad state of things is only desire less successful in gratifying itself.

Against this theory of ethics Mr. Huxley, in the Oxford discourse, has recorded his dissentient protest. In the world below ethical man he sees the cosmic process that has been named Evolution going on everywhere and carrying all things forward in circular courses towards culmination or extinction; but he will pay no homage to this process in the sphere of human conduct. That explanation of the evolvings of social duty out of desire he barely deigns to notice. He quietly says of it that it gives as much natural sanction to the immoral sentiments as to the moral. "The thief and the murderer," he continues, "follow nature just as much as the philanthropist. Cosmic evolution may teach us how the good and the evil tendencies of men may have come about; but, in itself, it is incompetent to furnish any better reason why what we call good is preferable to what we call evil than we had before" (p. 31). To Mr. Huxley, good is good and evil evil; and he recognises that good and evil are set before the conscience of man, and that he is imperatively bidden to choose the good, whatever suggestions the cosmic process may make to him about his actions. In this sphere the cosmic process is to Mr. Huxley what the flesh is to St. Paul : the cosmic process lusts against the moral ideal, and the moral ideal against the cosmic process, for these are contrary the one to the other.

Evil is positive, let speculators on the cosmos, materialist or theological, manipulate it as they please. "The universal experience of mankind," writes Mr. Huxley, "testifies that, whether we look within us or without us, evil stares us in the face on all sides" (p. 23). And again: "To the man with an ethical ideal, the world, including himself, will always seem full of evil" (p. 54). Disregarding more than, as it seems to me, is quite reasonable the argument which traces social morality directly to the one movement of evolution, he insists that "the cosmic process has no sort of relation to moral ends; that the imitation of it by man is contrary to the first principles of ethics" (p. 34). "Ethical nature may count upon having to reckon with a tenacious and powerful enemy as long as the world lasts" (p. 36). We are warranted in hoping for a large abatement of the evil of the world; but it is "an essential condition of the realisation of that hope that we should cast aside the notion that the escape from pain and sorrow is the proper object of life" (p. 37).

When we recall things we have read about man being an automaton, and a taste for morality being of the same kind as an ear for music, and about human life having for its teachers the inexorable laws of nature,—what welcome can be too cordial for Christians to give to the courage and resolution with which this great naturalist now defies the idols of evolution, and separates himself from the philosophy of Mr. Herbert Spencer, and pays homage to the old sanctities of conscience and duty and the ethical ideal?

In the second century of the Christian era many inquiring minds were much exercised by the difficulty of accounting for the evil in the world. Certain thinkers of that age, who came under the influence both of Christianity in its more Jewish form and of ancient Oriental speculations, occupied themselves in devising systems by which the mixed and baffling nature of things might be explained, or at least exhibited. To the Catholic Christians these systems were so many forms of seductive error, and they were denounced by them under the comprehensive name of Gnostic, from the Gnosis, the knowledge or speculative philosophy, of which they were the fruits. In general they represented all existences, divine and earthly, as issuing from a mysterious Depth, out of which powers or energies emanated; and it was a common feature of them that they assigned the making of the earthly world to an Artificer, a Demiurgus or demiurge, who was more or less evil, inferior to the highest powers, and in some opposition to them.

We are more familiar in these days with Agnostics than with Gnostics. The term Agnostic has been introduced into the discussions of our time—I believe by Mr. Huxley—in order to define the position of those who held that nothing can be certainly known concerning the supernatural world, and that it is wise to refrain from both positive and negative assertions, if not from all speculation, about it. But the Agnostic has been asked, and in some cases has been constrained to ask himself, "Are we, then, to throw over the recognition of duty and conscience and the moral ideal, with the hope which never fails to sustain and encourage those who look reverently upwards? That would be to deprive ourselves of the convictions and sentiments to which the world has evidently owed all that is worthiest in human existence. To know *ourselves* as well as we can is a knowledge which no Agnostic creed forbids. Are we, then, to know ourselves as automata worked by the cosmic process?" Mr. Huxley emphatically declares that he, for one, will not be a worshipper of Evolution on these terms. He believes in the cosmic process, but he believes with still deeper conviction in the higher law bidding the spiritual man renounce and defy the cosmic process, and in a power enabling him to do something to repel and to curb it. In this awakening discourse he may perhaps be said to be rather Gnostical than Agnostic. Like the Gnostics of the second century he has been fascinated by the brooding speculations of Asiatic sages on the eternal mysteries of the world. The Gnostic Deep or Abyss is named by him Nebulous Potentiality; the Demiurge or Artificer is entitled the Cosmic Process. Out of Nebulous Potentiality have come not only the Force which carries on the process of evolution, but also a Wisdom, and a Moral Energy, which incite the enlightened human spirit to combat the cosmic process and to aid in rescuing human society out of its grasp. In his language concerning human duty and the spiritual nature of man, however, Mr. Huxley is no complacent philosopher weaving a system of the universe; he falls back like the simplest of us upon the testimony of conscience and of experience, and allows it to inspire him to a confident utterance of faith and hope. In some of his words, indeed, we seem to hear the accents of the old simple Christianity, as when he says, " Ethical nature may count upon having to reckon with a tenacious and powerful enemy as long as the world lasts." Write enemy with a capital E, and it is Satan, that is, the Adversary; or the Devil, that is, the inspirer of falsehood and strife, the unscrupulously selfish motive in the struggle for existence.

Let me guard against misunderstanding by admitting fully that in this declaration of his mature convictions—which becomes even more interesting when we compare it with Mr. John Stuart Mill's similarly remarkable *Essays on Religion* — Mr. Huxley by no means professes to hold our Christian beliefs. On the contrary, he appeals in part to the original Buddhism of Gautama, but still more to the highest form of Stoicism, for proof that a noble and severe and humane morality may be held and practised apart from a belief in immortality. But so far as the opposition between the spirit and the flesh is concerned, he is Pauline and Christian. His faith in a moral ideal defies science; he calls on his fellow-men to live and be saved by hope.

How the evil in the world is to be reconciled with Supreme Goodness is a problem which is as much alive now as in the times of the Indian sages or of the Gnostics. It is thrown in the teeth of the Christian theology; it makes philosophical Deism a folly; it causes anguish to the inquiring Christian child. If we turn to the New Testament, we find there no attempt to solve the problem, no Gnosis about the origin of evil or its place in the world. What may often strike us as unaccountable is that the problem itself does not appear there, that it is not represented in its pages by any doubt or sense of perplexity, such as must have troubled, we should have thought, a mind like St. Paul's. According to our New Testament teachers, evil exists, and is a very serious matter. Essential evil is the willing surrender of the mind and conduct to falsehood, to ill-will, to the rule of the senses; and this evil is to be simply fought against as the enemy. It is in a very secondary sense that suffering and pain is spoken of as evil; and in suffering we may distinguish, though we cannot separate, that which is mental from that which is bodily. Mental suffering we are to do what we can to assuage in others; for ourselves, whilst not rebelling against it or running away from it, we are encouraged to hope that we may ultimately be delivered from its pangs and may enter into peace and rest. Bodily pain has still less of positive evil in it; certainly it is not to be abhorred by the faithful Christian; it may always in the human sufferer be turned to good. In Mr. Huxley's phrase, "the notion that to escape from pain and sorrow is the proper object of life must be cast aside" by those who look for guidance to the New Testament.

But though there is no Gnosis about Evil, any more than about Powers and Emanations, in our sacred volume, a principle bearing on the problem of evil is there laid down, which St. Paul delights to state in the most absolute terms he can find. All things are of God: from Him and through Him and unto Him are all things; there is one God and Father of all, Who is above all and through all and in all. And this principle appeals with irresistible force to our minds. A belief in Unity, though so penetrating a thinker and so consummate a man of science as Mr. Huxley seems to be rebelling against it and refusing to be bound by it, is one towards which all modern thought leads us. But if there is one God, from whom all things proceed, then evil also must be from God. What can we reply to this logical conclusion?

Referring to the ancient speculations upon this subject, Mr. Huxley observes, " Thus, brought before the tribunal of ethics, the cosmos might well seem to stand condemned. The conscience of man revolted against the moral indifference of nature, and the microcosmic atom should have found the illimitable macrocosm guilty. But few, or none, ventured to record that verdict" (p. 13). No: it seems ridiculous, as well as audacious, for a man to judge and condemn the Maker of the World. We all stand baffled and troubled before this mystery: all, that is, except those to whom Evolution is the one Divinity, to whom a man is as irresponsible as a tree, to whom good means nothing but the pleasure which comes by nature, and evil nothing but the pain which comes by nature :—to all but these the problem how to reconcile disorder, cruelty, falsehood, misery, despair, with the nature and work of an all-powerful and all-good Creator, is an insoluble one. Let not Christians persuade themselves that they can solve it; but, if *they* cannot, neither, certainly, can others. We are taught that God hates and condemns and punishes moral evil; we are taught also that all things are of God, and all things include sinful men, and the ape and the tiger in them, and suffering creatures and the pain which the course of evolution, for a time at least, may be thought to have increased rather than lessened.

Whilst it is feeble and useless to delude ourselves with attempts to explain away this contradiction, it is entirely reasonable and our Christian duty to make the best of things, so far as we honestly and candidly can. Mr. Huxley's cue was to put the difficulty in its most baffling form. He is too hard, if I may venture to say so, on the cosmic process. For us it is wise and pious to see all the good in it; and we shall not find ourselves obliged to regard the instinct of self-assertion, the pursuit of pleasure, as essentially evil. Evil, for man who can know good and evil, does not consist in being simply moved by that instinct; it consists in being a slave to it, in allowing it to have the dominion over him. This pushing instinct we may see to have been the cause, not only of progress, but also of illimitable vital enjoyment throughout the creation. Even in the lower forms it has largely promoted concord and co-operation, with the happiness that springs from these sentiments and habits, as well as strife and mutual injury. And it will apparently remain the mechanical force—the steam or electric fluid—of human life; not evil when it is kept well under control, evil when the mastery over inner and outer conduct is conceded to it. So in economic life, it seems idle to expect that co-operation will ever supersede and exclude the competitive impulse; what we may hope is that this impulse will be made a servant and not a master. It is not evil that we should seek each man his personal happiness; but we do wrong when we make the pursuit of happiness the supreme law of our existence. The evil which we name sin is what ought to be essential evil to us; let us admit this to be as hard to dispose of intellectually in God's creation as it is to overcome it practically in the moral life. Pain, on the other hand, especially bodily pain, may be comparatively made light of. The world as we know it—and we can have no real knowledge of any different kind of world—is essentially a world of inequality, of degrees, of growth or development: a world in which we, the highest of visible creatures, are to live by hope and desire and effort. In such a world pain is an absolutely necessary ingredient. Nor can it be otherwise than unequally distributed. Equality is no Divine law. One of the most confusing of modern errors is the identifying of justice with equality. Equality is an idol from the worship of which we ought to try diligently to free ourselves. Our world, I say, is one of Degrees; everywhere there is a lower and a higher, a past and a future, something to leave behind, something before us to which we may aspire. Our God is the God of hope; and He obliges us to look down with disapprobation upon much of what has been and is, in order that we may reach forward with longing to that which may be.

The moral ideal which offers itself to Christians and draws them onwards is not a fleeting image, magnified by some imaginative faculty, of our own virtues; it is the perfect filial nature looking to the perfect Fatherly nature. We see this living and acting in the Son of God, Jesus Christ. He is "our Pattern, to live and to die." In Him we see with assurance what our Maker, being our Father, intends us to be. In Him we see justified those unselfish impulses which all are compelled to honour and which Nature cannot adequately explain. We see before each man, as he stumbles on with his continual and pathetic failures, the ideal of human perfection, in a life of perfect devotion to the heavenly Father and of perfect association with our fellow-men. We know nothing better than that; towards that fulness we may always aspire and strive.

Social man has been made, and is still making, partly by that process of evolution which Mr. Herbert Spencer explains to us, partly by influences such as those in which Mr. Huxley believes. In all this we Christians are taught to see the working of the Spirit of God. A Divine energy, brooding and creative, enlightening as well as impelling, breathes like a heavenly atmosphere around all human souls; and the better life, the pure happiness of each is in yielding to it and being inspired by it. Nature, or the inferior cosmic process, urging the individual to pursue his own pleasure, is controlled and used and turned to its own higher ends by the Divine Spirit. The influence of the Spirit strives, not against Nature so much as against man's inclination to submit himself to Nature, and offers him the emotions and affections which are proper to a child of God. What each man needs is not exclusively or primarily Stoical resolution, but the filial disposition which shows itself in reverence, shame, trust, admiration,—in the qualities which are not for the enlightened few only but which are redeeming and vivifying affections for every man and woman and child. From these may best be generated the persevering and ever-renewed effort, the defiant resolution, which the moralist demands. And with these a man may most happily adjust himself to the actual conditions of life,—to the disappointments, the sufferings, the perplexities and contradictions, by which none can fail to be tried. When we look at such trials with something of the faith and hope which the Gospel inspired in St. Paul, they can be regarded even with thankfulness as the discipline with which the eternal Father is training His spiritual children. All things may be seen to work together for good to them that love God. We are made for hope and progress, to turn our backs on the past and our faces towards the future. How else is it that the cries Onwards and Upwards, every trumpet-call of spiritual battle, all invitations to hope, seem to *find* us, and speak to us as from a heaven which cannot deceive? Let us not be too dull to be stirred, or too proud to be helped, by such encouraging voices.

The good to which we shall thus be led to cleave will give us the most wholesome knowledge of the evil which we are to abhor. If we hold the good and define it well, evil also will be sufficiently defined. We shall be armed against the sophistries which so easily excuse what is wrong and bad. Sensuality, stupidity, indifference, vanity—these and the like will be to us things which our Maker hates, because they are contrary to the better things to which He is calling us. What we have known of our God enables us to believe in a glory for which it is worth while to work and suffer and strive, in a development of membership, of harmony, of common joy, of intelligence and admiration, of which the

Spirit is even now giving us rudimentary earnests. What should be the courage and patience, the readiness to help and be helped, the loftiness of character and steadiness of purpose, of those who believe that the God of hope is thus leading them onwards?

XIII

THE CHURCH AS THE FLOCK OF CHRIST[1]

"I am the good shepherd."—St. John x. 11.

THERE is one distinction between the ways of Oriental sheep and those of the sheep we know, which it is important to bear in mind when we read what our Lord says about the shepherd and his sheep. In this country the shepherd drives the sheep before him, keeping them together by the help of his dog; in the East the sheep have themselves some of the habits of dogs, and know the shepherd's voice, and follow him. Those who travel in Palestine to-day may hear the shepherd calling a particular sheep by name, and may see the sheep recognising the voice and coming to him. The Lord Jesus brings pointedly into view this feature of the pastoral life of His country. The true shepherd, He says, calls his own sheep by name; he goes before them, and they follow him, for they know his voice. And a stranger will they not follow,

[1] Preached at St. Philip's, Waterloo Place, on the 19th April 1896 second Sunday after Easter.

but will flee from him, for they know not the voice of strangers.

So that in the action of the shepherd and of his sheep that great principle was represented, which is brought before us many times in our services for this morning,—the principle, I mean, that Christ leads, and His people follow. We are reminded to-day that we belong to Christ, as a flock to its owner; that He is the Shepherd and Overseer, the Pastor and Bishop, of our souls; that He has gone before us, on the path of devotion to the heavenly Father; that He seeks us when we wander, and would bring us back to safety and submission; that our duty and happiness are to hear His voice and to walk after Him in His steps.

There is another name by which the flock of Christ is more commonly known: it is called the Church, the Catholic or Universal Church. Christ, we say, is the Divine Pastor and Bishop of His flock the Church. There is nothing, it would seem, important or definite to be learnt from the name Church, whether in its English form or in the Greek word Ecclesia which Church represents. What the name of the Church brought to St. Paul's mind was an organised body; God, he says, put all things in subjection under the feet of Christ, and gave Him to be head over all things to the Church, which is His body. A shepherd leading and guarding and feeding his sheep, a head presiding over the limbs and organs of a body, a foundation-stone on which the stones of a building are laid and adjusted together,— these are the Scriptural images of Christ and His Church. The using of quite different images has the advantage of hindering us from resting in any one image and substituting it in our minds for the spiritual reality which the images are intended to help us to see and understand. We should not doubt, I think, that the close and entire dependence of the Church upon Christ is one spiritual fact prominently presented by these images, and not least by that of the Eastern shepherd and flock.

The images given us by our Lord and His Apostles hardly suggest "the Church" of those to whom the flock of Christ is a Queen sitting on an earthly throne, receiving the homage of her subjects, and ruling them with autocratic dominion. The Roman Catholics would not only accept, but would glory in, this view of the Church. The question, according to them, for every Christian is, as to his belief, what the Church bids him confess, and as to his action, what the Church bids him do. The Church's authority is absolute; the Church's voice settles everything without appeal. Such a view leads naturally enough to the acknowledgment of a chosen man sitting on the spiritual throne of the world, in whom the absolute authority of the Church is incarnate, and through whose lips the voice of the Church is heard. To obey the Pope is to obey the Church; to obey the Church is to obey Christ. To those who do not obey the Pope the Roman Catholics cry, "What will become of you, if you do not enter the fold of the Church? There is no salvation outside the Church; the primary duty of all men is to submit to the Church."

No one has thus exalted the Church with more enthusiasm than the distinguished Roman and English ecclesiastic whose life has proved so interesting to so many Anglican readers. Describing a certain priest with entire commendation, Cardinal Manning sums up his merits by saying that he was [1] "ecclesiastical in every way." This is a tribute that may justly be paid to the Cardinal himself, and he would have reckoned it as the highest praise that could be given to him. He was altogether ecclesiastical. Even in his earlier life, before his anxieties about his salvation drove him into what he was led to conclude was the safest—because the most imperious—of Christian communions, the Church was everything. After he had submitted to Rome, his enthusiasm for the infallible Church and the Papal authority exceeded that of almost all hereditary Roman Catholics. His object in life was to exalt the Church, to win subjects for the Church, to advance by all possible arts and labours the cause of the Church in this country. He was ecclesiastical in every way. Except in the Church he did not know where to look for Christ; the Holy Spirit could have no existence if it did not speak dogmatically through the voice of an organised body.

Now think of Christ and His flock—that is, of the way in which Christ Himself speaks of the Church of Christ. His sheep hear His voice and follow Him; but they are in great danger of falling victims to the thief or the wolf. The thief comes to steal and kill and destroy; the wolf snatches them and scatters them. He, the true Shepherd, defends them with His life; His hope is to draw from all the world sheep that will follow Him and

[1] *Life*, vol. ii. p. 269.

become one flock under one Shepherd. You can hardly by any effort think of this flock of Christ as ruling its own members with absolute authority; you cannot think of the sheep setting up for themselves and seeing it to be their duty to follow with unreserved submission a sheep of their own number. The figure of a Divine Queen, receiving the homage of her subjects and ruling them with despotic authority, will not suit the flock of Christ. Listen to what Faber, himself a convert from our Church to that of Rome, is moved to say or sing as he contemplates Christ and His flock:—

> Souls of men! why will ye scatter
>   Like a crowd of frightened sheep?
> Foolish hearts! why will ye wander
>   From a love so true and deep?
> Was there ever kindest Shepherd
>   Half so gentle, half so sweet,
> As the Saviour who would have us
>   Come and gather round His feet?

Is it possible to see, in the flock thus imagined, the infallible Mistress of mankind?

What the worshippers of the Church say as to the despotic dominion of the Catholic Church, and the necessity for each Christian of submitting to the authority and guidance of the Church, is said in the New Testament of the Lord Jesus Christ and the Holy Spirit. Reading the Apostolic records, we find ourselves invited to believe that Christ is actually the Shepherd of His flock, now as when He was visible in Galilee and Judæa. He is shown to us beginning His pastoral work as a visible Leader.

When He went up to Jerusalem to make His culminating sacrifice, He, the Shepherd, went before, and the Apostles and other disciples, His sheep, followed Him; they followed Him in simple dependence and obedience, awestruck, not understanding, keeping close behind their Shepherd. Jesus knew well how different it would be for them when He had gone out of their sight. With warnings, with remonstrances, with tenderest assurances of love, with definite and emphatic promises, He sought to prepare His followers for the different kind of fellowship with Him which was to be their lot when He had returned to His Father. If they could only believe it, He said, it would be better for them, His presence with them would be of a closer kind and more constant, when they should no longer see Him. At first all this pressing encouragement seemed ineffectual. The Shepherd was smitten, and the sheep of the flock were scattered abroad. They reeled under the first blow. But they were beginning to recover a little from the shock, when they were favoured with those appearances of their risen Master which gave them a stage of transition from the visible to the invisible Presence of Christ. When the Spirit of the Father and the Son came in power on the Day of Pentecost, they felt the promises of Christ to be fulfilled. Thenceforward the Apostles of Christ lived in the consciousness that He was leading them and they were following. By their labour and ministry He began to gather together His great flock in all the parts of the world, and the new sheep were taught that they had in Him an actual effective Shepherd, who made use of various ministries

The Church as the Flock of Christ

and labours, but parted with none of His own authority.

That such a confession, the acknowledgment of Christ as the living effective Shepherd of His flock, makes an immense demand on our faith, who would be inclined to deny? Every one knows something of the feeling which is so often expressed,—" Who will tell me definitely and with authority what I am to believe, what I am to do? New difficulties perplex me, where am I to go to get them solved ? If you say that Christ is my teacher, that the Holy Spirit is my guide, I feel almost as if I were mocked. Do you mean that if I put a direct question to Christ, I can count upon getting a direct answer?" It is beyond denial that immense demands *are* made upon our faith. No one escapes from such demands, not even by choosing once for all to submit to the Church of Rome. It is hard to believe that it is good for us that our faith should be strained as it is. But the call which Apostolical Christianity addresses to us, that we should look to Christ Himself as our living Shepherd, and yield to the soft pressures of the Holy Spirit, is one which honours us, which appeals to and awakens all that is highest and most truly human in us, which—*if* it may be trusted, if only it may be trusted!—has infinite promise in it. And has it not an answering witness in every heart? Can we not imagine that it may be good for faith to have arduous tasks laid upon it?

It is not to be supposed for a moment that the invisible Shepherd declines the use of visible agencies. It is the part of good sheep, of earnest and dependent followers of the Divine Shepherd, to accept all that has come down to them, all that surrounds them, all that happens to them, with the fullest presumption that through these things Christ is guiding and guarding them. Let us be bold to claim that sons and daughters of England and of the Church of England have right, if any have, to utter the Psalmist's thanksgiving, "The lot is fallen unto me in a fair ground, yea, I have a goodly heritage." It is right for us, let us not doubt, to begin with believing what our fathers have told us. If Christ and the Spirit lead us, they do it primarily through all that is true and good in our sacred traditions. No doubt, if we say this for ourselves, we are bound to say it also for those who inherit religions differing less or more widely from ours. Let us say it freely. It must be right for all human beings to be humble, reverent, responsive, slow to give up what they have been taught until something that they are convinced is better has been shown to them.

In many ways and by many agents, let us believe, the Divine Teacher is instructing us and drawing us after Himself. He does not use only ecclesiastical methods of instruction and influence. Let us never think of the Head of the Church as interested in religion alone. Ecclesiastics and ecclesiastical bodies have by no means proved themselves safe keepers of truth. Religion has been largely corrected and purified, under the discipline of Christ and the Holy Spirit, by secular convictions and instincts. The knowledge of justice or righteousness, in particular, and therefore of the God of righteousness, has been greatly developed by the influences of civil life. They who would be loyal to the Divine Shepherd must keep their ears open to all that witnesses of righteousness and truth, whether the testimony comes from expected or unexpected quarters. And they must bear in mind that His voice is addressed to the inner spirit, that it always seeks to awaken and constrain and win that which is most spiritual and therefore highest in them, that the question which life puts to them is whether they will be docile as spiritual beings to the suggestions which seem to speak with most authority to their most human consciousness.

In our own day the path of practical obedience —if not the acceptance of a creed—is much easier in many ways than it was when Christ offered Himself to his countrymen in Galilee and Judæa as the true Shepherd. Then, the Lord Jesus was painfully impressed—we may venture to say—by the sacrifices which His hearers would have to make if they resolved to follow Him. By His gracious words, and the yet more attractive gracious works with which He supported the words, multitudes were drawn to Him. Many were ready to push with a certain eager violence into the Kingdom which Jesus proclaimed. But to this readiness He gave no encouragement. He continually astonished the multitude by repelling their willingness to become His followers. He was always bidding them count the cost of what they proposed to do. Recall what we have just been hearing in the lesson: "There went with him great multitudes; and Jesus turned, and said to them, If any man cometh unto me, and hateth not his own father and mother and wife and children and brethren and sisters, yea, and his own life also, he cannot be my disciple." You must not suppose these words, and others like them, to have been spoken coldly, as a general instruction to Christians to be at least indifferent towards those whom Nature teaches them to love. No, indeed! that was no teaching of Jesus Christ. It was because He felt so strongly how deplorable it was that divisions in families should be caused by the following of Him, and yet saw so clearly that thus it must be, that He dwelt resolutely and bitterly upon what His true disciples would have to face. He deliberately made the worst, in paradoxical forms of expression, of the pains and efforts of discipleship, knowing that He was doing what in the long-run would be kindest to the eager people around Him. And he was moved also, we may be sure, by the consciousness of His own yearning desire to win followers; yes, followers, but of the right sort: not such as would acclaim Him King and then fall away from Him, not such as would say to Him Lord, Lord, and not do the things which He bade them; but such as came with childlike hearts to the Father in heaven, rejoicing to have their sins forgiven them, and to leave their sins behind them, followers who would face everything, privation, torture of body and of mind, death itself, to be true to Him.

We, my Christian brethren, have been born into better times. Let us have no scruple in thinking as well of our times as facts will allow us to do; let us not suppose that we have to adopt all New Testament language as fitting our own circumstances equally with those of the first believers in Christ. We ought to be glad and thankful to recognise whatever blessed changes the Kingdom of Heaven has wrought in the world. If the path of loyalty to Christ and surrender to the Father is easy to us, let it be easy. If we can combine a happy social life with our discipleship, let us do so by all means with reverent thankfulness. We are under no obligation whatever to make ourselves and those around us unhappy for the Kingdom of Heaven's sake.

Only, let us understand clearly the imperious Lordship of the Divine Shepherd. If we are willing to be of His flock, let us remember that He claims us to be His own, absolutely His own, and that He will not be satisfied with us unless we know Him and hear His voice and follow Him. We are not to hold that He wishes us to forsake the world, in the sense of refusing to have anything to do with its business, its politics, its enjoyments; how much less in the sense of sitting loose to domestic obligations! We are to hold, on the contrary, that the kingdom of the world is become the kingdom of our Lord and of His Christ. But let us not make the fatal mistake of concluding that Christ is less exacting, less imperious, now than when He bade the rich young man sell all that he had and give the price to the poor, and called upon His followers to desert their homes. Let us believe that He would have us take a part in the work of the world; but then we must work in loyal obedience to the principles of His kingdom. To the pure all things are pure; yes, to the pure! Every creature of God is good, and nothing is to be rejected, if it be received with thanksgiving; yes, but we must enjoy with free inward thankfulness to the Father of Jesus Christ. Let those who can regard a Christian walk as easy in this good Christian country of ours do so by all means; but there will be many more, I take it, who will sigh under its difficulty than be complacent as to its easiness. To some it may even seem that the comparative outward easiness increases the inward difficulty; that the Christian who is called to come out from amongst his neighbours and be separate, and face reproach and opposition, and make painful sacrifices, has really a less arduous spiritual task than he who has to be in the world and to join with sympathy in all the movements and customs of his class and yet not to be *of* the world. Not to speak of those religious teachers who have exhorted earnest Christians to flee into the desert or into conventual seclusion, there were pious men who warned our grandfathers that if they were truly Christ's they must renounce many of the pursuits of the world,— that the converted could not go to dances, or theatres, or races, or play at cards, could hardly hunt or shoot, could not enter into the strife of politics. Was a heavier burden, or a lighter, laid upon those who accepted such teaching with reverence than upon our children who are urged to conquer all things for Christ by sharing freely in all things? The Divine Taskmaster alone knows perfectly about the relation of the tasks which He assigns to the souls on which He lays them. But what we have to understand is that the law of Christ does *not* vary with circumstances. In every condition of the world the Divine Shepherd will claim the entire devotion of the spirit and—with that—the presenting of the body as a living sacrifice. Compromise has a place in the work of the world; but there is no compromise allowed in the serving of Christ. In every age those who do not follow Christ with perfect obedience are withholding something of what He claims, are wandering to their own peril, are losing a part of the true happiness of their existence.

The Jesus of the Gospels was infinitely gracious; what more gracious words do we know or can we imagine than those—" Come unto me, all ye that labour and are heavy laden, and I will give you rest"? But there was a strange loftiness also in His bearing. He was disdainful towards irreverent questioners, He flung fiery words in the faces of the false and hard, He would have all or nothing from those who were willing to give him something. And He bade His envoys imitate His own loftiness; they were to offer the kingdom as a blessing to their countrymen, but to shake off the dust from their feet as a testimony against those who refused it. Let us, my Christian brethren, not forget either the grace in the awfulness, or the awfulness in the grace, of our Saviour and Lord. Let us fear to resist that tender sustained pressure with which Christ, exalted on the Cross, sitting at the Father's right hand, is drawing our hearts unto Himself.

XIV

THE NATURE OF THE CHURCH CATHOLIC[1]

THE discussions which have been so rife during the last year or two concerning the unity of Christendom, and the kind of action by which union might be promoted amongst the separated bodies of Christians, have necessarily involved assumptions as to what the nature of the Church is; and they have also stimulated inquiry into the authority and the truth of such assumptions. We in England may be said to have inherited two principal definitions of the Church of Christ. 1. The Church is defined by some as consisting of the aggregate of those Christian communions which have preserved a valid succession from the Apostles, and which may, on that account, be regarded as representing the one Catholic Church of the earliest ages. 2. It is defined by others as consisting of all the persons, belonging to any communion, whom God sees to be truly converted and to have the right character of believers in Christ. These persons are sometimes

[1] From the *Churchman*, March 1896.

said to constitute the "invisible" Church—not that they are themselves invisible, for they are as visible as their fellow-Christians—but because they are a select portion of those who outwardly profess to be Christians, and no man can claim to see with certainty who they are that belong to this select portion. The view of the Church which I am about to advocate, as having advantages for present thought and action over these two, and as the true Apostolic view, may be thus summarily stated:

The Church is a Divine structure, consisting of Christ the Head, and of men as His ideal members: this ideal Divine organism is not identical with any existing society or combination of societies, but is the order and life which all Christian societies and their members imperfectly and inadequately represent, and into which it is appointed to them to grow, and the spiritual reality which binds them all in one.

The difficulties which make it hard for any Christians to apply their doctrine of the Church to the actual circumstances of Christendom are so well known that I need only touch upon them briefly. The Roman Catholic position has the advantage—so highly estimated as an attribute of doctrine at the present time—of being the most definite. The Church of Christ is the Papal Church, and the definition of the Papal Church is that it is governed by the absolute authority of the Pope. A Roman Catholic might hold that view with entire comfort if there were no other Christians besides Roman Catholics in the world. But what is he to make of the non-Papal Christian bodies—of our poor Church of England, for one? At the opposite pole, the view of Evangelical Protestants—that the Church of Christ consists of all truly converted Christians in every communion—has also a certain simplicity. I need not dwell on the arguments which may be brought against it: the chief real difficulty which besets it in our day goes to the heart of it. The belief in a class of converted Christians, separated by a change of nature from the fellow-Christians who look so like them, has almost ceased to be a living one. The Congregationalist inherits the doctrine that he and the fellow-members of his congregation know themselves and each other to belong to such a class; but it is hard for him to hold it. He will protest that he does not pretend to decide who are true believers and who are not; but he would also prefer not to have to answer the question whether there is a division between the true and the nominal believers—in fact and in God's sight—so deep that all on one side of it belong to the body of Christ, and all on the other side of it are separate from Christ. Anglican Catholics have their own difficulties. Making much of succession, they cannot help being impressed by the prestige of the Roman Church, which—if the question of corruption of doctrine and practice be put aside— must be admitted to hold the best position in Christendom as representing the old undivided Church. Many Anglicans, as we know, have been disturbed by doubts whether a Church openly rebelling against the see of Rome and excommunicated by that see, like our own, may not have cut itself off from the Church Catholic. If they fall back on doctrine and practice, and are convinced that the pretensions of the Pope are extravagant, and that in many other things Rome has wandered far from the ways of the primitive Church, they seem to be constituting themselves judges, and to be approaching dangerously near to the position of the Protestant bodies which care nothing for succession, but are ready to maintain, as they do with various degrees of plausibility, that each of them is the most faithful representative of Apostolical Christianity. These Protestant bodies must be a perpetual difficulty to the High Anglican of to-day. He knows something of them, and he is constrained to confess that they seem to be endowed with every Christian quality. The Protestant communities have learning, saintliness, zeal; they abound in good works; the devotion they show to Christ is rewarded with remarkable successes in the converting of the heathen; but they have not the Apostolical succession; therefore, they do not belong to the Church Catholic—that is, to the body of Christ. What can this mean and imply? Will Christ say to them, "I never knew you"? If not, what sort of relation have they to Christ? Is the spirit of Christ given as freely outside the Church as within it?—to those who do not belong to His body as to His members?

To the philosophical observer, contemplating Christianity from the outside, there is no problem in the multitude and variety of the Christian communions. He is familiar with the tendencies to variation, and can trace with more or less of sureness how each of these bodies began to diverge, and by what causes it has been led to become what it is. It may interest him to make out how much there is of common Christianity in the creeds and sentiments and practices of all these sections and subsections of Christendom. But we Christians are not so free. We inherit this name of the Church; and the idea of a One Church clings to our Christian minds, and refuses to be overpowered and extinguished by all the divisions which force themselves on our notice. This tenacity of the idea of the Church depends, as we may see, on our belief in *Christ*. All who believe in Christ as at the Father's right hand are obliged to think of Him as the Elder Brother of a family, the Head of a body or society, the King of a commonwealth. The One Lord gives a necessary unity of some kind to those who belong to Him.

And this is precisely the view of the Church which we find in the New Testament. The Church there is a dependency of Christ. The unity of the Church is not derived from any circumscribing line. It depends on Christ the Head.

All Christians, including the Roman Catholics, in their appeal to the past and to authority reach back and up ultimately to the New Testament. In this volume we find the words of Christ and His Apostles, the history of the beginnings of the Church, the rock whence we were hewn, the hole of the pit whence we were digged. The Roman Catholics claim, indeed, that the Church has been developed, and that this development has been under Divine guidance, and that the Church of to-day enjoys the advantages of delegated Divine authority as much as the Church of the Apostolic days—a claim which represents, in a perverted form, what ought to be the universal faith of Christians; but this claim does not bar the appeal to the New Testament as preserving for us the original and essential principles of Christianity and of the Church.

Going back, then, along the lines of the historical Church till we cross the threshold of the New Testament, we come upon the Church as the Apostles founded it and left it. At the close of the Apostolic age there were a number of societies scattered over the cities of the Roman world, the members of which had accepted Jesus the Crucified as Lord and Saviour, and had been moved by a Spirit which they believed to have come from heaven, from the Father and the Son. They had all been baptized into the name of Jesus—that is, into the name of the Son and the Father and the Spirit. They had received the Gospel, directly or indirectly, from the Apostles or Envoys of Jesus Christ—the Twelve and St. Paul—and they were under the absolute authority of the Apostles. Every society had for administration and guidance under the Supreme Authority elders or overseers appointed by the Apostles, and in general some ministers or servers also to do practical work. All these societies counted themselves branches of one body, as being all united to Christ, the one Head, and as being moved by the same Spirit. In addition to the one baptism by which every member was received into the body, all the members were accustomed to meet regularly for fellowship, and at their regular meetings they partook of a sacred ceremonial meal—the same in all the societies— which fed a common union to Christ. The name

"Church" (ecclesia) came into use for each society and for the whole body. We read constantly of the "Church" and the "Churches," and of the "brethren," the "saints," the "called," the "faithful," who are the members of the Church. Besides what they were told concerning Jesus Christ by their teachers, the believers were taught that the body to which they belonged came into existence on a certain Day of Pentecost, through the action of an overpowering Spirit, which brought thousands of strangers into joyous brotherhood and partnership.

It is obvious that a line might easily have been drawn round this Apostolic Church. Let this be conceded to those who insist that some circumscription must be found for the Church, to separate it from the rest of mankind. The Church consisted of all the Churches, and these of the members who had been admitted by the baptism, and had not separated themselves or been separated from the communion, which were the badges of the society. There were no Protestants, no Nonconformists, no sects of heretics, in the age of the New Testament. But there were many persons included amongst the members of the Church whom we are surprised to find the Apostles allowing to remain within the fellowship. St. Paul, it is evident, could not have thought of the body of Christ as having its sanctity created by the faith or graces of its members. He refers to misbelieving, to immoral, to insubordinate Christians, without showing any desire to drive them out of the Church. He nowhere gives the least hint of making a distinction in his own mind between the truly converted as constituting the body of Christ and the other merely professing Christians as not belonging to the body. Believing, as he did, in the holiness of the Church, he could not have regarded this holiness as identical with, or dependent upon, the purity and devoutness of its actual members.

St. Paul may be said to be the theological exponent of the doctrine of the Church amongst the New Testament writers; and his account of the Church is chiefly to be found in the Epistle to the Ephesians. In the first half of the epistle he sets forth the calling of Christians, and in the second half the duties which spring out of the calling. The idea of the Church is closely associated with the calling —the calling being the expression of the eternal Divine purpose. The Apostle saw in Christ God choosing men to be His children, holy and without blemish before Him in love. That this purpose might be carried out, the Son of God was manifested, died, was raised to the Father's right hand, to be the Head of this family of God. Every one who accepted the Gospel was taken into this family; was joined to Christ as a member of His body. But the reality and perfectness of the family, the society, the body, were in God's purpose and idea. That which St. Paul saw in the Church was what God had made and was making. And he could, therefore, contemplate the Church without qualification as a perfect body with perfect members. The actual Christians and their societies had all sorts of deformities and weaknesses. But it was God's design that individual members and the several Churches should grow into the perfection of the ideal Church, of the family which God had prepared, of the body which was the proper fulness or completion of the Divine Head. The various institutions and provisions of Christian Church life were given in order that the actual imperfect members might be nourished, and trained, and adjusted into their proper forms and places.

I do not deny that there is a certain difficulty in forming a mental conception of this ideal Church—a Church which is more real than any actual society, because it is God's purpose and creation; but the difficulty seems to me to be of the same kind as that of all our truest theological thoughts. And I offer two or three considerations which may perhaps diminish the difficulty. (1) Christ, contemplated as we know Him, has the ideal Church, so to say, attached to Him. It makes a great difference whether we are looking about for a separate Divine Church on the earth, or are letting Christ in heaven suggest and bring home to us the Church which is His body. Christ evidently sought to hinder His followers from thinking of Him by Himself. He desired to be associated by them, on the one hand with the Father, on the other hand with mankind. It was a main part of the purpose of His coming, that He should attach men to Himself, and Himself to men. We know Him most truly when we contemplate Him as the Son of the Father and the Head of His body. And the body, thus regarded as completing Christ, becomes easily to our minds ideal, spiritual, prophetic: a vision of what should be and is to be, not made by our imaginations, but discerned in the will of God by our faith. (2) Again, it may be helpful to place the Church by the side of the kingdom of Christ, or of God, or of heaven. During the last generation or two we have been learning how much Christians have lost by falling into a way of identifying the kingdom of heaven with happiness after death. It is generally recognised now that the establishment of the heavenly kingdom on the earth is the key to the Gospel narrative. It is sometimes said that the kingdom of Christ is the Church; and there is substantial truth, I think, in the identification. The kingdom by no means occupies in the Acts and the Epistles the place which it does in the Gospels; and where it does occur, we might sometimes perhaps, without injury to the sense, substitute the Church for it. But this could not always be done. The name retains its own proper meaning, and suggests the ideas associated with a kingdom and commonwealth. It should set us thinking of the King, Christ the representative of God, the Son of the Father; of the laws, which are the impulses of the Spirit of Christ; of the franchises and possessions, which are spiritual; of the subjects, who are admitted into it and bound to be loyal to its authority and brotherly with their fellow-citizens; of the territory, which is the world of human feeling and action. We are referring to the same condition of things, whether we speak of Christ as the head of His body the Church, or as the Prince of the heavenly kingdom. And it seems to me that the idea of the heavenly kingdom, with Christ reigning in it upon the earth as King of kings and Lord of lords, does not demand or invite that circumscription and definition of its subjects which the idea of the Church has been thought to make necessary. (3) A third consideration is, that a parallel may be found for the ideal Church and the actual Church or Churches, in the ideal Christian and the actual man. Take such statements as those of St. John: "Whosoever abideth in Him sinneth not: whosoever sinneth hath not seen Him, neither knoweth Him." "Whosoever is begotten of God doeth no sin, because His seed abideth in Him; and he cannot sin, because he is begotten of God." A reader who knows the actual only must be perplexed by such sayings; he will understand the Apostle as implying that there are certain persons, the truly regenerate, who never fall into sin; as dividing mankind between the class of sinless persons, the children of God, and the class of sinners, the children of the devil. But he finds the same Apostle protesting, "If we say that we have no sin, we deceive ourselves, and the truth is not in us." What St. John means is, that the true son of God does not sin, and cannot sin. He knows that in the actual human beings whom the Father has called His children, there is also another nature different from that of the child of God. What St. John wishes to impress upon his Christian reader is that, when he sins, he is denying his true self, is violating the nature which he has received of the Father. It is right and well that sinful human beings should be called children of God; it is most desirable that every Christian should account himself a son of God. There is always the true man, of God's making, accompanying the imperfect sinning man; and to this ideal man the actual man must strive to conform himself. As Milton says in his grand style: "He that holds himself in reverence and due esteem, both for the dignity of God's image upon him and for the price of his redemption, which he thinks is visibly marked upon his forehead, accounts himself both a fit person to do the noblest and godliest deeds, and also much better worth than to deject and defile, with such a debasement and such a pollution as sin is, himself so highly ransomed and ennobled to a new friendship and filial relation with God" (*The Reason of Church Government*, chap. iii.). It seems not unlikely that when our Lord said of little children, "Their angels do always behold the face of My Father which is in heaven," He meant by the "angel" the spiritual double, the ideal heavenly form, of the earthly person.

If, then, we think of the One Catholic and Apostolic Church as the ideal Divinely-created organic structure into which actual Churches and their earthly members are to grow, how shall we be led to regard existing Christendom and its many Christian communions?

1. Our faith will be less shocked and disturbed by the split-up condition of Christendom. I say "less," than if we felt ourselves bound to identify the Bride of Christ with some one of the existing communions, or with the aggregate of so many of them, or with a body of select persons more or less hidden in them. There must be much to trouble us in the sight of Christian bodies disowning each other, as there is in the defects and faults of every Christian body, and in the immense non-Christian world still unconquered at the end of the nineteenth century. But we shall not refuse to see some advantages—as we often have to recognise with thankfulness good coming out of evil—that appear to result from

separation and diversity. Functions and powers of the kingdom of God, which might have been otherwise dormant, have been developed through the special energies and special adjustments to environment set going by the separateness of communions. The Christianity of the world may be perceived to be larger and richer than it might be if it were the religion of a single well-disciplined body. We are freed from the painful supposed duty of judging and disowning great Christian societies, and are encouraged, on the contrary, to discern all the good we can in them.

2. It is natural to members of the Church of England to value highly succession and order and authoritative institutions. Whilst there is nothing to forbid our admitting that the Church of Rome has advantages not possessed by ourselves or by the non-Episcopalian communions, we may reasonably congratulate ourselves on having Episcopacy with an unbroken succession, the Sacraments, the inheritance of the Christian literature of all ages. It may rightly seem to us a great gain that Christian Churches should be as national as possible. We may hold and contend that the kingdom of Christ is best established in any part of the earth where the ancient order has been preserved and the organised nation of the land worships God and cleaves to Christ in a Church of its own. But all that we may be obliged to protest against and to condemn in the Churches of Rome or of Eastern Europe will not bind us to " unchurch " them, or to pronounce them separated from Christ.

3. But we shall follow the whole stress of the

New Testament in looking reverently for the fruits of the Spirit, in person and society, and holding them to be trustworthy credentials of fellowship with Christ. Christ bade His followers "beware of false prophets." How were they to discern them? Did Christ say, "Take care that any one who undertakes to teach and guide you shall show himself to be authorised by Me, or by the Apostles whom I commission as My representatives"? The criterion He gave was, "By their fruits ye shall know them." Nothing could be more marked or definite than the commission which Christ gave to the Twelve. They knew themselves to have His commission, and they felt even their number to be important, and as the Twelve they ruled the Pentecostal Church. But if Christ had charged His followers, "Listen to no one but the Twelve, or those whom the Twelve may ordain," they would have been bound to treat St. Paul as a false prophet. Saul of Tarsus did, indeed, excite suspicion and misgivings in the Twelve and their adherents. He appeared outside of Christ's order, rendered no allegiance to the Twelve, took his stand on the commission he had received in a vision, and claimed to be known and judged by his fruits. His credentials, he boldly declared, were the Churches he founded—these and his own manifest integrity and devotion. The irregular Apostle did a greater work in spreading the kingdom of Christ than all the regular Apostles together. It is important, however, to notice that St. Paul was not indifferent to the unity of the Church. He laboured zealously and successfully to keep his Churches in fellowship with those of the Twelve. What more impressive testimony could we have than St. Paul and his work, that by the will of Christ there should be room amongst Christians for unauthorised service and leadership? Christ made solemn choice and appointment of the Twelve, and then, without giving any explanation or notice to the Twelve, sent a thirteenth, whom they were to accept as a colleague against their first surprise and misgivings, because they could not help seeing that he was doing Christ's work and had the Spirit with him. Such warrant have we for acknowledging the presence of Christ and the Spirit with the Christian societies which reject one part or another of the traditional order of the Church. We know these societies by their fruits.

4. Our own Church we may thankfully and reverently perceive to have a peculiarly important place amongst the aggregate of the Christian bodies. It is a great Church, with special privileges, and we may humbly hope that its work in the world is not altogether unworthy of it. But it is further important through the middle place in which it stands. If an unfriendly critic might taunt the Church of England with being neither one thing nor the other, neither loyally Catholic nor frankly Protestant, we shall prefer to believe that it is both. And it may be for the advantage of Christendom that we should not throw in our lot either with those to whom succession and order are everything, or with those to whom a Church is a collection of persons who happen to agree in the deductions they draw from the New Testament.

5. Lastly, if the perfect Church of Christ is

represented on the earth by those many inadequate and fragmentary and transitory bodies which profess loyalty to the one Lord and Saviour, and if each of the bodies has life and truth in proportion to its real loyalty to Christ the Head, then the royal road to unity must be through each drawing closer to Christ as a member to the Head. To be open to the light of Christ and so to drop errors, to study what the Son of man will approve in policy and conduct, to weigh interests and values in the scales of God, to understand that the aim of all Christians and of all Christian societies must be to grow into perfect fellowship with Christ—these are the ways of progress for the bettering of each Church in itself and for the uniting of Church to Church.

XV

REUNION [1]

In any consideration of the question of the Reunion of Christendom, the intermediate position of our own Church will be felt to have special interest and importance. We stand between the Church of Rome on the one side and the non-Episcopalian communions on the other. I am not forgetting the Eastern Churches, or their high claims on our sympathy and respect; but we in England are less closely in contact with these than with the great Latin Church and the Protestant bodies which have dispensed with the Episcopal succession. Those of us who yearn for reunion are looking, as our leanings incline us, either towards Rome, or towards non-Episcopalian Protestantism; we are considering on what terms we might consent to be joined again in some way to the Roman Church, or by what concessions any Protestant communions might be induced to coalesce with the English Church.

I think it will be universally admitted that negotiations aiming at actual reunion on either side are at the present time quite hopeless. As regards

[1] From the *Churchman*, December 1896.

Rome, *Roma locuta est.* The demands of the Papal See are more exacting than ever. Leo XIII. is the most benevolent of Popes, most anxious to commend himself and his Church to all non-Papal Christians; but in his recent Encyclical letter on the Unity of the Church he declares as positively as possible that he will hear of nothing on the part of those who are now separated from Rome but absolute submission to the chair of St. Peter, absolute acceptance of every dogma affirmed by the Vatican Council. And there is no movement in the Roman Catholic Church pretending to overbear the personal authority of the Pope. Anglicans may go over to Rome individually, as they have done; of no other way of reunion can they entertain at present the slightest hope. Nor is there any desire of corporate reunion with the Anglican Church, here, or in the Colonies, or in the United States, stirring in any single Nonconformist communion. Dissenters find it a simple matter to join the Church, and this way of reunion is the only one thought of.

At the same time it is reasonably urged that aspirations after reunion cannot be without effect; that if the sense of the unchristian nature of schisms in Christendom is growing deeper and more acute in Christian minds, such a feeling must be a breath of the Spirit of Christ; and that it is most desirable that we should let our hopes play freely about ideals of Church Unity. Ah, yes! Christians ought surely to be intolerant of disunion amongst professing Christians; they ought to be convinced that there is something wrong, something to be corrected, if believers in Christ cannot worship and labour in unison. I know what the sectarian spirit has found to say. This is the language it is accustomed to use : " It is no doubt very deplorable that there are so many of those who call themselves Christians who do not entertain right views in religion ; the fact is a mystery, and not the only mystery in human existence ; but truth is truth, and, whether those who hold the truth are many or few, the truth must be maintained firmly and without compromise ; those who have been taught by Christ and the Spirit cannot consent to associate with themselves any who have not been thus taught." What can sound more plausible? Thus have churches and sects and cliques wrapped themselves in cloaks of self-complacent separatism. But it is one good thing in our age, that the bulwarks set up to divide Christians from one another are being undermined. In all denominations we are not so sure of ourselves ; we see in those who are not of our communion signs of truth, proofs of goodness, which forbid us to assume that Christ has not taught them, that His Spirit has not moved in them. The Pope may still be obliged to tell us that he is very sorry, but he can only regard us as rebelling against Christ so long as we decline to accept the minutest particulars of what the Church of Rome teaches ; but good Roman Catholics do not feel like that. And we of the Church of England are happily not bound to "unchurch" Roman Catholics—whatever unchurching may mean. You may easily meet with delightful instances of intimate Christian fellowship between Anglicans and Roman Catholics, the letter of repulsion proving powerless against the spirit of attraction. And as regards Dissenters, when we see our High Churchmen, including bishops and archbishops, inviting dissenting ministers to join them in prayer-meetings, we want no other proof that Christian union can live and work underneath denominational differences.

The desire of reunion with Rome may indeed mean nothing but uneasy misgivings as to the safety of our Anglican position. Those who are always dwelling on the "Nulla salus extra ecclesiam" may well be anxious to know for certain what the true Ecclesia is. The question, "Is the Church of Rome the true Church or not?" has haunted and troubled many Anglicans until they have succumbed to the pretensions of the Church which at all events claims, as no other does, to be the one only Church of Christ. And those who cannot bring themselves to the point of going over would find comfort in getting their Church recognised in some way by Rome. But with this kind of craving for reunion I do not deal. I assume that we here are interested in, and sympathise with, that nobler Christian longing, which is troubled by the divisions of Christendom as violating the unity for which Christ prayed. As I have said, we can find no encouragement in the signs of the times to pursue any scheme of corporate reunion. But we do find encouragement, wonderful encouragement, to follow after Christian fellow-feeling, by cherishing a common belief that Christ is seeking all men, a common tenderness towards each other's pious prepossessions, a common desire and hope that all the world may be subdued to Christ. In that direction, we may confidently believe, Christ is pointing.

I can understand its being doubted whether it is

desirable to get over the repugnance to popery and the dread of Papists which have been the traditional instincts of Protestants. Such a change of feeling is a very serious matter, and mere indifference to dogma is not a state of mind in which earnest Christians can find comfort. But where Christ leads it is safe to follow, even if the path is an untried one. And to the simple and teachable Christian mind there is a great deal that is attractive and of high promise amongst Roman Catholics at the present time. There is a new interest in the Scriptures, a new desire to get at their real meaning, which may inspire the best hopes. And in a multitude of pious lives we may see that what is dominant, what is vital, is that devout, over-mastering reverence for the true Christ which makes all Christians one. With that it cannot but be right to sympathise; and when any mutual approach between Roman Catholics and ourselves is prompted by Christian sympathy, we shall not think it necessary to guard ourselves from misunderstanding or infection by some solemn repudiation of Romish error. The one thing that offers the best promise for the future is that in every section of Christendom hearts should be increasingly drawn towards Christ and increasingly influenced by the Spirit of Christ. It does not matter so much that errors of belief should remain in the formal profession, if they are tending to drop out of the real religion of those who profess them. Churches and denominations are terribly clogged with the mistakes of past generations, and it is difficult to see how false doctrines are to be got rid of; but the first necessity is that they should wither and grow dead—which is a thing that may easily happen.

But if Christians in all Churches and sects were to be moved to cultivate spiritual sympathy and mutual respect towards each other in Christ, might not this disposition tend to make them satisfied with a Christendom cut up into a multitude of denominations, and be dangerous to belief in that unity of the Church on which stress is undoubtedly laid by the Apostles, as well as by all the later Fathers of the Church? The fear of such an influence has given birth to that pathetic pleading on behalf of the unity of the Church which the Pope has addressed to the Christian world in his recent Encyclical letter. This manifesto is a declaration against the possibility of any kind of union of Christians except under one absolute earthly government. There is nothing new in the Pope's doctrine concerning the Church; he asserts, as he could hardly help doing, that there is but one Church, that the Roman Church is the one Church, that all who do not belong to it are cut off from the grace of Christ, and that if they call themselves Christians they are rebels against Christ; but we seem to trace in this letter a new shrinking from the old sentiment and language of Rome about non-Roman Christians. And there is a certain novelty also, if I am not mistaken, in the ground of the Pope's argument. "Christ the Lord," he says, "instituted and formed the Church; wherefore, when we are asked what its nature is, the main thing is to see what Christ wished, and what, in fact, He did. . . . It is so evident, from the clear and frequent testimonies of Holy Writ, that the true Church of Jesus Christ is one, that no Christian can dare to deny it. But in judging and determining the nature of this unity many have erred in various ways. Not the foundation of the Church alone, but its whole constitution, belongs to the class of things effected by Christ's free choice. For this reason the entire case must be judged by what was actually done. We must, consequently, investigate not how the Church may possibly be one, but how He who founded it willed that it should be one." That is precisely the modern method of inquiry, commonly called the historical method. And it is the Protestant method also, inasmuch as the appeal is to Holy Writ. And the inquiry to which the Pope invites us is of primary interest to all who are thinking about reunion. For we are anxiously asking ourselves what we are to make of a Christendom divided as we behold it. Is the one Church of Christ conceivable except as a single organised community? Is it the first thing for a Christian to do, to find out which of the competing communions is the true Church, and to "unchurch" all the rest? Or is it safe to hold that a Christian ought to respect the particular calling he has received in his birth, and that his first duty is to believe in and follow Christ to the best of his knowledge and power in the denomination into which he has been born? Let us welcome this appeal of the Pope. We cannot do better than go with him to the New Testament, to see what we can learn as to the original making and form of the Church.

But the Pope soon disappoints us sadly. To find out about the Church of the first days, we should look as a matter of course to the Acts, the Epistles, the Revelation; but all this larger part of the New Testament the Pope ignores, as completely as if he did actually in the more proper sense of the word ignore it—as if he was entirely unacquainted with it. He quotes the familiar words addressed by our Lord to St. Peter: "Upon this rock I will build My Church"; "I have prayed for thee that thy faith fail not"; "Feed My sheep." Disregarding his own principle, he lays down *a priori* that "Christ must have given to His Church a supreme authority, to which all Christians must render obedience"; that Christ "was obliged, when He ascended into heaven, to designate a vicegerent on earth"; and then he concludes that the supreme authority which Christ was bound to delegate was given to Peter and to his successors. "God confided His Church to Peter, so that he—Peter—might safely guard it with his unconquerable power"; "Jesus Christ appointed Peter to be the head of the Church; and He also determined that the authority instituted in perpetuity for the salvation of all should be inherited by his successors, in whom the same permanent authority of Peter himself should continue." But the Pope does not go on to exhibit to us even Peter, whilst he lived, exercising authority over the universal Church, and guarding it with his unconquerable power. What we do see in the sacred history is a very different state of things: we see Paul founding the Gentile Churches, defiantly declaring that he holds no commission from the Twelve, rebuking Peter, claiming to be the autocrat of his own Churches. The Pope makes no allusion to all this. Certainly nothing that Roman Catholics can say can explain away the fact that neither in the Acts, nor in the Epistles, nor in the Revelation, is there a single hint that St. Peter had any authority over St. Paul or St. Paul's churches.

To all Christians, and not only to Roman Catholics, there must be something very surprising and not easy to account for in the calling and ministry of St. Paul. It is undeniable that Christ in the Gospels bestows on the Twelve a most definite commission and a special training; that He promises them the twelve thrones of His kingdom; that He gives them much tender and solicitous instruction about the work they were to perform as His representatives and envoys. The Pope adds something, with the usual Roman freedom, to the facts when he says, "To the Apostles and their legitimate successors alone these words have reference: 'Go ye into the whole world to preach the Gospel'; 'Baptizing them'; 'Do this in commemoration of Me'; 'Whose sins you shall forgive, they are forgiven them.' And in like manner He ordered the Apostles only, and those who should lawfully succeed them, to feed —that is, to govern with authority—all Christian souls."

But it is evident that on the Day of Pentecost and for some time after the Apostles understood their commission as giving them jointly supreme authority over the Church, and that their authority was recognised without question. But in course of time Saul of Tarsus appears on the scene. He was not one of those to whom the Lord Jesus had given the special apostolic commission. He declared that he had a commission given to him directly from heaven. The Twelve were not informed by their Master that He was giving to another an extraordinary apostolic commission; and—as we should have expected— they regarded him who claimed this appointment with some suspicion and jealousy. St. Paul, for his part, desired to be as a Christian brother with the Twelve, but he would in no way put himself under them. After a while it was recognised by the Apostles and the Church in general that Saul or Paul had a calling from Christ to carry the Gospel to the Gentiles; and he did his work with such effect as to found churches, which included Jews and Gentiles, in a multitude of Gentile cities. He earnestly desired to preserve unity with the Christians of Judæa, and with the Apostles to whom they looked up; but he maintained his absolute independence. And he was led to do this with the more emphasis because his position gave great offence to many followers of the Twelve, and they denounced him as an unauthorised teacher, who rebelled against the authority which Christ Himself had set up in His Church. St. Paul's defence, as we know, was that his churches were themselves his credentials.

Well, then, when we ask Holy Writ to tell us what Christ willed and actually did in founding and constituting the one Church, it presents to us a number of societies, one section of which is subject to St. Peter and the Apostles, to whom Christ in His lifetime gave plenary authority and power, and the other to St. Paul, who professed to have received a commission of his own from Christ in heaven.

The Pauline Churches were in fellowship with the Petrine, but on a footing of independence and equality. That was the state of things which existed during the active period of St. Paul's Apostleship. It would seem that Christ, when He had sanctioned the principle of formal regularity and order in appointing the Twelve, and keeping the Church subject to them for some time, chose to violate that principle surprisingly and conspicuously in the interest of direct heavenly action and spiritual life, by making an irregular Apostle the greatest and most successful of the founders of the Church. I do not know what we can infer from this actual choice and operation of Christ, by which the Pope so rightly lays down that we should be guided, but these two conclusions: (1) That order and succession and transmitted authority are good; (2) that they are not so good as the Spirit and life.

St. Paul stands before us unmistakably a Divine exception, a heavenly justification of irregularity, an authoritative intimation that God may choose to interfere with His own ordinance. And we may find a great deal in human history that answers to this revelation. From all parts there arises evidence that order and transmitted authority cannot guarantee to men goodness and life; nay, that with all the benefits which it belongs to them to bestow, they have a dangerous tendency to ally themselves with lifelessness and corruption. The best external order may tempt men to look to it, rather than to God. Our Lord and those whom He called had known the Jewish priesthood, and had seen to what ungodliness the sacred institutions of Israel might be made to minister; and must we not believe that Christ foresaw that it would not be well for His Church that it should become one organised body, governed by one external authority? Let us thank the Pope for so emphatically putting before us the living action of Christ for our guide; and let us consider what was implied for the instruction of the future Church when He that wrought for Peter unto the Apostleship of the circumcision, wrought for Paul also unto the Gentiles.

Meditating on the true unity of the Church, in judging and determining the nature of which many —as the Pope says—have erred in various ways, let us note that Christ did not set up a vicegerent to rule the Church and the nations; that He kept the supreme authority in His own heavenly hands; that when the Twelve were actually governing the whole Church, in the belief that they had received from their Master a commission to do so, He did not will that this order should become universal and permanent, but sent another Apostle out of due course to be independent of the Twelve, and to labour more abundantly and with more success than they all; that it may be called a law of God's kingdom that, when order grows stagnant, life is brought in some irregular way from above; that no regulated credentials, no authorised transmission of power, should be so sacred to God's children as His own Spirit working in the hearts and lives of men.

If we can believe in Christ as the living Head, we may take His one body to be something more perfect than any of the earthly organisations by which it is so imperfectly set forth, and may see a true limb of the body in each of these organisations, just in so far as it is faithful to Christ and instinct with His Spirit. We are under no compulsion to circumscribe any one or more of the societies which profess allegiance to Christ, and to force upon ourselves the distasteful conclusion that Christ owns all within the circle, and disowns all without it. For ourselves of the Church of England, we may rightly prize and hold fast all the advantages that have come down to us, and especially our Church's unbroken history and national form, so long as these do not move us to arrogance, but to thankfulness and a desire to serve. I believe that St. Paul would say to each Christian society, See that you fill your place in the one body of Christ through earnest obedience to the Head, and submission of your hearts to the Spirit, and wait the time of Christ for such readjusting of the Churches as may be necessary to the perfect organisation of Christendom.

XVI

THE BIBLE AND THE CHURCH[1]

IF a number of persons belonging to our communion were to be asked, "How is it determined for you what in matters of religion you are to believe and to do?"—some would answer, "I receive my directions from the Bible"; others, "I receive mine from the Church." The adherent of the Church would be ready at the same time to speak with the utmost deference of the Bible; with more hesitation, and probably not without a cautious definition of the Church to safeguard the admission, the adherent of the Bible would admit that we owe much to the Church. To the Protestant, the Bible has primary and absolute authority, and the Church holds a strictly subordinate place; to the Catholic, the authority of the Church comes first, and the Church is the keeper and interpreter of the Bible.

There is a third answer that may be given to the question I have supposed to be asked, representing what I should venture to call a more excellent way. A Christian may fitly profess, "I look to the living

[1] Read at the Church Congress at Folkestone, 4th October 1892.

God as the source of the directions I receive for thinking and doing. His teaching has come, and still comes, through various channels; but I am bound to think of God Himself as the one supreme Teacher and Director, who keeps the instruction of His children in His own hands, and uses agents and methods according to His will."

Such a profession of faith would be pushed aside by many with a feeling of impatience. They would admit with due solemnity that God is the supreme Teacher and Director; but the practical question, they would promptly urge, is how He makes His mind known. "He Himself is out of our reach in heaven; where is His oracle on earth? If God's teaching is to be of any use to men, there must be some instructor on earth to whom they may go as to God's delegate." And some virtually say, "The Bible is *our* representative of God"; and others, "The Church is *our* representative of God." But is not God making it clear to us in this age, that He will have no power or person or thing to be a substitute for Himself, either to the conscience of Christendom or to the conscience of the individual Christian? If people will object that it is not practical to refer to God in heaven as our Teacher and Director, is it at all more practical to appeal to the Bible or to the Church? Whilst men were asserting for the Bible an exclusive infallibility, seekers after truth and reality have been led on to scrutinise this substitute for God, with the result that the priceless volume which has been deified by the Protestant world can no longer be worshipped as an infallible idol. The Bible seems to be failing us in these days; because it has been used as God will not have it used. Is it practical, again, to make *the Church* an oracle? Let us leave to the Roman Catholic the comfort he enjoys in having a Pope to give infallible utterances: but we Anglicans, if we depend on the living Voice of the Church for infallible direction, have a hardly soluble problem confronting us in the question where we are to find that Voice, and through what organ it is to be heard. Till there is more agreement amongst us as to the mouth by which the Church speaks, we do not gain much by holding that the Church speaks with infallible authority.

If we have any ear for what the living God is saying, we shall hear Him warning us in these days with an emphasis which compels us to listen, that there is no infallibility for us except in Himself, and that He will tolerate no substitute for Himself in the region of spiritual apprehension. It is an awakening lesson, if we have faith for it. In the light of this teaching we shall see that the first step in considering the authority of the Bible and that of the Church and the relation between the two is to have done with the assumption of any infallibility inhering in either. What, then, is the Bible? and what is the Church? Not substitutes for God, but instruments through which we believe, agencies used for our instruction and discipline by the one infallible Instructor.

There can be no merit or piety in blinding ourselves; it cannot be disloyal or irreverent towards God to look with as searching a gaze upon the Bible and the Church as upon the natural creation. The more searchingly we consider them, so long as it is with a reverent faith in God, the more likely we are to understand and appreciate their designed value and power and their appointed functions. The Bible, it is evident, is not in form a manual of faith and practice; it is a collection of various kinds of literature, each piece of which had what seemed at the time of its composition a natural origin—unless we are to except from this statement the Apocalyptic portions of it, which wise Christians have never valued more than a Gospel or one of St. Paul's letters. According to the old titles, the two volumes of Holy Scripture are the select literature of the two Covenants respectively. In various ways they help us to understand the revelation which God gave of Himself, first in the history of the Jewish race, and then in the coming of Christ and His exaltation to His kingdom. The New Testament leaves Christ, the Son of God and Son of man, reigning in the spiritual kingdom newly established for Him in heaven and on earth. The worth of the Bible is in the knowledge which it enables us to gain of God, of Christ, and of the Kingdom. According to our Christian belief, Christ has been reigning since the New Testament volume was closed, and is reigning now; we are subjects in His kingdom. There might, conceivably, be a select literature of this continuing reign of Christ; there is no such collection, and it is not probable that there ever will be; but if there were, it would be another volume of sacred records, and it might be called the Book of the Church. Such an imaginary book suggests to our minds the materials of which it would be composed; and we can see that it would incorporate the institutions and liturgies, the historical crises, and the theology, of the Church. From this point of view, the *antithesis* between the Bible and the Church tends to disappear and to resolve itself into a succession. The Scriptural books of selected records have been followed in the Divine order by a series and accumulation of records from which no recognised selection has been made. "The Church" often means chiefly this accumulation of sacred institutes of the Kingdom of Christ, the comprehensive tradition of the kingdom, the Christian ministry and sacraments, the history and the religious literature of the Christian ages. By means of the Biblical records, and by means of these various expressions of the Divine mind and will which have been given in the developing of Christ's kingdom, God, we hold, is teaching and training the Christian people of to-day.

What, then, are the authorities to which we owe deference as Christians and members of the Church of England? That authority, I should reply, has the first title to guide us, which commends itself to us most impressively, which is backed most strongly by circumstances, which seems for each and at the time to be most charged with the Voice of God, and which promises to bring us nearest to God. In any consideration of the authorities by which we are directed in believing and doing, that which rules us with the most of power and right ought not to be passed by without notice: I mean the authority of parents, including in a subordinate degree—according to the exposition of the fifth commandment given us in the Catechism—that of all whom the constitution of society sets over us. It is natural for children to think as their parents do, and to imitate them; and as soon as they begin to know anything about duty, the primeval command teaches them that they are bound to honour father and mother by rendering to them respect and obedience. The most fanatical Christian would not deny that the child of Mussulman parents ought to begin by trying to be a good Mussulman like his parents. Yet we do not regard parents as infallible. Here, then, we see the Divine principle as to authority in general, and the deference due to it, illustrated. It is not uncommon, nor is it an ungracious sign, for a young child to assume his father to be infallible. But as he grows older, he becomes aware of other authorities which prove his father to be fallible; and when he is well brought up, he is led to believe in a perfect God, whose will he is to find out by all ways that are open to him, and then to obey with absolute submission. The true man, as the child of God, defers to any authority which he finds to be claiming his respect and obedience, until he becomes aware of some other which he feels to be teaching him something better, and which he recognises as having a superior right over him.

> Lord, with what care hast Thou begirt us round!
> Parents first season us; then schoolmasters
> Deliver us to laws; they send us bound
> To rules of reason.

English children for many generations have had the Bible held up to them by their parents and teachers as the supreme authority for belief and conduct, and the Bible, when they have studied it, has won for itself their reverence. They have also been trained to respect the clergyman and the Prayer-Book—the clergyman chiefly as expounding the Bible, the Prayer-Book as agreeing with the Bible; and the Church of England, represented by the clergyman and the Prayer-Book, has been eulogised to them as an eminently Scriptural Church. Of the Church Catholic the Protestant generations have not known much. But Roman Catholics, and of late years Anglo-Catholics, have been trained in their childhood to look up to the Church, chiefly at first in the person of the priest and in the ceremonies of religion, as the authority directing them what to believe and to do. God, we are constrained to say, has been directing Protestants through the Bible, Catholics through the Church. In either case God ought to have been seen from the first as above the Bible and above the Church; but it has been a natural error to make the Bible or the Church a substitute for God, and to appeal to the one and the other as ultimate and infallible guides. Of this error the study of the Bible and of the Church should be the best corrective. The records of the two Covenants are throughout bearing witness of God—of God who called out Abraham, and governed and taught Israel, and who manifested Himself in His Son, so that a spiritual kingdom with Christ as its Head might be established for men. Therefore one who is truly taught by the Bible should have his mind possessed by the living God, the one Director and Inspirer of mankind and of men. As the New

Testament sets before him the beginnings of the Church, it ought to be profoundly interesting to him to observe how Christ has been ruling His kingdom, and how men have served Him as His subjects, since he was exalted to His throne down to the present time. On the other hand, one who studies the Church is led to think of it as the bride of Christ, as the Body of which Christ is the Head, as existing to serve and glorify Christ, as the Father's house in which men through the Spirit dwell with Christ and the Father. What can be so important, then, to one who looks up to the Church, as to know Christ? And how are we to seek the most authentic knowledge of Christ, the Husband and Head of the Church? Obviously it is in the Gospels that He is to be found, and in the rest of that volume which the Church has preserved as its most sacred and precious possession. All the literature of the sacred volume is charged with interest and authority for one who is led through the Church to Christ. So the Bible naturally sends its readers on through Christ of whom it bears witness to the Church, and the Church naturally excites, through Christ whom it worships, a profoundly reverent interest in the Bible.

It seems to be natural, also, that religious minds should experience more or less of pain in learning that the writings in the sacred volume have no guaranteed immunity from error, and that the societies on earth representing the ideal Church, the Bride of Christ, form a scene of so much confusion and imperfection. In making these discoveries, some will have a sense of losing their faith. But it is not faith in Christ, faith in the living God, that should be thus lost. Faith in the God of the Bible and of the Church, as in the God of our parents, may be quickened and called higher by discoveries of the fallibility of Bible, Church, and parents. The Bible and the Church have only been of use to us in so far as they have trained us to believe in the living God. And to those who can believe in Him, whilst they see that nothing can rightly take His place in the guiding of His people, all the means He uses for the revealing of Himself will have their appointed honour and value. Deference to parents, deference to the communion in which each is brought up, deference to the Scriptures of the Covenants, deference to the teaching of time, will by such believers be cherished for themselves, and instilled into the young. The last of these authorities is perhaps that in which the Voice of the living God speaks most decisively to each generation. According to an old saying quoted by Lord Bacon, "Truth is the daughter of Time." And what is Time but the living God leading His creation onwards? The Bible can uphold no statement, the Church can uphold no doctrinal propositions, against the revelations of time. But whilst time, or the Divine Evolution, is not to be silenced by Church or Bible, it is surely proving itself to be no enemy or scorner of either. Time means what God is doing and saying now, the Church and the Bible present to us what the same God did and said in the days of our fathers and in the old time before them. Not one of these instructors is authorised to teach us mechanically, or is permitted to appropriate our faith to itself. In learning from each, it is necessary that the mind of the Christian and the Churchman should strive to be spiritual and to discern the things that are more excellent, and should listen with filial docility for the heavenly Voice which alone imparts perfect truth. Whilst the Eternal Spirit uses these outward channels of instruction, He Himself, as Christians are encouraged to believe, speaks directly to the listening ear, and leads by secret guidance the obedient soul. But these spiritual touches cannot be made the basis or material of common agreements as to belief and practice. Only we have this confidence through Christ to Godward—that those who look up to God with inward humility and teachableness will be led on by His kindly light, and will be enabled to make a profitable use of the methods of teaching which He employs. But the Bible, the Church, and the progress of mankind—each of the three will be an effectual help to us in apprehending what is best and of highest authority in the other two. Working together for our instruction, they will cause us to increase and go forwards in the knowledge and faith of the Father and of the Son by the Holy Spirit; because they are all from the one God who was and is and is to be, and who gives the knowledge of Himself as the prize and crown of our lives.

XVII

CHURCH PRIDE[1]

"Since ye are zealous of spiritual gifts, seek that ye may abound unto the edifying of the church."—1 CORINTHIANS xiv. 12.

LOOKING over the texts from which one was to be chosen for this morning's sermon, I noticed that they refer almost without exception to the ministrations of preachers of the Gospel. As the sermon is to be a warning against the sin of pride, it would seem that the founder of it was anxious that the ministers of Christ and all who work with them should be warned against any form of pride to which they might be specially liable, and which would hinder and damage their efficiency as builders of the Church. In accordance with this indication I am taking as my subject what I will briefly designate as Church Pride.

Whenever we reflect upon pride, we find ourselves obliged to recognise at the outset that there is pride which is the opposite of sinful. We often speak of a proper pride. And this is not one of the cases in which the same word happens to be used for two things which are easily distinguishable from each

[1] Preached at St. Mary's, Oxford, 20th November 1897.

other. The two kinds of pride appear to have a good deal of sentiment in common, and it is by no means obvious how the line is to be drawn between them or what makes the one sort good and the other bad. If a person whom we do not know is described to us as being proud, we are likely enough to be in doubt whether we should approve of his pride or not. Sometimes a personal pride which would be resented by a vulgar appreciation might be held in honour by a more discriminating taste. Englishmen know what it is to have a pride in their country. We do not feel ashamed of showing it. It is not without some complacency that we read the couplet in which Goldsmith characterised his countrymen—"Pride in their port, defiance in their eye, I see the lords of human-kind pass by." But there is an English pride which reasonably excites anger and aversion in the people of other countries, and of this we cannot think well. So there is pride in a family, in a school, in a college, in a university, which may be either proper or improper, which shows a generous nature and is of high value, or which is objectionable and gives just offence. Never was a fine regimental pride more nobly illustrated than by that speech of a few words which bids fair to carry down the name of the Gordon Highlanders with honour to a remote posterity; but there is an empty-headed pride in belonging to a crack regiment which does not commend itself to general admiration. If there is thus pride and pride in the feelings with which we regard ourselves and all the fellowships into which our lot may throw us, it must be thought probable that pride in the Church—the communion which enfolds all other relations—may also have the twofold character.

In the case of personal pride we are accustomed to express our approval or disapproval by the use of terms which have acquired a distinctive connotation, such as self-respect, self-esteem, arrogance. By self-respect we always mean something good, but self-esteem is not commonly used in a good sense, and arrogance certainly never. But these terms in themselves do not help us to understand the difference which they indicate. The true explanation of it is given in some lofty words of Milton, which occur in his treatise on "The Reason of Church Government." "There is," he says, "an esteem whereby men bear an inward reverence toward their own persons. And if the love of God, as a fire sent from heaven to be ever kept alive upon the altars of our hearts, be the *first* principle of all godly and virtuous actions in men, this pious and just honouring of ourselves is the *second*, and may be thought as the radical moisture and fountain-head whence every laudable and worthy enterprise issues forth. . . . He that holds himself in reverence and due esteem, both for the dignity of God's image upon him and for the price of his redemption which he thinks is visibly marked upon his forehead, accounts himself both a fit person to do the noblest and godliest deeds, and much better worth than to deject and defile, with such a debasement and such a pollution as sin is, himself so highly ransomed and ennobled to a new friendship and filial relation with God."[1] If every man has,

[1] *English Prose Writings* of John Milton, edited by Henry Morley, pp. 168, 169.

besides the actual nature which expresses itself in his daily doings and experiences, another form, the image of him as God's plan and purpose would have him be, the redeemed filial nature which cannot sin; if he has a calling which plainly puts before him what he ought to be, then he can cherish this ideal of himself with what Milton does not hesitate to name an inward reverence. And it is something of this reverence which gives its quality to all proper pride.

We may be the more satisfied with this explanation of the right kind of pride when we see that it also explains the right kind of humility. If the ancient codes of ethics did not include humility amongst the virtues, no one can doubt that Christians are bound to seek it and cherish it as a heavenly grace. The notion that the just estimate of ourselves is the mean between pride as one extreme, and humility as the other, will not bear a moment's consideration. But when a man has a deeply rooted consciousness of himself as made in the Divine image and redeemed by the sacrifice of Christ, and called to be a true son of God—and how could he have a higher estimate of himself than that?—he will be unable to shut out the secondary consciousness that he is not feeling and living as one so made and redeemed and called might be expected to feel and live. The difference between his appointed perfection and his actual life and mind will often make him ashamed and conscious of unworthiness. He will be very little inclined to think complacently of himself or to boast of his doings. To glory in the Lord will be to be humbled in himself.

We may trace this double consciousness, as in the individual man, so in the man as a member of a community. It is right for us to be proud of our country. The most sensitive Christian amongst us will not reproach himself for the pleasure with which he may be thrilled by those famous lines of Wordsworth :—

> In our halls is hung
> Armoury of the invincible knights of old ;
> We must be free or die who speak the tongue
> That Shakespeare spake, the faith and morals hold
> That Milton held ; in everything we are sprung
> From earth's first blood, have titles manifold.

But the poet, at the very time that he thus gloried, was reproaching his countrymen for being unworthy sons of such a country ; he called his England "a fen of stagnant waters" ; he feared that plain living and high thinking were no more. He was at the same moment proud of his country for what it had inherited, and ashamed of much in the Englishman of his day which did dishonour to its glories. And that will often be the double feeling of the fervent patriot. There will be in his mind a proud appreciation of the calling and ideal of which the past history of his country bears witness, and a keen sensitiveness about opinions and sentiments, it may be an attitude and a policy, of his countrymen, which seem to him to fall below his country's honour. He will sometimes ask himself whether he is doing, for his part, all that a proud and grateful Englishman ought to do. Is not *that* the patriotism which we should desire to cherish in ourselves and to see strengthened in our fellow-countrymen ? We can easily recognise a vulgar pride, the pride against which Christians ought to be on their guard, in the patriotism which gloats over the extent of our empire and the amount of our wealth, which finds a pleasure in making men of other nations feel our superiority; and we can see that such a pride knows nothing of any correlative humility. But think of our England in its relation to the God who makes every nation of men to dwell on all the face of the earth, determining their appointed seasons and the bounds of their habitation; think of it as having a calling legibly interpreted by the signs of that favour with which the Lord hath hitherto helped us; imagine to yourselves the part which a nation so uniquely blessed might be expected to play in the world-wide developments of the Divine counsels, and then you will understand how any English exhibition of arrogance, instead of elating us, should make us wince; how anxious we should be that the international virtues which are time's latest birth, magnanimity and courtesy, equitable estimation of rights, consideration towards the weak, generous readiness to assist less fortunate races, should be the proudest elements of our country's glory; what an ambition it should be for us to show to the world the spectacle of a people united and contented, with their minds set upon righteousness, a true people of God throughout the length and breadth of our dominion.

Yes, the lesson that will rightly instruct us about all pride is contained in that short word of St. Paul's, "He that glorieth, let him glory in the Lord." Let us meditate, not arrogantly on what we may claim for ourselves, but with reverence on God's purpose claiming *us* for its fulfilment, both as individuals and as tied together in our smaller and our larger associations.

I have suggested that it may be possible, even with regard to the Church, for the pride we ought to feel as members of this highest of our social organisms to be adulterated with some infection of the improper pride. If there is such a danger, it must be one of which we ought to take serious heed.

It is well understood that the Christians of our time are much more interested in the Church than those of some former generations have been. We who belong to the ancient Church of our land are none of us content that our thoughts of the Church should be confined within the limits of the Church of England; the time for that sort of narrowness has gone by. It is with the Church Catholic that our minds are occupied, and we think of the Church of England as a part of the Church Catholic. However we may define the Universal Church, we shall all admit that our definitions leave difficulties outside them which give no little trouble both to our minds and our hearts. These difficulties, added to that craving for definition by which so many minds are possessed, make Church questions the more interesting to anxious Christians.

In the Apostolic language about the Church we recognise a parallel to that twofold view of the individual Christian which I have illustrated from our Milton's writings, but which we also find in the New Testament. St. Paul, during his imprisonment at Rome, was much occupied with contemplation of the Church. In the Epistle to the Ephesians, an outpouring of peculiar Christian enthusiasm, he gives three distinct images of the Church, two chiefly illustrating its unity, the third its purity, and all setting forth its close relation to Christ. The Church is a Body, all the members making but one Body, and Christ is the Head. From the Head is derived the law and form of the Body, and also its life. The Body is well proportioned; it has ligaments binding limb to limb, and special functions for every part and organ; it is a perfectly adjusted framework, with love for its principle of life and growth. The Church is a Bride, loved by her Husband Christ with a perfect conjugal love; He gave Himself up for her, consecrated and cleansed her that He might present her to Himself in her glory, not having spot or wrinkle or any such thing, but that she should be holy and without blemish. The Church is a Temple, a house for God to dwell in; Christ Jesus is the chief corner-stone; the first confessors and witnesses of Christ are primary foundation-stones; each individual believer is a stone; associations of believers are so many chambers of the whole building. So St. Paul and his fellow-believers conceived of the Church, and so they desired that all Christians should think of the society into which they were taken. But when they looked at the daily doings of the Churches in the East and in the West, did they behold the unity and the glory of which they had visions? What they saw filled them with conflicting emotions. They were moved to give fervent thanks to God for the faith and hope and love which were everywhere bearing undeniable fruit; but the vanities and jealousies and immoralities which were continually breaking out amongst the Christians filled them with shame and grief. Perfect harmony, spotless purity, were by no means characteristic of the actual Church of the Apostolic age. So there was abundant reason for the double consciousness; to glory in the Lord was the privilege and duty of the Christian society—a privilege to be enjoyed without misgivings, a duty not to be neglected; to glory in itself was what facts forbade it to do. Pride and a sense of unworthiness not only had to be combined; each sentiment aided and nourished the other.

But that the actual Church, composed of frail and sinful members, should glory in itself, and should take the unity and purity and attachment to Christ of its heavenly image as entitling it to glory in itself, has not proved to be an impossibility. There has been an assumption, running down through the ages, and penetrating into every part of the Christian community, that the actual Church must have some method or other of asserting itself to be what it is called to be. The obstacles put in the way of such an assumption might have been thought to be insuperable. That a Roman Catholic, reading the history of the Papacy, should have to believe the aggregate of those who submit to the See of Rome to be, one and alone, the spotless Bride of Christ, is enough to excite our pity. The theory that the spotless Bride, the perfect Body, consists of those persons in every Christian communion whom God sees to be truly converted, has a certain elusiveness in its favour, but it is greatly discouraged at the present time by the many objections which can be brought against it. The doctrine of those Anglicans who hold that the Church, the perfect Body, the spotless Bride, is made up of the Church of England, the Church of Rome, the Oriental Churches, and any other communion which has the Episcopal succession unbroken—a doctrine which seems to require that races sunk in superstitious idolatry shall be regarded as more vitally attached to Christ and more truly fellow-members with ourselves than the best of non-Episcopalian Christians—can hardly be an easy one to believe.

Whether inspired by this doctrine or not, there are certain visible stirrings of English Churchmen's pride in their Church, about which, if there is always spiritual danger attending pride, I hope it may not be disloyal to express some apprehension. I speak in the belief that the proper pride and the wrong pride are not easily to be separated and marked off from each other.

1. An opinion is being expressed in favour of refusing Christian baptism to infants where there is no trustworthy security for their being brought up as members of the Church. It must be admitted to be true that a large number of English people are not leading regular Christian lives, most of whom have been baptized in their infancy, and nearly all these in the fonts of the Church of England. This is especially true of the populations of our large towns, though it is not without truth in our country districts also. Many of these baptized persons are very ignorant of Christian doctrine; some of them do not even profess to hold the Christian faith. Not a few are openly immoral in their conduct; many more are rarely seen inside a church. We are all of us

incessantly deploring this state of things, and considering and consulting how we may win these careless and alienated persons to real membership of the Church. We feel and acknowledge that the non-Christian lives of persons who were brought to Christian baptism as infants are a standing discredit and reproach to the Church. The proposed remedy for this evil, to which I am now referring, is that we should relieve ourselves of a considerable part of such discredit by declining to baptize those who seem likely to be brought up under bad conditions, and declaring that we do not know them and are not responsible for them. We are reminded by this proposal of what I presume to be the arguments of those whom we call by a shortened name Baptists. They think it safer and more in harmony with the character and claims of the Church of Christ not to baptize infants at all. Assuming the Church to be a holy body, they seek to preserve its holiness by admitting into it only such persons as give trustworthy evidence that they have been changed and made new creatures in Christ. That certainly seems the more thorough policy, if it is the credit of the Church as a holy body that is to be kept in view. It is perhaps believed by those who recommend that we should decline to baptize the less favoured infants, that it will be better even for the rejected that they should not be baptized. There is an oppressive doctrine of post-baptismal sin which represents the condition of the baptized sinner as only the worse and the more hopeless for his having been baptized. But when we consider what sinners we all are, this doctrine would seem to make it kinder not to baptize any infants at all, and would even suggest the postponing of baptism not merely to the years of discretion, but to the *articulus mortis*. On the whole, where this plan of selecting and rejecting infants finds approval, it will probably be not on account of the lessened danger for the rejected, but in the interest of the Church's character; and what will seem to many of us decisive objections to the plan will be neutralised by the feeling of pride in the Church.

2. We hear it contended, again, that ecclesiastical discipline over the laity should be restored. What can be thought of a Church, it is asked, which does not dare to exercise such discipline over its members? As we try to imagine what this would mean, the suggestion seems a sufficiently bold one. The penalty brought into action would be, it may be presumed, exclusion from the Sacrament of the Body and Blood of Christ, and therewith from all ecclesiastical offices and rights. Only communicants would be recognised as members of the Church, and by exclusion from the Holy Communion the Church would purge itself of unworthy members. Soundness of belief, as well as decency of moral conduct, would be required in communicants. The introduction of such discipline would be a serious matter. It will occur to some that our Lord did not think better of Pharisees, whom discipline would pass by or stamp with approval, than of the sinners whom discipline would cast out. So far as the Sacrament is concerned, it has little need at the present time to be protected from outrage. I have heard of its being a custom in the Presbyterian Kirk of Scotland that the minister should "fence the tables" by a

preliminary address, in which he warns his hearers against unworthy partaking of the communion; and the address, it is said, has sometimes been so telling, that only a few, and those the most hardily self-righteous, have ventured to present themselves. Many of us may think that in the Church of England the Table is already fenced, even to excess, by the prevalent feeling about the Sacrament. But as in the movement concerning the other Sacrament, all arguments against the restoration of effective Church discipline will count for little, with some, in comparison with the demands of the honour of the Church. And therefore it is that I venture to suggest a doubt whether the pride in the Church which has this working is entirely of the right sort.

3. Once more, there is a movement, which has been sweeping Diocesan Conferences before it, in favour of demanding self-government for the Church. And the force of this movement is due partly, indeed, to a hope that abuses may be more quickly and effectually remedied by a representative Church Body than by Parliament, and that new forms of spiritual activity may be developed, but mainly to a feeling of tenderness for the honour of the Church. When the scheme of a self-governing Church comes to be seriously considered, it will probably be seen that, if the self-government is to be real and vital, the change will be a revolutionary one. Some of those who support the movement have been stipulating that the independence of the Church is not to be absolute, but is to be controlled by the veto of Parliament. We have examples of independent

Anglican Churches in the Colonies, in America, and in Ireland; but a self-governing Church subject to a veto of the State upon all its actions is one of which we have no example; and we might reasonably expect such a constitution to start a struggle between the ecclesiastical independence and the civil veto which would continue until one triumphed over the other. As the Dissenting bodies become more and more indifferent to the special doctrines or methods which brought them into existence, it is probable that the Church will grow stronger, both in the country and in Parliament; and the people and their representatives will the less see the need or advantage of surrendering the powers which they and their forefathers have exercised for so many generations. At this early stage of the movement, however, it is the Church sentiment that supplies the motive force. Churchmen look at other religious bodies, and see them enjoying the privilege and the dignity of governing themselves, and they say to one another that it is a humiliation to the Church of England to be subject as it is to the State. The self-governing bodies are able to reproach the Church of England as Erastian, and there is no word of reproach so stinging to Church pride as Erastianism. Churchmen ask why they should not now at length be delivered from Erastianism, and be as the Roman Catholics, as the Methodists, as the Positivists. It may surely be asked, on the other hand, why we of the Church of England should wish to be as the Dissenters and the Roman Catholics. Are they so much better than we? I hope it is not a wrong pride in the Church that would compel us to ask this question. Are we bound to acknowledge that we see in them a higher spirituality, proofs of a more abundant blessing of God upon them, such as we can distinctly trace to their not being subject to State control? The assumption that the Divine Spirit is specially pledged to guide ecclesiastical government has no little historical experience to contradict it.

It is no doubt a telling argument for the change that is demanded that in this our day the Parliament has come to contain many men who are not Churchmen, and that there is no security that the Prime Minister should even be a professing Christian. But Englishmen have learnt not to be much affected either by existing anomalies or by anticipations of what may happen in the future. Our explanation of the many anomalies with which we may be taunted is that they represent the living forces of our national history. Pious men have faith to believe that the irregular-looking conditions which the Hand of God has prepared for us out of the various elements of the past are to be preferred to a regular man-made constitution. We find that in general that which is of God in human experience and human life is marked by contradictions. It will hardly be denied that a Parliament including unorthodox members may be a better body to control Church matters, and more likely to act with reverent right feeling, than some Parliaments and kings that have been formally orthodox, as even the heathen Cæsar, ordained of God to govern, was a truer instrument of God's will than the orthodox ecclesiastical Council of the Jews. Are we sure that it must be a godly pride in the Church that chafes under civil government, and insists that for the honour of the Church its government must be made purely ecclesiastical?

Not that we are bidden by loyalty to the God of our fathers to believe that whatever is, is right, and that our part is simply to let things drift. Assuredly we are placed here to improve our inheritance, to confess what is wrong amongst us, and to do our best to put it right, to shrink from no change, however revolutionary, which the glory of God and the cause of the kingdom of Christ may seem to demand. I am only pleading that, with regard to the Church, we may not be misled by plausible notions of honour and dignity; that we should endeavour to make our improvements with insight and with a wise use of the opportunities afforded to us. What I suppose we have to do, as faithful Christians and students of the Apostolic teaching, is to keep the true image of the Church as the Bride of Christ, arrayed in fine linen and bright and pure, continually before our minds, and to glory in it, whilst we look with humility, and with such self-reproach as we deserve, upon the Church as it now exists upon the earth. We are not to begin by taking for granted that there is no Church but what is to be seen somewhere in the societies of sinful men here below, and therefore to try how we can impose all the features of the heavenly Church by theory and arrangement upon some one or more of such societies. We can say to ourselves with the conviction of faith, "All Christians ought to be one in a holy fellowship, all the societies of those who bear the name of Christ ought to be moved and restrained by the Spirit of Christ"; and in the power of that conviction we can work and strive towards perfection, daring to give thanks for all the good things of our inheritance, and holding ourselves the more responsible as members of the Church of Christ for every advantage that has been given us. We shall be kept in mind that all true Church progress must be spiritual, whilst we shall understand that the inward spirit will issue into outward forms, and that outward things are made by the Divine law subservient to spiritual life. We may well be appalled by the greatness of the task laid upon Christian England, and by the manifold and far-reaching opportunities of our English Church. But the calls which fill us with awe should also inspire us with hope and energy. For God does not show us a duty without also giving the strength to fulfil it.

XVIII

THE MORAL USE OF MONEY[1]

"Make to yourselves friends by means of the mammon of unrighteousness; that, when it shall fail, they may receive you into the eternal tabernacles."—ST. LUKE xvi. 9.

THE Authorised Version of the New Testament is still predominantly in use amongst us, and it is probable that an indefinite number of readers continue to be misled by its way of rendering this passage. It is constantly assumed in popular speech and in the newspapers that to "make friends of the mammon of unrighteousness" means to make friends with mammon, to come into some sort of alliance or compromise with mammon. It is not to be supposed that the translators intended to convey that sense. To make friends of mammon could hardly be the same thing as to make a friend of mammon. There are other sayings of our Lord in which the word "of" is misleading; as in "My kingdom is not of this world," "I speak not of myself." In these places "from" would express the sense better to our ears: "My kingdom is not from this world," "I speak not

[1] Preached before the University of Cambridge, 16th February 1890.

from myself." In our text we need the unambiguous form which the Revisers have given us. What our Lord said was, " Make friends for yourselves by means of the mammon of unrighteousness," " Let the mammon of unrighteousness be to you a means of making friends."

It is important that this saying should be rightly understood, for it is of singular significance and value. It does not indeed give us, what many of us may often have craved, practical directions as to the manner in which we should deal with money or money's worth which may come into our possession. Our Lord took care to avoid putting into the hands of His disciples what they might regard and use as a directory of conduct. When He delivered practical precepts they were often in such a form that they could not be, and were manifestly not intended to be, observed in the letter. A vivid precept of action may be the most telling expression of a principle; and our Lord would have us look through every precept of His to the principle, the motive, the reason behind it. What He sought to do, and did, was to declare principles to those who would accept Him as Master. And in this moral of the parable of the unrighteous steward Christ gave to His disciples a profound and comprehensive law for the employment of money. They were to make friends by means of it. In what particular ways they were to seek this end He does not lay down; He leaves to them the duty of finding out the best ways. But for every generation and in all kinds of circumstances it is a luminous principle that those who have money are to aim at making friends by the ways in which they use it.

The story of which the parable consists was probably told for the sake of this moral only. A parable may, or may not, be susceptible of interpretation through all its parts. We are not at all bound to assume that the rich man stands for any one in the spiritual world, or the steward, or the debtors, or that the acts of the story—the wasting of the goods, the calling of the steward to account, his dealing with his lord's debtors—have spiritual acts analogous to them which they are intended to bring to our minds. Our Lord called attention to the one lesson which He desired to convey. As the dishonest steward had sought by dishonest means to provide himself with friends against the time of destitution which was coming upon him, so the children of light were bidden to provide themselves, by a worthy use of money, with friends for the time when money should fail them. Without pronouncing that the parable has no other less obvious interpretation, it is reasonable that we should give our attention first and chiefly to the lesson to which our attention is called. And the reflections which follow this lesson will be seen to support the view that our Lord intended to declare not merely one use to which money might well be put, but the comprehensive purpose for which money is entrusted to men. "If ye have not been faithful in the unrighteous mammon, who will commit to your trust the true riches? And if ye have not been faithful in that which is another's, who will give you that which is your own?" Every man, according to the teaching of Jesus Christ, is made to be a slave of God. God entrusts to each certain possessions, of which he is allowed to have the control and disposal. He is bound to be faithful in the administration of these. And what the true Lord of the possessions and of the man sets him to do with them is to make friends by means of them.

It is a noticeable feature of this teaching of Jesus Christ that He speaks of money—for we may conveniently designate all external possessions by the name of money—as the mammon of unrighteousness, the unrighteous mammon. Mammon, it is said, meant simply riches, and is a neutral word; and money would therefore be a fair equivalent of it. To us it might be said, ye cannot be slaves to God and to money. But our Lord, in His expressions, makes money the natural ally or instrument of unrighteousness. Obviously He must have meant to recognise, or to complain, that this was as a matter of fact a character of money. "Let money," He says, "which is so habitually associated with unrighteousness, be in your hands a means of making friends." This is one example of that open and direct prejudice against riches which the Lord Jesus entertained and expressed. The Pharisees, who hated Him, and whom He defied and denounced, had it for one of their characteristics that they were rich and loved money. Poor men, it was seen, could more easily become followers of Jesus than rich men; and He took note, with anger and emphasis, of this fact. "It is easier for a camel to go through the eye of a needle, than for a rich man to enter into the kingdom of God—to become my true disciple." Those whom He addressed were familiar with the unrighteousness—the dishonesty, the strifes, the worldliness, the inhumanity—of which the pursuit of money was the cause or occasion. And Jesus had no desire to palliate these evil fruits or to make the least of them. He thought it expedient, and rather safe than dangerous, to refer to money as if it were itself an evil thing. He sought to encourage what we might call a prejudice against it in the minds which were open to His teaching. He taught those who wished to do the will of the Heavenly Father with regard to money to look at it with suspicion.

In this day of ours we may hear riches and the rich denounced by champions of the poorer classes with a freedom which is sometimes compared with that of Christ. Bold and generous spirits, chiefly of course amongst the young, instead of treating money with the traditional respect, are assuming it to be the root of almost all the evil in the world. By money I mean the personal owning of possessions. To get rid of this, it is held, would be to reform the world, to make all men happy. Some, in a half and half way, would stop short at the abolition of the personal owning of land; others are more thorough, and would forbid the owning of things in general. It is clear, indeed, that the maleficent power of money would be in no degree broken by the abolition of property in land. And the philosophical speculators who anticipated the extreme Socialists of to-day, and who—seeing the many evils which might be referred to the influence of money on the senses and imagination of men—were tempted to take the short course of destroying the occasion of such evils, undertook to construct commonwealths in which no man should have anything which he could call his own. There is

The Moral Use of Money

no Hyde Park demagogue who condemns private property with more decision than Plato, the scorner of the demos, or Thomas More, Lord High Chancellor of England. Let me quote a few sentences from a bishop's translation of a Lord Chancellor's book. "I must say that, as I hope for mercy, I can have no other notion of all the governments that I see or know than that they are a conspiracy of the rich, who, on pretence of managing the public, only pursue their private ends, and devise all the ways and arts they can find out—first, that they may without danger preserve all that they have so ill acquired, and then that they may engage the poor to toil and labour for them at as low rates as possible, and oppress them as much as they please. . . . Yet these wicked men, after that they have by a most insatiable covetousness divided that among themselves with which all the rest might have been well supplied, are far from that happiness that is enjoyed among the Utopians; for the use as well as the desire of money being extinguished, much anxiety and great occasions of mischief are cut off with it. And who does not see that the frauds, thefts, robberies, quarrels, tumults, contentions, seditions, murders, treacheries, and witchcrafts, which are indeed rather punished than restrained by the severities of the law, would all fall off if money were not any more valued by the world? Men's fears, solicitudes, cares, labours, and watchings would all perish in the same moment with the value of money; even poverty itself, for the relief of which money seems most necessary, would fall." " When I balance all these things in my thoughts, I grow more favourable to Plato, and do not wonder that he resolved not to make any laws for such as would not submit to a community of all things; for so wise a man could not but foresee that the setting all upon a level was the only way to make a nation happy, which cannot be obtained so long as there is property." The Utopians are said to have been attracted to Christianity by the fact that Christ and His followers lived by their rule of having all things common, and that the rule was still kept up in some communities amongst the sincerest sort of Christians. And it is charged against the later preachers of Christianity that "they, observing that the world would not willingly suit their lives to the rules that Christ has given, have fitted His doctrine, as if it had been a leaden rule, to their lives, that so some way or other they might agree with one another."

It cannot be disputed that Christ saw and noted the evils which have been associated with money no less seriously than those who before Him and after Him have advocated as the only effectual cure of those evils the extinction of money. His example also may be claimed in that He and His band of followers had for a time a common purse. And there cannot but be the most solemn significance in the impulse which moved the thousands of believers on the Day of Pentecost to throw their possessions into a common stock. It is equally true, however, that Christ did not ordain that His followers should have all things common. There is no evidence of His having issued any such command. The precepts of conduct which He did give to His followers expressly imply that they would possess personal property. A man could not give alms, could not lend, could not invite the poor, the maimed, the lame, the blind to a dinner unless he had means of his own.

It would be unwise to infer from this legislation of Christ that the substitution of a universal community of possession for separate ownership, such as Plato and Sir Thomas More and the most extreme modern Socialists have advocated, is necessarily forbidden by Christianity. The suppression of selfish desires and the setting of the general good above the gratification of the individual may be justly regarded as characteristically Christian principles; and any change of the institutions of society which should be suggested by these principles, and should commend itself as likely to establish them amongst men and to promote the universal well-being, might claim the authority of Christ as in its favour, although it might alter customs which Christ recognised and to which He adjusted His exhortations. In accordance with this view we do not hesitate to regard the abolition of slavery as a Christian movement. But Christians have as much right—nay, are as much bound—to be rational and to see their way as the most worldly; and to almost all Christians it seems certain that community of possession has not, for mankind in general, the sanction of the Divine Ruler of the world, and that the attempt to establish it would introduce confusion and would end in ruinous disappointment.

Our duty therefore is to attend to what Christ teaches us with regard to the use of possessions, on the assumption that God still grants separate ownership to each of us. He leaves us, we understand, still to be tempted. It is by this method of discipline that we can see the human race throughout its history to have been governed. The great appetitive force has been always and everywhere at work in human nature. The modern exposition of the natural history of man gives a place of supreme importance to this force; there are some naturalists, indeed, who see nothing but this in all human history from the beginning. Each man, according to their description, is seen to have been pushing himself forward, struggling to keep himself alive, seeking to gratify the desire that works in him, trying to get hold of as much as he could for himself. The drawing together of men, and their submission to social restraints, may be traced to this one sovereign impulse, because the individual has derived strength and security, as well as pleasure, from association with others. There is so much undeniable truth in this doctrine that we ought to beware of contradicting it. It is a vulgar error to suppose that Christians are taught to make friends with mammon; but it is assuredly good policy for our creed to make friends with evolution. We must be ready to see the hand of the Creator in this primal appetitive force, or we shall be obliged to put a great deal of creation out of the hand of our God. What the Bible teaches is that there was always something in man, more or less developed, which was intended to control appetite and self-assertion; that temptation is the great moral process to which men have been subjected, and the invariable condition of spiritual progress; that the Creator gives to man the desires of the flesh, in order that he may learn to rule them with the sense of duty and the affections of the Spirit. It may be admitted that human beings, in the consciousness of their weakness, do wisely when they shun temptation, and put it so far as they can out of the way of the weak; this is the reasonable action of that self-distrust which we ought to cherish. But the God who is training us will not let temptation be put away from us; and the Bible has not taught us to look for progress through the exclusion of temptation. We pathetically plead with God that He knows us to be set in the midst of so many and great dangers that by reason of the frailty of our nature we cannot always stand upright; but, knowing this, God sets us in the midst of the dangers, and we must believe that He sees it to be better for us that we should be tempted and fall, than that we should not be tempted. But His will is that we should be tempted and *not* fall; and this is the issue upon which we should set our minds and our hopes.

We recognise, then, in money, in the owning of little or much, an extremely serious instrument of temptation. It may cause us to fall, it may do us harm, and we may do harm with it. What is our Lord's counsel with regard to it? Not that this occasion of evil should be destroyed; not that each should for himself refuse to take it, but that we should make friends by means of it.

It is God's will that men should be friends together; so the Son of God reports of His Father's mind. Yes, the God who made money to tempt men, wills that they should make friends of each other. Across all the jealousies and strifes and hatreds and mutual injuries which have seemed so natural to men, this higher law has at all times been felt and even discerned. The divisions have been the more superficial; the uniting forces have been the deeper and more permanent. Every man, it has been acknowledged, ought to be a friend to every man. There is something wrong when men quarrel and try to harm each other. The true Maker of men has willed, and continues to will, that they should not be enemies, that they should not be indifferent to each other, that they should be friends. All the natural occasions of mutual assistance, all the reasons for combination, all the gratification that one is able to afford to another — these are indications and works of that higher purpose which designs that men should be drawn together by ties of sincere goodwill and desire of each other's welfare. Before Christ came, the chosen people had been hearing a voice saying to them, Thou shalt love thy neighbour as thyself. This old commandment was issued again as new by Jesus to His disciples; for they were to love one another as He had loved them; their love was to be an imitation of the love which the Heavenly Father had shown in Christ, a response to that love, a fruit of it. Jesus said to His disciples, Love not your friends only, but your enemies also; love them whilst they are in the act of injuring you. The purpose of the Creator of mankind was to be fulfilled by a universal goodwill between man and man, and for this end a persistent Divine influence was to work in men's hearts, which would not suffer itself to be quenched by any ingratitude or malice, but would resolutely set itself to conquer evil with good. If friends were to be made by the use of money, it was because to make friends was to be the aim of all communications between man and man, because every man was intended to feel as a friend towards his neighbour, and to desire that his neighbour should feel as a friend towards him. Only through the relation of men to God, and of men to each other in God, is human life in any of its parts to be thoroughly understood.

But it may be said that to make friends was not the final object set by the Lord before His hearers, but to obtain admission into the eternal tabernacles. According to the parable, if the dishonest steward tried to put certain persons under an obligation to him, it was with a view to his own advantage. It cannot be denied that our Lord's precept might with some plausibility be thus interpreted—Give money freely to pious persons, that you may win the reward of going with them to heaven. Most of us would not willingly, I think, lower the Lord's precept to such a sense as this. We have learnt to regard the habit of giving to the Church and of doling out alms for the sake of gaining an entrance into abodes of bliss after death as an unworthy kind of religion. What St. Paul would have thought of it we may infer from the vehement protest, "If I bestow all my goods to feed the poor, but have not love, it profiteth me nothing." Yes, and what Christ would have thought of it may be inferred from another parable of His, with which He enforced another lesson. His eager disciple, Simon Peter, having heard Him speak with unusual emphasis of the hindrance which riches put in the way of those who might have followed

Him, reminded his Master, "Lo, we have left all and followed Thee: what shall we have therefore?" And this claim of reward grieved the Lord Jesus. All genuine surrender, He replied, would be richly rewarded; but there might be apparent surrender which would not win God's favour. There were first that might be put last. And the disciple who should plead "I have sacrificed much more than most men, and hope I may be proportionately rewarded," would find himself rebuffed. The Divine rewards were not to be given according to any external scale of labour or surrender, but would pour confusion upon such measurement. We shall not readily believe, therefore, that our Lord taught His disciples to give largely for the sake of securing happiness after death.

It seems probable, certainly, that our Lord was referring to what might happen after death. If the old reading "When *ye* fail" had held its ground, the failing would be taken as a matter of course to mean disappearance from this life. And the failing of the mammon may be most naturally supposed to occur at the moment of death. There are other sayings of our Lord which point in this direction:—To the rich man who planned the comfortable enjoyment of his riches "God said, Thou foolish one, this night is thy soul required of thee; and the things which thou hast prepared, whose shall they be?" "When thou makest a feast, bid the poor, the maimed, the lame, the blind: and thou shalt be blessed; because they have not wherewith to recompense thee: for thou shalt be recompensed in the resurrection of the just." "If thou wouldest be perfect, go, sell that thou hast, and give to the poor, and thou shalt have treasure in heaven." I admit, therefore, that in these words "that, when it shall fail, they may receive you into the eternal tabernacles," we shall reasonably read a promise of reward after death. What I would urge is that we must understand the promised reward in the light of our Lord's teaching concerning service and recompense, and that the emphasis of the precept is upon the making of friends. A faithful administration of possessions as a trust is what Christ demands, and He indicates a higher gift which will reward proved faithfulness. "If ye have not been faithful in the unrighteous mammon, who will commit to your trust the true riches? And if ye have not been faithful in that which is another's, who will give you that which is your own?" This higher endowment, which is much, is true or genuine, is your own, must be spiritual treasure; it must consist in knowledge of God, in godly affections, in pure fellowship, in worthy joy. And it is not our Lord's custom to speak of such treasure as belonging exclusively to the life after death. Spiritual endowment is not withheld from men in this life; the kingdom of heaven was for this world as well as for the next. We should not therefore be departing from the characteristic method of Christ's teaching if we were to adopt an interpretation of His precept which understands Him as saying, "Use the money which God gives you for Him, not for yourselves, and it will bring in friends who will not merely give you the temporary refuge which the cast-off servant sought, but will receive you in your hours of weakness and sorrow into their very heart of hearts, will bear you with them when they are kneeling in the presence of their Father." Whatever Christ promises for the future life has a foretaste possible in this life. "Make to yourselves friends," Christ says, "with whom you may have the fellowship of the higher world; friends to whom your relations will be not of a worldly but a heavenly kind. And use money, which may be so easily misused, to knit such friendships."

But how this is to be done, by what use or uses of money human friendship of the nobler kind is to be created, our Lord left it to His hearers in that generation, and in the generations which have followed, to find out. And the art which so long ago He bade men learn proves to be a much more difficult one than any one supposes it to be until he gives his mind to it. The little progress that has been made in it may be due in part to the entirely inadequate appreciation of its difficulty which has prevailed up to the present day. When we look back through the ages of Church history, we perceive what we may call a simple but unreflecting acceptance of the New Testament teaching on this subject. Preachers have recognised the dangers to which money exposes the possessor of it; they have glorified the surrender of it; the general strain of their teaching has been, "Give to the poor; give to the Church; in either case you will be giving to God, and God will amply repay you for the gift." For special societies, like those of the religious orders, the entire renunciation of personal property has been thought a highly Christian rule. Some speculators, as in the Utopia of which I have reminded you, have made the universal abolition of personal property an object of aspiration. In our own day more study has been given to the Christian use of money than ever before. The penetrating investigations of economists had succeeded in dispersing what might be called universal errors on purely economic questions; and those who desired that, from a moral and Christian point of view, money should be well applied, have perceived that the study of processes and effects was very necessary for their purpose also, and that common opinion and practice were at least seriously impeached by what study began to bring to light. People are asking what good can be done by great wealth—an interesting and important question; but many who are not wealthy are more exercised by the question what is their own duty with regard to money than by solicitude about the duty of the great plutocrats. For, indeed, no one can touch the matter closely and sincerely without perceiving that there are problems, as there is duty, for those who have little, no less than for those who have much, for those who have the hundreds a year, no less than for those who have the hundreds of thousands. And this direction of anxious thought I take to be an evidence that the Spirit of Christ is giving a somewhat new impulse to the minds of men in this our day; and I have hoped that on this Quinquagesima, or Charity Sunday, we might usefully look for the great principles and aims by which we may see our Master guiding us towards the right employment of our means.

That our money is not our own, but is entrusted to us for the chief purpose of making friends in the kingdom of heaven, we have heard Christ teaching us.

It was inevitable that hearers of Christ and readers of the Gospels should assume the obvious way of making friends by means of money to be the giving of it to the poor. No one can listen reverently to Christ without taking the duty of giving to the poor into his heart as one of the most solemn of obligations. But the first thing we have learnt from the study of beneficence is that to give to the poor is very likely to do them harm. It would be a faithless wish— but how one is tempted to wish that this knowledge had been kept from us! It would have been so simple to give, and go on giving. There would have been no problem; sincere Christians would have known what to do, faithful preachers of the Gospel would have known what to urge. Undoubtedly thoughtful persons have been restrained from free giving by a prevision of the harm it would do, before these days; but it is wonderful how little recognition there was in former times of a fact of experience, a connexion of cause and effect, which has been so clear to many of us now. Even now the knowledge is very unwillingly received, and there are those who will insist that it must be right to give to the needy, and that it is the duty of the Christian to obey the commands of Christ without regard to consequences; and if you urge that it can hardly be Christian wisdom to shut your eyes, and that you have only to look round the corner or into next week to see the results of your giving, they will perhaps treat you as the doctrinaire devotee of an inhuman science. They ought to know better. The truest friends of the poor, the men and the women who have given up the most of their lives to the considering and helping of them, are those who will entreat you to refrain from attempts to help them which experience proves to be weakening and injurious. It is a most Christian and human regard for the poor that forbids free giving, and that would look with dismay upon the distribution of thousands and millions—even if it were in bread and coals and clothing—amongst the neediest of the population. Nor is the giving of alms a sure way of making true friends. I have myself known givers of alms to be spoken of very disrespectfully by those who have taken advantage of their benevolence or misguided sense of duty. So that we find ourselves stopped from doing what Christian instinct and the words of Christ would first prompt us to do. No considerable portion of the riches of the world could be advantageously laid out in adding directly to the comforts of the poorest. As much as we can venture with our eyes open so to apply ought of course to be given with joy, and nothing ought to put a limit to almsgiving except the real interest of the poor. It would be a shame indeed that in this country and this age our almsgiving should be limited in amount by anything else.

But the largest amount of almsgiving that a regard for the poor could sanction will leave the bulk of our means still in our hands. And we should like to take the precept of Christ as referring to more than a small percentage of what we have. We are accustomed to think ourselves bound to make gifts, not only to the needy, but to the Church and to the general interests of the community. If we speak of anything as given to God, we do not mean to imply that it is not also given to our fellow-men. And though the gifts to which I refer are not intended to relieve destitution, it is almost always assumed more or less distinctly that they have in view the advantage of the poorer and less-favoured classes. A far larger amount is given, and rightly given, to public objects than is expended in the direct relief of the poor. May we not say that those who use money in such ways are making friends by means of it, and are so fulfilling the Lord's precept? They are acting as themselves friends to their neighbours and fellow-countrymen, and they assuredly succeed in winning a great deal of friendly feeling in return. Indeed, the general appreciation of munificence is so ready and fervent, that large giving might have been expected to be more attractive to members of our wealthy class than it actually has been. There are some social reformers who, by taxation or otherwise, would extinguish rich men and prevent them from existing. They could not easily persuade us that the result would be a gain to the community, or find a way of accomplishing it which would not be disastrous to an industrial commonwealth. But the wisdom of making friends by applying their wealth in some visible way to the service of the public and diverting a substantial portion of it from themselves, will perhaps be brought home increasingly in the immediate future to our rich men and women. The preachers of Christ may tell their fellow-Christians that in so doing they will not only be acting prudently, but will be fulfilling their Lord's command. And though munificence is for the rich, and great wealth has in a special degree to excuse and justify itself, and the task of considering how to appropriate thousands and hundreds of thousands is a burden which may help the less rich to be content with their lot, we are none of us exempt from the duty of thinking how with some portion of our means we may best serve the higher interests of mankind. For we are daily learning what may be done by combination. And what could more fitly be one of the dominant social thoughts of a Christian democracy than to be always considering by what express efforts of the few and of the many together the highest well-being of the community and of mankind may be most effectively promoted?

But let us suppose that Christians in general, after giving generously to religion, to education, to public art, to the health and recreation of the people, to social fellowship, continue to use the larger part of what they have in private expenditure. Must we hold that in that proportion they are disregarding the law of Christ? that they are assuming themselves to be absolute owners and not stewards, and are not compelling the mammon of unrighteousness into the service of true friendship? I would rather believe that the common instincts and customs and conventions of mankind have more of the will of God in them than such a conclusion would imply. Let him who sees his way to it lay down the law about expenditure in positive regulations for loyal Christians. A Count Tolstoi, who himself walks in the way which he marks out, is entitled to sympathetic respect, and such devotion cannot fail to be a beneficial testimony. But the impulses and habits which have brought the races of men up to their present level must not be hastily assumed to be altogether evil; and those who find themselves unable to frame a scheme of life to supplant them are thereby warned to make the best rather than the worst of them. We may be too hard on the money-making and the money-spending which constitute— shall I say?—the brute stuff of the world's life. Look at them without hatred, and you will admit that they have an immense effect in the way of making friends. What a significant thing it is that every operation of trade, every industrial compact, so far as it is free, implies the advantage of both the parties to it! The excessive laudation of trade as sure to establish the peace of the world and the universal friendship of men, which expressed the hopes of our great free-traders, may have been discredited. A great deal of evil, including wars, must be put down to the account of trade or traders; but so must, undeniably, a great deal of good, and in particular an immeasurable development of friendly relations and friendly sentiments amongst men. And how would it be if all money-making and money-spending were simply honest; if there were no fraud, no overreaching; if even bare legal justness of dealing were observed; if men knew that in matters of business they could trust one another? Think of the occasions of intercourse that are created by pecuniary transactions, of the opportunity which they afford for the growth of human sentiments, of the multitudinous crossing of lines of demarcation which they involve. But when we suppose it to be a loyal Christian who is making money and spending it, we must credit him with more than a shrinking from fraud. Let him be a clever energetic man of business, liking with the hereditary human instinct to see the profits of his talent and industry, going in general by the haggling of the market, not imagining that he can escape out of the range of competition; let him allow himself to be drawn on by the traditional custom of expenditure, spending more freely as he grows richer upon the ordinary objects. But he will never have anything to do with any man without the Christian feeling that he ought to be friends with him; he will shrink not only from being but even from seeming to be unkind or ungenerous; he will be possessed by the continual desire that nothing which passes between him and another in buying and selling may have a tendency to make Christian brotherhood between them impossible. As a matter of fact, one who in spending money or making it creates an impression on the minds of those around him that he is always honourable, always liberal, well on his guard against being cheated, but not suspicious, not in the least purse-proud though he may be rich, knowing the superiority of man to gold, a master of mammon and not its slave—such a one does win confidence, esteem, affection, does make friends, more than if he kept for himself the bare necessaries of life and got rid of the rest of his means in gifts.

God forbid that I should be one of the preachers who may justly be reproached with making the law of Christ a leaden flexible rule, to fit it to the actual worldly lives of men. What demand indeed can be more exacting than that men living in the world, getting and spending, should cherish an altogether unworldly mind? It is in truth a weaker and less arduous advocacy of Christian morality to assume that it is to be followed by a few who can break away from the world and lead exceptional lives, rather than that it is the law for all practical progressive human life. If we accept Jesus Christ as the Father's Son, who reveals to us the mind of the Maker of the world, we must hold that His commandments can be obeyed by all to the world's advantage, and are equally binding on all who profess to believe in Him. If He has declared that money is a trust, and that it is to be used for making friends, the preacher of Christ must testify to every man, whether he has much or little, however he may be getting or have got it, that what he has is not his own, and that he is responsible for giving and spending it in such ways as to win esteem and confidence and goodwill. Entire giving away, absolute renunciation, is the ideal Christian mind for every one who has and spends, and until a Christian attains to this he has still to pray and strive: If he quails before such a *demand*, the Gospel *offers* that mind to him as an emancipation and a happiness, and promises the Spirit of God to create it in him. To be in bondage to mammon is bad for a man; to exchange bondage to mammon for bondage to God is the only way to escape out of an evil condition, and is perfect freedom. "Blessed are the poor in spirit"; happy are they who inwardly divest themselves of possessions, and could bear without murmuring the loss of them.

How such a law of inward renunciation would operate on outward life, no moralist, no theological casuist, is competent to pronounce beforehand.

Every one can see that it would quickly reform away many of the disgraces, most of the insincerities, of ordinary human conduct. But the Divine Spirit has reserved to Himself the ultimate direction of practice. It is only by the study of circumstances and by experiment that the way of realising the will of God is to be found out. Different persons will be led to act in different ways, and wisdom will be justified by her children. It would be interesting to see how the principle of stewardship, the law of friend-making, more thoroughly accepted and followed, would tell upon our social system. There would be cases, as there are now,—more, probably, than there are now,—of total abandonment of possessions; not a more difficult form of obedience, but requiring more enterprise, and such as we call more heroic. We have the examples of the Apostles before us. "Lo, we," said St. Peter to his Master, "have left all and followed Thee." They had made the renunciation first in heart and mind, and then it had seemed right for them to carry it out straight into visible act. They left their boats and nets and homes, and went after the Master who attracted them. They had one great aim and one great reward. They sought to make a friend, and they gained a Friend. "Ye are My friends," said the Lord Jesus. And an apostle even greater than the Twelve tells us that he had gladly suffered the loss of all things that he might gain Christ. Our Church has taught us in its collects to regard the Apostles as our leaders, and to set their renunciation as an example before us. Let us keep the same goal in view as they did. The precept of Christ will not be altered in its bearing, and it may obtain greater force over our hearts, if we change it slightly and read, " Make to yourselves a Friend by means of the mammon of unrighteousness ; that, when it shall fail, He may receive you into the eternal tabernacles."

XIX

PEACE AND WAR[1]

"If it be possible, as much as in you lieth, be at peace with all men."
—ROMANS xii. 18.

THERE is a line in the *Faery Queen* in which Spenser notes the unshrinking resolution with which loving pity faces darkness, filth, and foul smells, in setting itself to rescue a half-dead captive out of a dungeon. "Entire affection," he says, "hateth nicer hands"—hands, that is, too nice or fastidious to put themselves to such work. Similarly, we are insisting in some of these lectures, whole-hearted Christianity hateth nicer hands. There have been persons, even divines of high reputation, to whom war has seemed too repulsive a fact for Christianity to have anything to do with. They have regarded wars between nations as inevitable; they have not been able to understand how the course of the world could dispense with them; but war is so dreadful to Christian feeling, that they have concluded that the only thing for religion to do is to pass by on the other side. To us the spirit of Christ is bearing witness that our faith must not pass anything by on the other side.

[1] Preached in Lent 1895, as part of a Course of Sermons organised by the London Branch of the Christian Social Union.

The worst and most impracticable things in the world are those which belief in Christ is specially called to affront and to attack. We have no right to turn away from blood and carnage, or to admit that, if war is wrong from the Christian point of view, it is to be allowed to go on. And though it may seem honourable to the gospel to affirm that its morality is peremptory and will have nothing to do with compromises, we can see that the method of Christ in His ruling of the world does not disdain the partial remedying of evils, the gradual improvement of human society.

I should be making but a futile use of the opportunity given me to-day if I were to content myself with repeating Christian commonplaces about peace on earth and good-will amongst men. It is the wish, I am sure, of those who have organised these lectures that the preachers should in all practical questions come to the point. It is true that international relations belong to "high politics"; but in a democratic age those who are but units of the population cannot entirely divest themselves of responsibility, and may perhaps exercise some influence, even with regard to matters that must be practically dealt with by experts of administration. We are warranted in assuming that international peace is not only a Divine ideal, commending itself to all the good aspirations of mankind, but also a proper object of the efforts of statesmen and the policy of governments. During centuries of almost unceasing war between the nations, all who have gone to church have been bidden to pray that it may please God to give to all nations unity, peace, and concord.

But the Christian Church has not in old time done much—has hardly even laboured with conscious endeavour—to prevent wars from occurring. George Fox and his followers have made protests, with a sincerity which they have attested by voluntary sacrifices, against the causing of bodily pain to any one either by individuals or by nations, as an act altogether forbidden to Christians; but the understanding of Christ's precepts in the letter is mischievously confusing to the Christian conscience, and it is doubtful whether such repudiations as those of the Society of Friends and of Count Tolstoi have not done more to discourage than to stimulate intelligent and general efforts to avoid war. In our own age, however, many causes have been cooperating to awaken the conscience of Christendom on this question, and to set people thinking how peace between nations may best be preserved. Our eyes have been in some degree opened to the kingdom of heaven as a living reality, and we have been léd to see that this spiritual kingdom claims all the earth, with its kings and its nations, and all provinces of human life, for its own; and it is evident that when two nations are fighting with each other they are breaking the *pax cœlestis*, and that one of them certainly, if not both, has been showing disloyalty to its heavenly Lord. The idea of the Catholic Church has at the same time begun to shine with more of steady and attractive light before the minds of all Christians; and the song has a new music to our ears in which the four living creatures and the four-and-twenty elders pay homage to the Lamb, saying, " Worthy art Thou to take the book "—the book of destiny—"and to open the seals thereof: for Thou wast slain, and didst purchase unto God with Thy blood men of every tribe, and tongue, and people, and nation, and madest them to be unto our God a kingdom and priests; and they reign upon the earth." And then the immense increase of intercourse and the growing complexity of interests between the different countries on the face of the globe make war more unnatural and more ruinous: whilst the development of the machinery of destruction causes the imagination to quail before the terrors of the battle-field and the siege. So that whilst the childish doctrine that Christians ought never to consent to go to war at all takes no hold of men's minds, many earnest persons are much occupied with anxious thought as to the ways in which war might be superseded, or the chances of its occurring be diminished, or its horrors, if it should occur, be mitigated.

The suggestion that nations should be persuaded to contract together for a proportional reduction of their armaments does not seem to be entitled to much serious consideration. But the movement in favour of referring differences between nations, such as have so often ended in war, to impartial arbitration, is undoubtedly what we call a practical one. The method of arbitration has been actually tried with success; and it is admitted by the most unromantic statesmen that there is promise in it for the future. Apart from the particular cases in which irritating and threatening differences have already been thus settled, the very fact of nations submitting their claims to what they hope will be just judgment, and then acquiescing in any concessions which the judgment imposes upon them, is likely to exercise a very important moral influence. And this submitting of differences to independent judgment is the line which the historic progress of peace in the world has hitherto taken. The savage way of settling quarrels is to fight them out, till the weaker is killed or has had enough. The interest of the community, as soon as a community of the most elementary kind has existed, has always sought to restrain the free indulgence of personal anger, and with that view the ruling power has undertaken to see any complainant righted and to punish the wrong-doer. The ruling power forbids the members of the community to avenge themselves; it pronounces judgment, and enforces its judgment upon all the parties concerned. And so peace is preserved, in a greater or less degree, in a tribe or a nation. Not only are individuals thus kept from trying what one can do to injure another, but combinations of persons, sometimes embracing large numbers, bring questions of right and wrong into the courts, and submit to the judicial settlement of them. It has been easy to ask, Why should not nations, which are large combinations of persons, have their differences similarly adjusted? And the answer has unfortunately been equally obvious. Nations are not subject to a ruling power. If Europe were divided into a hundred small countries, it might be possible to establish a European federal government, with an adequate force to maintain peace amongst the federated States. But, as things now are and tend to be, we cannot even imagine a central European force that would undertake to treat—say

France and Germany—as subjects, and to prevent them from fighting. And we are obliged to admit that the internal peace of communities would have had a poor chance if it had depended on voluntary submission to arbitration.

With regard to the apparent hesitation on the part of the United States to act on the judgment given by the Court of Arbitrators in a recent controversy, it is impossible that the American people could be guilty of such treason to the cause of peace, and so dishonour themselves, as definitely to repudiate the obligation which they have incurred. But the very hesitation is greatly to be deplored.

Whilst, then, the lovers of peace will do all that they can to promote the international use of arbitration in particular cases, and to establish such a custom of submitting disputed points to arbitration as may have some constraining moral influence over statesmen and people, it is idle to hope for any such success in these endeavours as will warrant a great Power in disarming. When national safety and national honour are at stake, it will not do to trust unreservedly to the kindness and unselfishness of other nations. Arbitration may do mankind the great service of preventing some wars, but no sensible person will persuade himself that it lies in arbitration to abolish war. There are questions which no English statesman would think of referring to arbitration, unless he meant to surrender altogether his country's independence, and to make England the vassal of some Power or Powers outside itself. Our occupation of Egypt is a living example of such a question. Frenchmen, it is said, will never be heartily friendly to us so long as we retain our control of Egypt. I am afraid there is truth in this statement, and it is a serious one for us to keep in mind. But we cannot imagine any earthly judge or jury to whom we could be expected to submit the simple question whether we are to retire from Egypt or not. It would be equivalent to saying to the court, "You must undertake to govern Egypt, and the British empire, and the world." For there is a second question which would require an immediate answer, "What is to happen in Egypt, not to speak of other parts of the world, if we withdraw?"

But my business in this place is to ask what our Christianity prescribes with regard to international peace; and the direct concern of our faith in Christ is not so much with expedients as with tempers and affections. And the properly Christian spirit, if it responds to the heavenly voice which is bidding it claim public affairs as one sphere of its duty, cannot fail to be a powerful influence in the promotion of international peace.

Magnanimity seems to be the name that will best describe the temper proper to a great Christian nation in its dealings with other nations. A state differs from an individual, and national duty is not quite the same as individual duty. But it is a great point to recognise that there is such a thing as duty towards a neighbour nation. To the Christian eye, not only are men of all races members of the universal human race, but the nations are under one heavenly law, and each one has its place and its calling in the great Divine economy. As regards sacred precepts of policy, we are at a disadvantage from the fact that the New Testament age was not an age of independent nations, but of an empire with subject provinces ; and every precept of Christ and His Apostles possesses the reality and life of being meant for those to whom it was first addressed. The New Testament is the book of the Catholic Church, of redeemed mankind. But the New Testament is supplemented by the Old, which is the book of a nation. And even in the New Testament there is enough to make nations honourable and sacred to those who see, as we do, that God is at this time constructing the world out of them. I must take this for granted, and I will ask, Have we in England, we English Christians, acquired thoroughly the habit of honouring the nations with which we stand side by side in the world? Do we always bear in mind that they are entitled to our respect, to our good will, to our friendly consideration, to a favourable construction of their sentiments? Do we feel it to be wrong, an act to be ashamed of, a violation of God's law, though there may be no human tribunal to punish it, that one Power should behave unjustly or offensively to another Power?

There are those who persuade themselves that wars are the wanton work of kings and diplomatists, ·and that if we could only get the populations consulted before coming to blows, there would to a certainty be an end of war. But most of us do not so read history. A population often has more passion, a hotter sense of outraged pride or interest, less prudence, than sovereigns and ministers of state. And with us in England, there is no great danger of the Government hurrying us into a war which the people would judge to be unnecessary and unjustifiable. At all events, a gracious and magnanimous feeling on the part of the general population towards foreign nations would quickly tell on the policy of our Foreign Office : nay, why should we not congratulate ourselves on its having told already? For I do believe that in the general mind of England there is more of a desire to act justly, considerately, peaceably, towards all other nations, great and small, than is abroad put to the credit of perfidious Albion. If we venture to think fairly well of ourselves in this respect, let us try earnestly to justify our self-esteem. By our own habitual temper and way of speaking we should let our representatives know that we wish them, not to weaken our fighting force, not to lessen our influence for good in the world, but to refrain carefully from all that an impartial judge would pronounce to be aggressive, insolent, vexatiously exacting, and to make liberal allowance for national susceptibilities.

I have admitted that, as regards Christian duty, we cannot transfer the principles of conduct straight from the individual to a nation. The Christian law of personal duty is that a man should surrender himself absolutely to the disposal of the heavenly Father, so that by him and through him the Father's will may be done : not—as sacrifice is sometimes perversely misunderstood — that he should throw himself away, or make himself less serviceable to the Father's purposes than he might be ; but that he should offer himself, the best he is and the best he can make of himself, to the doing of the Father's will. And this we may believe to be also the true principle of a nation's conduct. But an individual may easily be called, in this sacrifice of himself, to give up his life or his property: for a nation, on the other hand—while we may refrain from laying down that it can never be conceivably a nation's duty to give up its life—it seems to be almost an absolute duty to cherish and defend its life. It is not a selfish feeling in a citizen to rejoice in his country's independence and greatness.

And such a feeling will of itself dispose the wise patriot to desire that his nation should cultivate an unaggressive and respectful policy, a policy of goodwill and consideration, towards other nations. For a nation may take to itself the encouragement given both under the old covenant and the new to individuals: "He that would love life and see good days, let him refrain his tongue from evil, and his lips that they speak no guile: and let him turn away from evil and do good; let him seek peace, and pursue it. For the eyes of the Lord are upon the righteous, and His ears unto their supplication; but the face of the Lord is upon them that do evil." It cannot be hurtful to a nation in the long-run that it should endeavour, at the cost of some self-restraint and of any reasonable concessions, to be on the best possible terms with its neighbours. I am far from advocating a feeble external policy, but before and beneath any duty of going to war and of trying to be victorious in war, the Christian must set, for his country as for himself, the great ideal of peace and good-will amongst men. The Lord, whose slaves we Christians are, is the Prince of Peace. If He forbade us absolutely to strike with the whip or with the sword, to deal death with rifle or artillery, we should be bound to obey Him. When He bids us fight, it must be because the true peace which He loves, and which He came to establish, is to be better attained by fighting than by submitting. Inasmuch as the Son of God is the heavenly Peacemaker, there is a blessing on all who anywhere make peace, and they shall share His name, and be called sons of God.

But St. Paul's precept admits that the keeping of peace does not depend upon one party only. The most peaceable of men may be forced into a contention, into an appeal to the law which may result in bringing serious punishment upon his adversary. And a nation may be forced into war more easily, according to Christian principles, than a single person into a quarrel; because kings and ministers of state, and all citizens in their degree, are trustees for large and high interests, which it is not within their right to surrender as men may surrender things which are privately theirs. At present there is no way of securely preventing war. That a great nation should make it known that nothing will provoke it into war, and should let its high spirit run down and its weapons of attack and defence grow rusty, is unquestionably the way to invite treatment from other powers which no self-respecting nation could tolerate. If you could imagine England persuaded by blind letter-worshipping Christians to disarm itself, totally or partially, that would be the worst service that could be rendered to the cause of peace.

We have to reckon upon war as possibly inevitable. I do not enter into argument with those who hold that a Christian man is not allowed in any circumstances, in a private or a public cause, to lay a finger of force upon a fellow-man. I believe that they entirely misread the New Testament; but they are few, and almost silent. A far more injurious notion is that of those who assume that war is an unchristian sort of thing, but also that it is a necessity in such a world as this. If it is necessary to go to war, it is not unchristian. Nothing that is necessary is forbidden by Christ. And if we can enter upon war with a clear conscience, it is foolish to urge that we should disable ourselves beforehand for the conflict. The chance of having to go to war implies to a rational mind our making ourselves ready for war. What can we think of the good sense of those—and there are such persons—who in the same breath will denounce armaments and demand that our Government should instantly protect Armenians from the cruelties of Turks and Kurds? It is not for me to express an opinion as to what our armies and ships of war and defences should be, and I do not know that there is any slackness on the part of our people in making such preparations as their responsible advisers tell them are necessary. Every one can understand how important it is to protect our trade and guard our dense population from being starved. But it does not appear to me to be unsuitable that I should appeal to our Christianity as not merely permitting but enjoining us to keep ourselves well armed, and to nourish a courageous spirit.

I remember being present a good many years ago at a meeting for religious discussion, at which Mr. Henry Richard was invited to plead the cause of peace. Mr. Richard was a good man, who drew to himself the reverent esteem of all who knew him. We listened to him with sincere respect as he dwelt upon the horrors of war, and made appalling calculations of the money spent on armaments. And we were then constrained to ask him what his counsel was with regard to our armies and fleets. He protested rather warmly that he had never maintained that we ought to disarm ourselves altogether. What then? Did he contend that we were spending four times as much, or twice as much, on armaments as we ought to do? But he disliked being thus questioned, and replied that he was sorry not to meet with more sympathy from his audience. No doubt we ought not to blind ourselves to the wounds and deaths and destruction of property which war causes, nor to the fact that the millions which we spend on our army and navy might be otherwise spent on various good objects. But a nation which spends what it deems necessary, however immense the sum may be, on self-preservation, may rightly ask, " Is not the life more than meat, and the body than raiment?" An accurate description of a field of battle, of a rout, of a siege, of an army wasted by disease, may be painful beyond what we can bear. But it is not amiss to remember that there are other human sufferings which would not form a pleasant picture. These soldiers who have been killed or badly wounded were not otherwise going to live for ever in perfect health. How many of them might not have suffered as much or more before they died, if they had not been victims of war? And the lives of many of them, if they had been prolonged, would not to a certainty have been of great value. Human life is not all golden. We often express without misgivings a deliberate wish that there were not so large a quantity of it upon certain areas as there is. But if we decline to go into uncomfortable comparative estimates of this kind, the horrors of war and its expensiveness, honestly and sternly faced, may produce another impression upon our minds than that of daunting us.

If there are any lessons characteristic of Christianity, this is one of them—that we are to set the things of the spirit above the things of the flesh. There is no amount of fleshly ease that can be weighed in the scales of Christ against even a low spiritual value. And the honour and consciousness of a nation are spiritual things. It has often been alleged by free critics that the morality of the New Testament is defective in not including patriotism amongst the Christian virtues. But Christianity puts no slight upon the Jewish patriotism, that supreme virtue of the Old Testament, which is a part of our Christian inheritance. If you could bring together under one view all the deaths and wounds that Englishmen have suffered and inflicted in war, and make one colossal addition sum of all the moneys spent on war by English governments from the days of Alfred till now, can we set the pain and the cost for a moment against what England has been and is in the realm of the spirit to her sons? The truth on which I am insisting has been expressed in some vivid sentences by the author of *Ecce Homo:* "War is frequently denounced as unchristian, because it involves circumstances of horror: and when the ardent champions of some great cause have declared that they would persevere although it should be necessary to lay waste a continent and exterminate a nation, the resolution is stigmatised as shocking and unchristian. Shocking it may be, but not therefore unchristian" (p. 278). Whilst he condemns religious persecutions as deplorable mistakes, carried on with much evil passion, he is yet bold to testify—"the ostensible object of such horrors was Christian, and the indignation which professedly prompts them is also Christian, and the assumption they involve, that agonies of pain and blood shed in rivers are less evils than the soul spotted and bewildered with sin, is most Christian" (p. 280). I do not see how we can refuse our assent to these statements; and in days of softness, when an absurd value is set upon human life as mere existence, it must be well that we should steep our minds in such convictions. At the same time, it is a comfort to know that Christian humanity has done something, and may probably do more, to mitigate the horrors of war, as well as to make its occurrence less likely. Under international rules, which it is the interest of all Powers to observe, non-combatants have now a degree of protection which formerly they could not claim; and to the fighting men war is made by various prescriptions less exasperating than it used to be. Here is a field on which our Christianity is bound to push its influence to the furthest possible point.

Some of those who denounce war would meet the argument that there are spiritual values for which we must be ready to suffer and inflict the pains involved in war by asserting that war necessarily degrades the contending nations by the unspiritual passions which it stimulates and lets loose. I find it alleged, for example, that "the moral deterioration and the depraving of right principle involved in war are much more serious than the visible and immediate results of this abysmal evil." I believe that actual experience calls for some modification of this judgment. There is a terrible war, producing hideous slaughter, now going on between China and Japan. It looks as if it were an aggressive war on the part of Japan. But I feel little doubt that the Japanese people are raised in the moral scale rather than lowered by this war; that they hate the Chinese less now than they did before the war began; that the patriotic sentiment inspiring the whole people to make joyful sacrifices for the sake of the safety and aggrandisement of their country is on the whole an elevating one. The most shocking war of my lifetime was the American civil war; and I do not believe that any American who lived through the war in either Northern or Southern State would admit that the general moral tone of the population was lowered by it. As to the moral effect of the Crimean war I can speak with more knowledge. Some of my hearers may think that I am making myself an apologist for war; but I am conscious of no other desire than to do justice to the good I have known. It is impossible for those who lived during that war to forget how deeply we were all moved by it; and every emotion that it stirred, of hope, of anxiety, of awe, of grief, was a nobler one than the habitual feelings of ordinary life. We had no malignant hatred of the enemy. The luxurious class sent out its men in larger proportion than any other class to die and to suffer cruel hardships for their country. I was then living and working in Whitechapel, and I had much to do with correspondence between families there and soldiers in the Crimea, and I could not help seeing how humble lives were exalted by the demands and the dangers of heroic service. I had a friend who was with our army as chaplain in the Crimea, and who saw all the miseries of that terrible campaign without the stimulus of being a combatant; and after his return he told me that, as he reflected on the past, he was sure he had never lived in so good a spiritual atmosphere as that of the English army on those blood-stained heights. Do not suppose me to say that we should do well in going to war for the sake of the moral advantages that we might gain by it; I have sufficiently declared that I count it a sin to bring on a needless war : but I hold myself warranted in believing that, if at any time we felt that as a self-respecting nation we had no alternative but to accept a challenge to battle, we might expect a fine thrill to go through every section of the population, waking up unselfish aspirations, drawing us into mutual sympathy and united effort, and teaching us to value more worthily the glories and blessings of our national heritage.

As I am asking you to look at the question of international peace and war in the light of resolute uncompromising Christian faith, and especially with reference to the personal duty lying upon us as citizens of a Christian country, I do not dwell at any length upon the aspects of war which have presented themselves to historical inquirers, when they have endeavoured to estimate the effects of particular wars upon the nations which have been engaged in them. But if we reject the doctrine that a war has always been sin and wickedness from beginning to end and on both sides, and hold that a nation may be obeying Christ in taking up arms, there may well be some Christian satisfaction in recognising the service which war has been made to render to the progress of mankind. We rightly desire to see in the history of the world as many signs of a beneficent governing Hand as we can discern. Looking back upon the period which comes within living memory, we find results of primary importance ascribed by political observers to almost every great war of the period. There seem to be knots in human affairs which cannot be untied by negotiation, and which require the violence of war to cut them. I suppose there is no American, even in the Southern States, who does not now recognise that the sufferings and losses of the civil war were a price that it was worth while to pay for the deliverance of the continent from slavery, and for the higher and closer unity which binds the several States and their people into one great nation. On the soil of Italy rivers of blood have been shed in our time; but the result of the carnage has been to change Italy from being a geographical expression into a united nation and an important European Power. As to the terrible war between Germany and France, it is impossible that Germans can regard it as a baneful and fruitless crime; whilst even Frenchmen, smarting under the humiliation of their country, have been able to recognise great compensating advantages in the downfall of the Second Empire and in the forcing of wholesome thought into the minds of the French people. Those who value trade highly, as most do of those to whom war is entirely evil and absolutely wrong, will not be able to blind themselves to the good which may at least be occasioned by evil, if victorious Japan should compel the Chinese to open their whole empire freely to foreign trade. This will do the Chinese themselves more good, in the mere maintenance of physical life and well-being, than they will have suffered harm in the slaughter of their worthless armies and the disabling of costly vessels. A war is sharp, but it does not last long, whilst these vast boons go on spreading their influence from year to year and from generation to generation.

Such historical observations may make us doubtful whether the time has yet come in the counsels of God for the superseding of war, and therefore less willing to risk the honour and greatness of our country on the chance that no foreign Power will ever offer us an insult or do us an injury : but they ought not to persuade statesmen—and I do not believe that they would—to speculate in war as a means of gaining something for their country and for mankind. I would echo the doctrine of the Quakers, that where duty is clear, the results of doing it are to be left in God's hands. God knows better than we do how His world is to be governed. He must have ways, whether we can imagine them or not, of governing the world without war. He must know how to save a people from being engrossed by money-getting, or surrendering themselves to the excitements of frivolity and carnal pleasure, or being turned into sheep by the dull and comfortable routine of a quiet life. And nothing can be clearer than the Christian duty of doing what makes for peace. It can never be right to be insolent, grasping, false to engagements. We ought to be lovers of our country, and it cannot be wrong that a blush of anger should come into the cheek of a Christian citizen if the honour of his nation should be outraged or its rightful interests assailed ; but it is still more certainly right that the blush should turn itself into one of shame if the country that he loves should be betrayed by its Government into aggressive or justly irritating action, especially towards a weaker state. The ideal bearing of a Christian Power in international relations seems to be that of a high-spirited gentleman of the old time—of a person, that is, trained to the use of arms, ready to resent a purposed outrage, but mindful of the obligations of courtesy and honour and social harmony, conscious that his station pledges him to self-restraint and magnanimity, *un*willing to wound yet *not* afraid to strike.

XX

PUBLIC SPIRIT[1]

"Not looking each of you to his own things, but each of you also to the things of others."—PHILIPPIANS ii. 4.

I AM about to speak of Public Spirit as a Christian virtue, included in the comprehensive sum of Christian duty. Before I do so, let me refer to a way of thinking about it which may be thus expressed :—
"Public Spirit is a civic virtue which has nothing to do with religion. When we study it where it has existed in greatest force, we observe that it is bred, or at least strongly stimulated, by particular circumstances. It is often made a part of a strictly human and secular morality. It may indeed, especially in the form of patriotism or love of country, be a whole religion in itself. If religion be, according to Matthew Arnold's definition of it, morality touched with emotion, then a patriotism like that of the Greeks of to-day has seriousness enough to be reckoned a religion. But the Greeks, or at least many of the most fervid of them, are not thinking of their duty to God or to Christ when they are giving themselves up for their country."

[1] Preached at St. Edmund's, Lombard Street, in Lent 1897.

Well, but suppose we want to urge public spirit as a duty, to say to people, "You ought to have more public spirit than you have,"—how are we to do it? It is not enough to tell them that public spirit is bred by particular circumstances. To believe that, and nothing else, about it, seems to make all exhortation foolish. Say to a man, "If you wish to be moral, you will be public-spirited; for the moralists of highest authority include public spirit in morality," he will not be irrational if something within him replies, "But suppose I do not wish to be moral! You may tell me that I shall then incur so much disapprobation, or at least fail to win so much admiration; but I may be able to put up with that disadvantage."

It is a different thing when we can assert, as the Christian does, a supernatural claim upon us. Morality, when it appeals to no superhuman authority, has to make the most of opinion and interest to back it, for it has nothing to say to the conscience. The conscience has no meaning without a God to whose voice it is an ear. We Christians have nothing to say against morality; we claim the very best morality, the most refined, and comprehensive, and universal, as ours by right. What we do is to put a foundation under it to give it something to rest upon; or, to use a better figure, to show and bear witness to the living root from which good human conduct grows. It is not a case of morality on one side and Christianity on the other, but of Christianity beneath and morality built upon it. The morality that chooses to be of this world only may be as good as possible, but to us it wants support and force; and Christianity on its part is artificial and worthless if it does not quicken and shape all conduct.

It is with the Christian principles of life, with the Christian revelation which gives us those principles, that we here, I in the pulpit and you in the church, are properly concerned. Let us look to the New Testament for these principles as they bear on the subject which is to occupy us.

You will easily recall what supremacy and power the idea of communion had in the first days of the Church. "The multitude of them that believed were of one heart and soul; and not one of them said that aught of the things which he possessed was his own; but they had all things common." You remember how this idea is insisted on as the governing principle of life by the Christian teachers, and especially by the chief Christian teacher, St. Paul. The believers were to regard themselves as the many members—the various limbs and organs—of one body. "We that are strong," said St. Paul, "ought to bear the infirmities of the weak, and not to please ourselves." We ought: that is, such fellow-help is required of us by the claim which God and Christ make upon us, and by the constitution in which we are set together; and our God holds us responsible for it. Say that this is religious teaching; so it is: but what kind of action does it prescribe? That is the question. It bids every Christian—every one who desires or is willing to be reckoned a follower of Christ—regard himself, not as an isolated individual, but as a member of a body, bound to fill his own place and do his own work in the interest of the body as a whole; it forbids him to say that anything that he has is his own; it constrains him to look, not only to his own advantage or pleasure, but also to the advantage or pleasure of others; it calls upon the strong to bear the infirmities of the weak, and not to please themselves. The dispositions thus enjoined cannot but take the form of civic or public spirit, in those Christians who belong to a country and are citizens of a commonwealth. True Christianity, it is evident, will go a long way in furthering social happiness; it subjects and coerces the individual more inwardly, and therefore more thoroughly, than any secular socialism can do, to the service of the community.

"Zeal for the public good," wrote Addison two centuries ago, "is the characteristic of a man of honour and a gentleman." An excellent maxim which ought still to be taken to heart by those who hold themselves to be under the obligations of men of honour and gentlemen. But our age is a different one from Addison's. We do not see why other men should not have a zeal for the public good as well as those of the upper class; and we have plenty of evidence that poor men may have as much public spirit as the rich. It is sometimes assumed that, under a democracy, the many will be, more or less excusably, bent upon getting as much as they can of the good things of the country for themselves; if they are, they will not be unlike the classes which have gone before them; but democratic movements have always had much more in them than the coveting of personal advantage. The largest element in the active democratic spirit has always been sympathy: and the masses of the people are easily moved by a common generous impulse. What we are now recognising is that zeal for the public good is characteristic of the Christian citizen, whether he be rich or poor, a person of influence or one of the many.

Patriotism and public spirit do not seem to be quite the same thing. In England there has always been an inexhaustible reserve of patriotism to rely upon in all classes. Englishmen have known at the bottom of their hearts the claim that their country has upon them; and during Queen Victoria's reign our country has greatly multiplied and strengthened its claims upon the whole people and on every class. When the occasion comes, it will once more find Englishmen ready to make any sacrifices for the safety and the honour of this inviolate land. But in the century now drawing to its close there has been more of individualism—to use the modern phrase—amongst us than in any other time or place. Circumstances have favoured the struggling of each individual to get on in life; and it is admitted that the amazing increase of the wealth of the country, and some other important advantages, are in great part due to this freedom and energy of competition. Together with this success of individuals, the sentiment and assumptions of individualism have become prevalent. People have clung tightly to what they have obtained by energy and adventure and toil. It has been thought that a man has an absolute ownership of what he happens to possess, a right to enjoy it himself as he pleases, and to leave it to be enjoyed by others after his death as it may please him to dictate. It has been assumed to be rather hard upon the individual that he should have to contribute to the public needs. The right of a man to do what he likes with his own has been thought to be at the foundation of society, at the very roots of things; the right of the country to take from a man for the benefit of the community to be very secondary, and a claim which it has been legitimate to regard with suspicion and hostility. There has been a certain amount of liberal giving; but it has been treated as something exceptional, and made so much of that one would have thought there would have been more of it for the sake of winning the admiration accorded to it.

The result of these influences is, that we are behind no country in private wealth and its personal and domestic expenditure, but are behind many countries—I rather think, behind all other countries—in the scale of what is applied to the service and enjoyment of the community. Now public expenditure is really better, more reasonable and more Christian, than private. If this statement seems doubtful to you, consider it. Imagine St. Paul, or any other honoured teacher of mankind, visiting two countries. In the one, let us suppose, he finds the private houses modest, personal luxury moderate, but all things belonging to the public—edifices, lands, institutions, administrations—showing signs of pride and care and free expenditure; in the other, let us suppose, he finds individuals and families vying with one another in cultivating the pleasures and exhibiting the adornments of life, but whatever is to be held and used in common starved and looked at in a jealous and grudging spirit. Which of the two nations, think you, would be pronounced to be the wiser and more Christian? To our forefathers, in this England of ours, the claim of the community was stronger than it has been to Englishmen of recent generations. The magnificent cathedrals, our precious parish churches, the ancient colleges and schools, remain as evidences of what was dedicated to God and the public in ages which had not, I daresay, the hundredth part of our wealth; and in those same times the demands made on property and lives for the incessant wars at home and abroad were what we should call ruinous. Even the castles of the great were public fortresses more than private pleasure-houses.

Those were not democratic ages, as regards forms of government. But in our time, democratic institutions seem to be specially successful in calling forth public spirit. Those who travel in the United States tell us of the many proofs of public spirit that America exhibits: in the newest settlements, the places of worship, the schools, the institutes, the libraries, surprise the English visitor by the amount spent upon them. That direction of effort and expenditure is due to the strong hold that the common life and the public interest have upon Americans in general. The voluntary gifts of wealthy Americans are on a splendid scale; but the rates or taxes levied for public purposes are also on a scale not known in this country. A rate may be a gift, as really as a subscription, from those who agree willingly to impose it upon themselves; and amongst the members of a self-governing community a liberal public spirit will show itself in generous rating for the common good.

There are signs of progress in this direction amongst ourselves. We see something of democratic self-respect stirring in our large populations. Whilst we retain, with universal acquiescence and satisfaction, the forms of our ancient monarchy, and Queen Victoria sits on the throne of Queen Elizabeth, we do not disguise from ourselves what the reality of our Government is. Gradual changes have spread the powers of legislation and administration more and more widely amongst the people. So far, under these changes, our country has prospered. The comforts of life were never so widely diffused, contentment and concord never prevailed so universally, as at this time. You will not suppose me to be stating that all is with us now as it should be: what I do affirm is that things are better, in the most important respects, as regards the country in general and all classes in it, than they ever were before. There is a general willingness that legislation should occupy itself with attempts to improve the condition of the classes which most need legislative help. We have every reason, as Englishmen and Englishwomen, to be thankful and to be hopeful.

In order that things may go better and better in this dear country of ours, we especially want two good things to be given to us in richer measure: that public spirit of which I have been speaking, and intelligence. I have maintained that the true public spirit is essentially a Christian virtue.

On the one hand, I cannot imagine the Christian consciousness to be strong in any man—and by the

Christian consciousness I mean devotion to Christ and thankfulness to the Father—without its making him public-spirited. I have reminded you that by the Christian calling every Christian is to regard himself as a member of a body, as having received from God whatever he possesses, and as holding it all in trust for the common good. A man who is arrogant or exclusive, a man of selfish ambition or close class-feeling, has not been mastered by Christian convictions.

And, on the other hand, I believe that political public spirit will show itself wanting in depth and permanence, unless it is rooted in the religious awe, and sense of brotherhood, and power of sacrifice, which we know as Christian. We want an increase of the Christian public spirit in all classes. Our richer people have nothing like the sense of duty to the public, the *communis sensus*, which has been shown by the rich in other ages and in other countries. They do not understand how largely they owe what they have inherited or what they have acquired to their nation. They and their property are created by their country—by its past, by its laws, by its greatness; and they owe to their country not only their lives, but the best use they can make of their possessions for their country's good. And as Christians they are bound to regard all that they have as not their own, but as held by them in trust. And the classes that we should not call rich, the working people and those not much above them, these need public spirit also. No doubt the class-feeling amongst the working people, which is admittedly strong, may almost claim to be public spirit, because they form the bulk of the population, and because the poor need sympathy and help more than the well-to-do. But so far as it remains class-feeling, it has not the full virtue of public spirit, and cannot claim to be that Christian civic feeling by which all the sons of Christian England should be distinguished. We all want a stronger conviction that the general good has a divine claim upon us, upon soul and body, persons and means. We must learn to take a pride and grateful pleasure in the places to which we belong, and which have ministered so largely to our happiness as well as to our existence. It is always honourable to a city when its people show that they care for it, and do not grudge making sacrifices for its credit and advantage.

And then we want intelligence. That apostolic saying will come into Christian minds, "If any of you lacketh wisdom, let him ask of God, who giveth to all liberally, and upbraideth not." It is important that in trying to serve the public in the Name of Christ, we should have the best aims before our minds, and should pursue them in wise manners. We have one great warning, that we cannot trust for guidance to our sympathetic impulses only. What is more natural for those who hold themselves responsible for their fellow-countrymen and brethren than to wish that public relief should be given freely to the needy, and especially to those who excite our compassion the most? Many persons are taking for granted that a Christian liberal spirit in a community cannot be better shown than in insisting that the utmost relief now allowed by the law should be given to the poor, and in helping to get the restrictions imposed by the law abolished. But experience gives a strange rebuff to this desire. All those who have studied the question practically and in the most Christian spirit are convinced that there is no surer way of lowering and injuring the poorest class than that of encouraging them to look to the rates for relief. Wherever relief is given freely, there to a certainty pauperism, with all its degradations, will be promoted. I do not know anything that so forces a Christian to reflect, and pause, and look up as this surprising fact. It obliges us to recognise and keep in mind that it is a higher duty to lift up the character of our poorer and weaker brethren, and to care for their independence and human dignity, than to give them what is needful for the body. We want our population to consist of persons who, down to the very lowest, maintain themselves and those who belong to them in honourable independence; and therefore we must beware of doing anything which experience shows to be hurtful to their self-respect and moral strength.

We want our population also to consist of temperate persons, and—if there are some who see their way confidently as to the best methods of securing universal temperance—there are many who feel strongly the need of being guided wisely by experience and knowledge in this important matter. Again, we want our population to be well educated ; and for doing the best that can be done towards this end also, we need similar guidance and readiness to follow it. Who, once more, will doubt that we want a keen and temperate intelligence, as well as courageous sympathy, for the development of the new conditions of labour in the new epoch on which we have entered?

The true social feeling, welcoming light and guidance from above and from around us,—that, my Christian brethren, is what should be strong in a Christian community. Through *that* the Spirit of God will work out the divine purposes in this favoured land. Let us open our hearts with awe to His gracious influences; let us lend ourselves to be instruments and ministers of higher than selfish aims, of nobler interests than those of personal enrichment or ambition; let us be glad to give each his help in whatever promises to make us a more united, a more intelligent, and a more Christian people.

XXI

THE NATURE OF JUSTICE: AN EXPOSITION ADDRESSED TO WORKING MEN

IN taking for my subject the nature of justice, I am attempting to deal with a question which may perhaps put some strain upon your attention; but it is manifestly a very important one, and, whilst in many ways it comes home to us all, it has a special interest for those who have anything to do with industrial operations or with political affairs. We are to ask why it is that any arrangement or mutual dealing between man and man is pronounced to be just or to be contrary to justice. I can understand, indeed, that some may be inclined to say, " Any one can see, without going into the reason why, that some arrangements that prevail now, and some things that are done, are unjust. What we want is that the injustice may be redressed without delay, and that things may be arranged more fairly, so that we may all have our rights." But thinking men find it a great satisfaction to know the reason why; and whilst there will be always differences of opinion as to what is just, the differences are likely to be aggravated if we are unable to explain what makes anything just. It is not enough to go by feeling; there will be different feelings on different sides; we want to understand, if we can, what justice means.

There is a very general disposition to catch at the notion of *equality* as explaining justice. It has been affirmed that all men are equal, and that perfect justice would consist in their all having equal advantages. "Why," it is asked, "should one man have more than another?" But what ground is there for saying that all men are in any sense equal? The statement seems utterly inconsistent with fact, and I know of no sense in which it can be made out to be true. The person who asks, "Why should one man be rich and another poor when all men are naturally equal?" might go on to ask, "Why should one man be tall and another short? Why should one man have better health, better looks, more talent, a nicer wife, finer children, more virtuous parents, than another?" The truth is that inequality exists everywhere in the world, and that we should be extremely puzzled to make a world upon the principle of all being equal. And it is never equality that we really want. You may be struck by the different degrees in which health is distributed amongst men. It pains us to think of the amount of ill-health that there is in the world. But you would not wish to bring about equality by making some less well whilst you make others less ill. You would aim at making the sick more healthy, not for the sake of equality, but for the sake of their being happier and being able to do more. If any one objects that it is Nature or the Creator who makes all the other inequalities, but that it is man who makes some rich and others poor, and that man ought to refrain from imitating Nature by the promotion of inequality, that is a distinction which will not hold good. Men become richer than others by nature, as we may say—by being clever or lucky or parsimonious, much more than by any artificial arrangements created by law. No, the foundations of the world are not laid on equality, nor will the perfection of society be found in making men equal. Harmony of various and unequal parts, not equality, will characterise the perfect society.

Another explanation of justice, which puts equality altogether aside, is of special interest because it issues from that great doctrine of evolution which is characteristic of our time, and has been expounded by the illustrious philosopher who is the chief authority on evolution, Mr. Herbert Spencer. Justice is defined by him to be the social equilibrium between the desires of the individual and the desires of the many. He accounts for its production in this way:— The one creative principle in the history of the world, from the beginning till now, is asserted to be the desire of every living thing for preservation and gratification. It is to this desire that all progress is due. Like Oliver Twist in Dickens's story, who, on a celebrated occasion, "asked for more," every living creature is always asking for more. But it so happens that each may often get the more—may gain safety and possessions and enjoyment—through the combination of individuals in a society. Social unions make rules for the advantage of their members in general, and these rules, whilst they have their origin in the desire of each for gratification, yet restrict the efforts of each to obtain gratifications for his independent self. Justice, teaches Mr. Herbert Spencer, is the balance or equilibrium which has established itself at any time between the self-seeking activities of the individual and the rules made by society for the protection and benefit of its members. Laws are attempts to register the equilibrium, and to enforce the observance of it on all; and the object of the best laws and most advanced justice is to secure the largest freedom for the individual to assert himself and to gain advantages for himself that is compatible with the interests of society—that is, of the other individuals around him. This is an interesting theory, to a considerable extent fitting the facts of the case; but it fails to explain why we should *reverence* justice as we do. It reduces justice to a casual result of competitive self-seeking. Each individual may be forced to conform himself to this justice by the power of the many; but what is there in the equilibrium produced by the power of the many restricting the desires of the one, to strike awe into the conscience, or to constrain us to moral obedience?

When conflicting interests are disturbing the equilibrium which has for a time prevailed,—say when there is a struggle between labour and capital, there is a general feeling that if we could only find out what is just, a new equilibrium might be established in accordance with justice. The name of justice is always invoked by the workers as supporting their demand for higher wages or better conditions of labour. But Mr. Spencer's theory knows of no justice but the equilibrium itself, which will be attained when the conflicting forces have agreed in a compromise or have otherwise come to rest.

Now, to urge that justice demands that workers should be paid so much is surely to say that some law or authority to which all men owe deference enjoins that so much should be paid. When you can say, "This is unjust," "That would be just," you do so with confident assurance that those who are concerned in the matter ought to, are bound to, conform to what is just. You assume that there is an authority of some kind over them, regulating the matter in question, to which, as good and reasonable men, they ought willingly to submit, and to which, if they are not willing, they should be made to submit. Let us say, then, that social justice in general is what this law to which all men owe deference prescribes as to their dealings with one another. What the supreme or Divine law ordains for the mutual dealings of men, *that* is just.

We find in this view a recognition and a partial explanation of the deference which we all pay to justice. We all confess that justice has authority over ourselves—that we are bound to seek and do what is just. We hold also that justice has authority over other men; that we are right in enforcing justice upon our fellow-men, whether they like it or not; that justice is something to live and to die for. The simplest explanation of the deference thus due to justice—and I know nothing else that adequately explains it—is that we recognise in justice the will of the good Maker and Ruler of mankind.

I am well aware that devoted worshippers and champions of justice are to be found amongst those who do not profess to acknowledge a God. But in worshipping justice they are really worshipping the nature and will of Him whom they refuse to acknowledge by name. Why are any of us bound to reverence justice, and to submit to it, and to do it, unless it is the law of the Power that makes us and is above us?

In the book entitled *Paris*, written by the French novelist whose trial has lately attracted the attention of the world, the author advocates atheism and justice as against Christianity and charity. Charity has had its trial, he says, and has failed—has failed to produce social happiness. Science, taking the place of Christianity, is to bring about a justice which will make mankind happy. But whenever he approaches any explanation of justice, he implies that it is what would come to pass if men were to act wisely and well in accordance with the true laws of life. We can get no notion of a justice other than the mere will of the stronger, a justice commanding our respect, without thus implying that it is what the Maker of men ordains. But how are we to know what the Divine law ordains?

In this way. You need not look far back upon human history to see that there is progress in the world, and progress along certain lines. You perceive that the Supreme Power is building up mankind, or—to use the more frequent language of the day—developing the human race. During the last half-century improvement has been wonderfully rapid and general, in this country perhaps more than anywhere else, but also throughout the world. Ask any old man with a good memory to tell you how things were sixty years ago with regard to the wages of the working classes, their food, their dwellings, their education, their self-respect and manners, the feeling that prevailed between different classes of society, and you will get some notion of what the improvement has been in the condition of the largest part of the population. You would receive a similar impression if any one were to describe to you the chief changes in the laws which have taken place during the same period.

Now, in all social improvement we read the purpose of the Builder of mankind. A machine does not grow as society grows; but continual improvements are made in machinery, by which it becomes more complicated, more effective, and more admirable. So it is with mankind. Human society is at its best when its members are severally happiest, and the largest variety of elements are contained in it, and these elements or members are most in harmony and fellow-feeling with each other. The Supreme Power has been mysteriously content with slowness of progress; but the great commonwealths of to-day are on the whole far happier and more socially perfect than those of any former day.

By social justice we mean, then, the plan, the whole system of relations, according to which the Supreme Power is building or developing the human world—the living order which the Maker appoints for the good of society, and which therefore has the Maker's authority to back it.

By far the largest and most important part of

social justice is to be found in the law of the land. The law fixes and enforces those regulations of mutual intercourse and exchange which have so far been found by general consent to be most satisfactory; and by doing so it confers inestimable benefits on mankind. It enables people to get on together without friction, and so it provides free play for the affections and charities of human nature. The law lays down for us what we can depend upon, and makes it possible to provide for the future; and so it cherishes that sense of responsibility without which a man can have no dignity, and that quiet confidence without which a life of responsibility cannot be a happy one. A population that understands what it owes to the laws will be heartily a law-abiding people. And what we call men's rights are for the most part what the law gives and secures to them.

But we are continually amending our laws. That is one of the proofs that the human race is made for progress. It is the evident purpose of the Maker of mankind that the communities of men should grow more perfect, that improvements should be made without ceasing in their social machinery. Society, or the energetic portion of it, is strongly possessed at this time by a belief in improvement and a longing for it, and a readiness to make changes in order to obtain it. We often say that some arrangement differing from what the law now fixes and enforces would be just, and that we can appeal to justice in demanding it. What do we mean by affirming it to be just, and by urging that it ought to be adopted with universal consent because it is just? I have contended that social justice consists in the best arrangements with regard to mutual dealings that men have been led to make for the good of society. Well, when we see plainly that some new arrangement, to be enforced by law or by opinion, would be to the great advantage of some, and would also promote the general well-being, and could be introduced at once without such disturbance of possession or ease or feeling as would neutralise its value,—then we can believe confidently that this is what the Father of men is desiring and intending to bring about, and we claim His authority for it by affirming that it is just. Nothing but this appeal to an unseen authority can account for the difference which we hold ourselves bound to pay, and which we call upon others to pay, to justice. It often takes some time to see what is just. You observe that I said that we pronounce a new arrangement to be peremptorily demanded by justice when it is practicable. It is not till we see it to be practicable that we have the inner confidence that the authority of the good Lord of society is backing it, and can therefore challenge the world to deny that it is just.

Let me take an illustration from a province outside labour questions. During the last half-century some of the most inportant social changes that have been made have concerned women's rights. The changes have been made slowly, but surely and progressively, and with remarkable general assent. They are partly legal, and partly they depend on opinion. They have been promoted by Conservatives as well as by Liberals. The law now gives to married women, for example, a control over their property which they did not formerly possess. It was urged that it was just that they should have it, and that it was their right. The interpretation of this contention was that the control of their property would be good for married women themselves, and that it could be conferred on them with advantage to society in general. It has also been demanded, as you know, that women should have the same votes that men have; and it is asserted by most of the advocates of women's suffrage that justice requires that they should have votes, and that women are kept out of their rights till they get them. Some votes, such as those for municipal administration and the working of the Poor Law, have already been given to women, but the parliamentary franchise is still withheld from them. If you are in favour of women's suffrage you will probably say that a woman has a right to vote as well as a man; and opponents will reply with evident force that they do not understand a natural or inherent right to vote; that the law does not give the vote to every man, but to such men as it chooses; that it makes the young man of twenty-one years a voter and disfranchises the young man who is only a day younger, and in other ways asserts the right to select and to reject at its discretion. The fact is that, when people say that it is only just that women should have votes, it is not because they hold women to be equal to men—which is no more true than that men are all equal to one another—but because they believe it to be clear enough for every one to be able to see it, that the extending of the parliamentary franchise to women would make women more satisfied and happier and better, and would not be to the injury but rather to the advantage of society in general. Having this confidence, they unconsciously or consciously recognise the authority of the Maker and Ruler of mankind as on their side, and then they feel that they can appeal to justice.

You will kindly bear in mind that I am speaking of the proper interpretation of the words just and justice. Using the term in the largest sense, I should say that justice is the whole *Order*, spiritual and external, of the human creation; the Order or system of relations which we are already able in part to apprehend, and towards higher perfections of which the Supreme Power is leading mankind onwards. The just or righteous man will be he who studies and respects this Order and sets himself to do his part in fulfilling it.

I have said just or righteous. In other languages, including Greek, which is the original language of the New Testament, and Latin, and the modern languages derived from the Latin, such as French and Italian, there is only one word for justice and righteousness. Our fathers and we, taking advantage of our having the two words, one from the Latin and one from the Saxon, have given them different shades of meaning. When we use the word righteousness, we think more of the whole of life, and take more definitely into account our spiritual nature, than when we speak of justice. Righteousness includes all our duties, all that it is right that we should do. But it refers, as justice does, to the Order which God has appointed and has confirmed by the sanctions of experience and law, to the relations in which He has placed us towards Himself and towards one another. St. Paul says, "Children, obey your parents in the Lord, for this is just." Justice requires that children should obey their parents. In this and like cases we should prefer the word righteous or righteousness. But, whichever be the word used, we are to understand St. Paul as implying that the relations of parents and children, of husband and wife, of fellow-members of the same community, are of the Creator's appointment, as well as those of employer and employed, of buyer and seller. And the complete justice or righteousness of human life is the due fulfilment of all divinely appointed relations. The laws do what they can to secure the performance of what is due from one to another in those various bonds; but law cannot regulate the affections; and we generally use the word justice to denote what the law is able to enforce.

It is to the well-being of society, understood as well as we are able to understand it, that we are to look for instruction in what is just; I mean the well-being of any parts and of the whole taken together. No benefit that could be acquired by a class to the inevitable injury of the whole could claim the support of justice, because it would not have the authority of Him who is building up mankind into harmony and well-being. It is natural for those who are enamoured of justice, as every Christian ought to be, to set their minds at work upon such perfecting of the social order as they can imagine. Their thoughts will naturally be arrested by those parts of the complex machinery in which they perceive special suffering and bondage; but they can never be regardless of the general well-being and harmony; and they will necessarily desire that when a change is made there should be as little friction and disturbance, and as general and willing a consent, as possible. It is always a living and progressive Order, the growing well-being and happiness of mankind, and this issuing from the highest source of authority, that draws to itself the hearts of the just, and makes them desire to live and die as its servants.

Let us dwell for a moment on the question of the due share of labour in the profits of industry. Imaginative minds have found no difficulty in picturing to themselves a state of society in which there should be no rich or poor, but all should work and all should be well-off. Where they have chiefly differed amongst themselves has been with regard to the apportionment of remuneration for work; some have thought that all the members of the community ought to be made as equal as possible, without consideration either of the kind or of the amount of the work they do; some that the less agreeable work should be more highly rewarded—that a street-sweeper, for example, should be better paid in honours and comforts than an inventor or a judge or a minister of State. Mr. Ruskin, who has done so much admirable work, and to whom we are so profoundly indebted for much of his teaching, is somewhat fancifully speculative in economical matters; and his view is that all who do the same kind of work ought to receive equal wages, fixed by some public authority. He states this view with characteristic courage and confidence. "The best labour," he says, "has been, and is, *as all labour ought to be*, paid by an invariable standard. ' What ? ' the reader perhaps answers amazedly, ' pay good and bad workmen alike ? ' Certainly. You pay with equal fee your good and bad physician and Prime Minister, why not your bricklayer ? So far as you employ it at all, bad work should be paid no less than good work." These speculators do not in general propose any method of making people work if they are disposed to be idle. I think they assume that when the social order which they devise comes into play, human nature will be altered and every one will hate being idle and be eager to do the work he is wanted to do. But how far will each creator of an ideal commonwealth be able to claim that his social order is *just*, and that any order which differs from his is unjust ? If he believes that his system not only will make every one happy but is one which men might set themselves immediately to carry out with safety and advantage, he will have for himself the satisfaction and support of holding it to be *just;* but until it comes nearer to actual life, so that many persons who have knowledge and a cool temperament think of it as immediately practicable, he and his partisans will not be able to claim publicly the support of justice with the confidence, say, of those who demand a " living wage."

Those of us who are less imaginative, or who do not set a high value on dreams of this kind, may easily put before our minds less revolutionary improvements in the condition of those who contribute the manual labour to industrial operations. We might think it not unreasonable that every one employed in great and thriving industries should have a clear £3 a week. Would this be too much, we may ask, to keep a skilled artisan and his family in decent comfort, and to enable him to provide for the future? You may feel in your minds that this would be no more than just. But you are hardly prepared to demand so much in the name of justice for all workers, or to complain that they are wronged or kept out of their rights in not having it. And you know why you are not. If companies and other employers had to pay much more in wages than they are paying now, they would not be able to tender at such prices as would bring them orders. A large and universal rise in wages, however desirable it may be, and however we may hope for it in the future, does not seem to be immediately obtainable. Sober and practical persons see no way of getting it. If enthusiasts say to the working masses: " You have the physical strength, you have only to upset society and take possession of what you ought to have," they do not succeed in persuading many that they would be able to get what they desire in that way. But those who insist on a minimum wage in any department of industry, do so in the belief that it can be had without seriously imperilling the industry, and therefore the whole means of living of the workers. The law authorises men to ask as high wages as they choose; and justice supports them in demanding as high wages as they can get. The more the condition of the whole labouring population can be improved, even if it be at the cost of reducing the luxuries of the rich few, the better; and we may be sure that such improvement has the authority of the Builder of mankind to back it; and therefore we say confidently that it is a just and righteous thing that the condition of those who are worst off should be improved to the utmost possible extent. But it is where the wages are lowest that there is the greatest practical difficulty in insisting on and obtaining a living wage; and before we denounce the *injustice* of those employers who pay miserable wages, we must be sure that they would be able to go on giving any employment at all if they had to pay better wages. How the position of the worst-paid part of our population is to be improved is a very large question, on which I do not enter here. We are now speaking about justice; and I say that an improvement is supported by justice, and may claim to be just, when it is seen to be not only desirable all round, but also such as can be immediately and safely carried out. As Browning says—

> The common problem, yours, mine, every one's,
> Is not to fancy what were fair in life,
> Provided it could be: but finding first
> What may be, then find how to make it fair
> Up to our means.

If I may, however, add a brief exhortation or two to my general argument, I would ask you to be on your guard against thinking too lightly of what we owe to the law; I mean to the law of the land, as administered by our courts and enforced by penalties. It is true that the law is essentially imperfect; it has to deal with external facts, and the courts often have great difficulty in ascertaining what even the external facts are; it sometimes costs a good deal to go to law for our rights; but our laws are better than those of any other generation or any other country, and it is the well-founded boast of our land that they are administered honestly and without favour. Such a state of things has been described in old times as a condition of almost paradisal felicity. Under the silent and unobtrusive protection of the law we can in general go about our work and enjoy our pleasures without hindrance or molestation, no one making us afraid. Some think we have already more *protection* from the law than is altogether good for us, and that it is too much the habit in this age to ask for laws to regulate everything. That may be said to be a proof of our confidence in the law. We may perhaps expect even too much from it. At all events let us be thankful and proud to be citizens of a country that has such good laws, such effective government, and such uncorrupt tribunals.

Let me ask you also to have faith in progress. Christians are bound to believe in it, because they believe in the heavenly Father, in whose hands are the destinies of mankind, and who is ever leading His creation onwards. Let no one despair about any improvement of which he can distinctly realise the form and the bearings. But if it is our belief in the heavenly Father's kingdom and righteousness that gives us hope, we must bear in mind that He cares more for the souls than for the bodies of His children, and that the progress which He chiefly desires is that of personal character and mutual affection and spiritual aspiration. The highest part of the Divine order consists in the relations of spiritual beings to God and to each other; and in the eyes of God the ease of the body will always be subordinate and subservient to the freedom and dignity of the inward man. First that which is spiritual, then that which is natural or physical. There is eternal truth in the precept which our Lord gave to the poor and suffering multitudes who crowded to hear Him—" Seek ye first the heavenly Father's kingdom and His justice; and all the things which the Gentiles seek, the meat and the drink and the clothing, shall be added unto you."

XXII

JUBILEE ADDRESSES, 1897

I

"Out of them shall proceed thanksgiving and the voice of them that make merry: and I will multiply them, and they shall not be few; I will also glorify them, and they shall not be small. . . . And their prince shall be of themselves, and their ruler shall proceed from the midst of them; and I will cause him to draw near, and he shall approach unto me. . . . And ye shall be my people, and I will be your God."—JEREMIAH xxx. 19.

IT is well within the truth to say—what is in the minds of all the subjects of the Queen, and of their fellow-men throughout the civilised world—that the history of mankind does not exhibit in any part of its annals such a national period as that which we are contemplating on this memorable day[1]: such a time, we mean, of happiness, of peaceful progress, of expansion; such a time lasting over so many years. Great deliverances, trying wars, splendid achievements of genius, have more power to thrill the heart and kindle the imagination than these special blessings of the Victorian era. The Reformation, Shakespeare, Elizabeth, Cromwell, Trafalgar,

[1] 20th June.

and Waterloo are names of light in our history to which our sixty years show nothing comparable. But for the triumph of peace, for growth in all the features and functions of national life, for diffused happiness, there has been nothing in the past—we can hardly suppose there will be anything in the future—to outdo the reign of Queen Victoria.

We are giving thanks to-day for the good things thus lavished upon us—we older persons who can remember for ourselves what the things around us were at the beginning of the reign, and you of younger age, to whom the noble works have been declared which our God has done for us in these two generations. What a thought it is—this of the vast volume of thankfulness going up from the earth to the throne of heaven! Let us think with gladness of the millions and scores of millions of fellow-souls with whose thanksgivings ours—ours from this Westmorland valley—are blending in these festive days! "It is a good thing to sing praises unto our God; yea, a joyful and pleasant thing it is to be thankful." It is a breath of God, rich with health and life, that thus moves us all, and constrains us to confess, "Not unto us, O Lord, not unto us, but unto Thy name give the praise, for Thy loving mercy and for Thy truth's sake!" In the larger part of to-day's services you all are the actors; yours are the minds, yours are the voices that here worship the God of our fathers; but you have heard some passages of Holy Writ which have power to feed and to lift your thoughts, and it is the preacher's duty to set before you as best he can some of the reasons which are universally felt to justify and call for the general thankfulness. These are well stated in the special Thanksgiving of the day. "We thank Thee for progress made in knowledge of Thy marvellous works, for increase of comfort given to human life, for kindlier feeling between rich and poor, for wonderful preaching of the Gospel to many nations." You will perceive these words of the Thanksgiving to be carefully chosen, and I am glad to follow the guidance that they offer.

But you may have observed that this thanksgiving includes no recognition of the Sovereign's personal goodness as one of the blessings by which we have been favoured, nor is there any direct praise of her to be found in the appointed services. That is well, if it were only because these services are appointed by the Queen's own authority. But her subjects are not ungrateful for the advantages which her whole empire has derived from her high and endearing qualities. It is matter of common knowledge that she has steadily used her great influence in support of seemliness of life ; that she has spared herself no labour, and has shown a trained patriotic intelligence in the performance of her constitutional duties ; that she has interested herself heartily in the well-being of her distant subjects, in India and elsewhere ; that she has submitted with dignity and cheerfulness to the modern English restraints upon Royal power of action ; and, what has touched her people most, that she has shown a peculiar tenderness and readiness of sympathy with suffering. I limit myself to what is, as I have said, matter of common knowledge. It is easy to see that a genuine enthusiasm of loyalty has been called forth by the virtues and kindnesses that have adorned the long life of the Queen, an enthusiasm chastened into reverence by the domestic sorrows with which that life has more than once been darkened.

The personal character which we thus thankfully recognise in Her Majesty has worked in a gracious harmony with the movements which we perceive to be characteristic of her reign. I do not dwell upon the vast extension of the territorial dominions, or the corresponding increase in the number of human souls subject to the British Crown. I ask you to consider that fourfold advance of which the Thanksgiving takes note, in knowledge, in comfort, in social good feeling, in evangelistic work.

1. The knowledge of God's marvellous works has been increased, in that much more has become known about them, and also in the sense that knowledge has been spread more widely.

The greatest name in science for the last sixty years is that of an Englishman, Charles Darwin. The idea which took possession of his mind, and which was verified by his wonderfully acute and patient observations—that of the gradual variation of living creatures under definite influences, and especially through the struggle for existence ; that is to say, the idea of gradual and not sudden creation—has proved so far-reaching and fruitful that our ways of looking at everything have been modified by it. For the large extension of astronomical knowledge within recent years, and in particular for the knowledge of the sun and other heavenly bodies which has been obtained through spectroscopic analysis, we may claim, I believe, the chief honour for subjects of the Queen. To Englishmen, again, is mainly due the discovery of the fact that energy or force can change its form, passing, for example, from heat into electricity, but does not perish. The germ theory of disease may be counted one of the triumphs of French science, having been clearly apprehended and verified by M. Pasteur. This is not the place, however, nor am I the person, to enlarge on scientific discoveries. These brief allusions may serve to indicate a progress in which every branch of human knowledge has, I believe, had a part during the last half-century or the sixty years of Her Majesty's reign.

But the reign has also been distinguished by an unprecedented *diffusion* of knowledge. It has been a great educational epoch. One important feature of it has been the admission of women to all the higher studies. A student who traces her parentage back to Kirkby Lonsdale has taken the highest mathematical place of the year at our chief seat of mathematical study, the University of Cambridge. Elementary education, so far as the law can secure it, has been made universal, and has been considerably raised in character and aim. Education in all its branches has been the object of unceasing attention and effort on the part of patriots and philanthropists. Our rulers will not be allowed to rest until the national provision for secondary and for technical education has been made more complete. It has been one of the steady convictions of the Victorian era that we ought to become to the utmost of our capabilities an educated people.

2. The " increase of comfort given to human life "

is largely the result of the extension and diffusion of knowledge. All kinds of inventions, and especially the new facilities of locomotion, have been adding incessantly to the comforts enjoyed by the mass of the people. These same causes have operated indirectly in making the general life more comfortable by promoting prosperity. Wages and prices are the powers which increase and diminish the ease of life for the working population; and if you want to know what has been the history of these during the reign of Victoria, ask any aged person whose memory is good to tell you about them. It is certain that there is no section of our working population that is not better off than the fathers and the grandfathers of the present workers were. The two most powerful causes of this prosperity have been Free Trade and steam. The setting of trade free and the application of the force of steam have combined to make the wealth of this country grow by leaps and bounds during the last two generations. And though some who contemplate the needlessly great riches of the successful few may be inclined to complain that even more of the new wealth has not been divided amongst the poorer producers of it, it is evident beyond contradiction that these poorer producers have everywhere had a share of it. Wages are worth what they will buy, and their real value depends not only on what they are in the current coin, but also on the current prices of the necessaries of life. Cheaper food and cheaper clothes mean more of comfort for the poor. And we have solid grounds for rejoicing that the poor are able to live more comfortably now in all parts of the Queen's dominions than the corresponding class could do when she began her happy reign.

3. And the fact that the lot of the poor is easier accounts in part, no doubt, for that kindlier feeling between rich and poor in which we may also rejoice. " Behold, how good and joyful a thing it is, brethren, to dwell together in unity!" And who will say that we are not now dwelling together in unity? Amongst ourselves, for example, here in Westmorland, what is there lacking to a wholesome and reasonable concord between class and class, between party and party, between Church and Dissent, between one school in the Church and another? We are using to-day an old Prayer for Unity which expresses an excellent sentiment, but of which the language is blessedly out of date. It speaks of great dangers, such as we ought seriously to lay to heart, which we are in by our unhappy divisions; it assumes that there is hatred and prejudice to be taken away from amongst us. Such language was appropriate when the prayer was made; but it has almost lost its truth now. It is not godly to make ourselves out to be worse than we are; rather do we glorify God's grace by making the best of ourselves. We are glad to use old prayers and old psalms, but we use them with a necessary freedom. The new prayer fits the circumstances of to-day; and if our forefathers perceived that there was serious danger as well as a reproach to their Christianity in their unhappy divisions, it is our duty to thank God with all our hearts for the kindly feeling prevailing amongst us and making our England a country that it is at unity in itself, and to be the more ashamed of the individual pettinesses

of jealousy and the like which ought to find no home in the breasts of English Christians.

4. Lastly, we give thanks for "wonderful preaching of the Gospel to many nations" as a blessing which has marked the Queen's reign.

It has been common of late years to speak of the loosening of old religious beliefs and the free rejection by many of the Christian theology as one of the most serious signs of the time. Undoubtedly there has been much in the literature of the day to disturb and alarm religious persons. The question, how far Christianity was losing its hold upon educated minds, has not been an easy one to answer. All persons of more than middle age are aware that the Christianity of our land has undergone some change. But there are reasons for believing that the change, being a change for the better, and at the same time a reversion to the real theology of the New Testament, has helped a large number of persons to be the truer Christians. Our Thanksgiving notes one remarkable piece of evidence as to the permanence and force of Christian faith amongst us. It does not refer, I imagine, to the efforts put forth in this country to draw the careless part of the population to Christ, though there is no section of the land in which these efforts, made by Churchmen and non-Churchmen alike, have not been hearty and sustained. The preaching of the Gospel to many nations must mean what we especially call missionary work. And this has certainly not flagged during our sixty years. Our missionary annals speak not only of large outlay, but of enthusiastic personal service, of lives cheerfully and heroically laid down in the cause of Christ, of the readiness of men and women to step into the breaches made by pestilence and the sword, and of the successes granted in recompense to these sincere Christian efforts. Yes, the flame of faith must still be burning in Christian England, or we should not see all Churches seriously bending themselves to the task of conquering the world for Christ. The Gospel, purified as it has been from conceptions which did dishonour to the Divine Nature, has not lost its power over hearts and consciences and lives. Christ as the Son of the Father, Christ as the Lord of the heavenly kingdom, Christ as the Builder of human society, is more simply believed in and proclaimed than when His Divine Figure was obscured by doctrines which have been seen to be inconsistent with a high morality as well as with scientific and literary discoveries. The larger views about other religions and the Divine government and care of all the races of mankind, which belong to our age, are now represented freely and fully in the preaching of Christian missionaries, and are not found to kill the desire of believers in Christ to bring all men to the one Saviour. The remarkable encouragement given to the preaching of the Gospel through the breadth of Africa from Uganda southwards, must make it seem to us all worth while to do more and more for missions, whilst the difficulties to be overcome in China and in India, and the very limited success in making converts in those countries, have rather the effect of stimulating enterprise and determination than of daunting hope and endeavour amongst the Christians of the world.

Let us not mingle, therefore, any down-hearted

apprehensions, as Christians anxious for the interests of the kingdom of Christ, with our patriotic thanksgivings. Let us not be slow of heart to believe that it is Christ who is leading our world onwards in that progress of which the steps are so cheeringly visible, whilst it is so difficult to understand its final goal. There remains, and will long remain, a sad abundance of things to be sorry for, to be ashamed of; there is work enough for the servants of Christ to do with their might. Alike for patient perseverance in well-doing and for heroic devotion, the heavenly service has its demands. All the voices of the past and of the present are calling us to go forward. "Onward!" they are saying to us, "Onward, Christian soldiers, Marching as to war, With the Cross of Jesus going on before."

XXIII

JUBILEE ADDRESSES, 1897

II

"Then Samuel took a stone, and set it between Mizpeh and Shen, and called the name of it Eben-ezer (*i.e.* the stone of help), saying, Hitherto hath the Lord helped us."—1 SAMUEL vii. 12.

ALREADY on Sunday, the anniversary of the Queen's Accession, we have assembled in our churches to render our thanksgivings to God for the blessings vouchsafed to this nation during her long reign, and to offer up our prayers with more than usual earnestness for our Queen and our country. We meet together again to-day,[1] as fellow-countrymen and fellow-citizens, to keep time, here in Kirkby Lonsdale also, with that wonderful procession which is representing to its countless spectators the greatness and the unity of the Empire. No Englishman can think unmoved of that winding train which is now following the Queen along the great arteries of London. This is a day, let us not shrink from saying, of pride for Englishmen; a day, let us also acknowledge, on which our responsibilities may well fill us with awe.

[1] 22nd June.

We should know still better the consciousness natural to the people of an empire not too vast to be of one heart and soul, if we were called upon to defend our honour and our liberties and the multitudinous interests committed to our charge against enemies that would assail them. Then there would be an electric response to the call. This round world would be girdled with defiant English resolve as with bands of flame. Such a call might come; and we ought to be prepared for it. This is, thank God, a time of peace; and we are thinking almost exclusively of the blessings and triumphs of peace. The Queen of our Empire is not an Alexander or a Napoleon, nourishing dreams of the conquest of the world. We are all anxious to be on friendly terms with our neighbours, and we are welcoming at this moment as the guests of the Sovereign representatives of all thrones and republics. But we are not omitting from our demonstrations of this week the evidences of our readiness for war. The head of our State, a woman venerable for age as well as for peaceful virtues, is to review a fleet which, like other products of the time, surpasses all that has been known or imagined in magnitude and costliness, in novelty and variety of expedients. Englishmen do not mean to be backward or grudging in the maintenance of their Navy. We may find comfort in the reflection that it is good for the peace of the world that England should have a strength to be respected. But let no one be troubled by the notion that Christianity, or the Sermon on the Mount, or the love of God in Christ, forbids us to face the horrors of war. War, when justifiable, is not unchristian; and it cannot be Christian to reduce armaments without abolishing them, any more than to have a weak woman as the only policeman in a town. Let us freely allow ourselves an honest English pride in being strong as well as in being rich.

It is not necessarily wrong to be proud. There is a pride which does not ape humility, but which actually begets the genuine humility. It is right that we should say to ourselves, "We are citizens of no mean city." It is not a small thing to be an Englishman; the England of these British Isles is no insignificant country. We may well be proud that Canada, Australia, South Africa, India, pay homage to the Crown and Parliament of Great Britain and Ireland, and that their representatives are amongst the most enthusiastically loyal of the Queen's subjects. But can you not understand the feeling that came into the heart of Solomon when he was set on the throne of David his father? It was a grand position for an Israelite, and Solomon did not think lightly of it; but the greatness of it made him feel his own inadequacy. "O Lord my God, Thou hast made Thy servant king instead of David my father: and I am but a little child; I know not how to go out or come in. And Thy servant is in the midst of Thy people which thou hast chosen, a great people, that cannot be numbered nor counted for multitude. Give Thy servant therefore an understanding heart to judge Thy people, that I may discern between good and evil; for who is able to judge this Thy great people?" If there is one general impression to be left by the pageants of this week, and by all that is written in our journals and preached in our churches and spoken at public dinners, to be left on the minds of the people who through the Parliament and the Ministers of State govern this unprecedented Empire, ought it not to be a deepening of the feeling expressed with such simplicity by Solomon?

It has been the common belief of political philosophers that such a thing can hardly be imagined as the successful governing of a vast and complicated empire by a democracy. Well, the Lord God, in His providence, has called a democracy to the government of this British Empire, and so far the task has been performed with some success. Hitherto hath the Lord helped us. One of our Victorian poets, comparing England to the fabled giant Atlas who was said to carry the globe on his shoulders, spoke of our country as staggering under "the load, Well-nigh not to be borne, Of the too vast orb of her fate." That was thirty years ago; now the load is a heavier one; the orb has grown vaster; but there is no sign yet of our country giving way under the burden. The colonies that call England mother are not now gathering round the couch of an age-stricken and enfeebled parent; rather do they remind us of the quiverful of arrows that enable their possessor to speak unashamed with enemies in the gate.

The question is not so much whether the ruling power consists of one, or a few, or of the many, but of what quality the ruling power is. A God-fearing people ought to govern better—if there were the whole world to govern—than a self-pleasing monarch or a corrupted aristocracy. The point of infinite importance for us English and for mankind is that the people who elect the British Parliament and set our statesmen on high should be a wise and religious people.

1. And one quality which a God-fearing people will cherish is that of a reverent and thankful feeling towards the past. At this moment we are looking back over an integral portion of our national history, but our thankfulness is dwelling chiefly on the *progress* which God's goodness has enabled us to make during the last sixty years. We are thanking God, not at all in a godless spirit, that we are now greater and even better than our fathers. We are reminding ourselves how much smaller the England of the Queen's Accession was than that of the sixtieth anniversary of it; how many things that needed to be altered have been reformed. But we must remember that we who have thus grown greater and better are the children of a noble England of the past; of an England whose history is full of inspiration for us, and should keep us reverent, and steady us with a sense of responsibility. As our own Wordsworth has grandly put it, "In our halls is hung Armoury of the invincible knights of old; We must be free, or die, who speak the tongue That Shakespeare spake, the faith and morals hold Which Milton held:—in everything we are sprung Of earth's first blood, have titles manifold." The old commandment promised a long continuance in their land to a people by whom father and mother were honoured. And experience has proved that there is nothing so likely to enable a nation to command the future as pious reverence for its past. Englishmen can say without bated breath, "Let us now

praise famous men, and the fathers that begat us. The Lord hath wrought great glory by them through His great power from the beginning." Let the thought be ever present with us that we have high traditions to honour and to carry forward.

2. And when we put our hands to the governing of our Empire, if it be but by the showing of a feeling and the utterance of a sympathy, let us hold fast the conviction that a God-fearing people must govern in accordance with its faith. One of the surest and happiest evidences that our God is leading us onwards is that it is affirmed with increasing confidence, and more persons are coming to see, that what we believe as Christians we must act upon not only in private life, but in politics. Two bad old notions are still delaying the general acceptance of this principle—one, that the life of nations is necessarily the brute struggle for existence, and that what each nation has to do, if it would not fall out and be thrust aside, is to contend unscrupulously for its own advantage; the other, that religion is a private matter between a man and his God, and means the saving of his own soul in the way in which he happens to think that souls are to be saved. But the true Christian, with the pious Hebrew, addresses his God thus: "O God of my fathers, and Lord of mercy, who hast made all things with Thy word, and ordained man through Thy wisdom, that he should have dominion over the creatures which Thou hast made, and order the world according to equity and righteousness, and execute judgment with an upright heart!" Is not that a fine aim for a great ruling power—to order the world according to equity and

righteousness? My hope is that this is becoming more and more the desire of the English people, of the democracy which chooses our great administrators and makes them the instruments of its purposes. Those who represent us have duties towards the subjects of the Crown and duties towards other nations. It is their business to study to preserve God's people committed to their charge in wealth (or well-being), peace, and godliness; to see to it that by their endeavours all things may be so ordered and settled upon the best and surest foundations that peace and happiness, truth and justice, religion and piety, may be established among us for all generations. Other nations they are bound to know as portions of the one great family of God, and to treat them to the utmost of their power and wisdom with fairness, courtesy, and good-will. It is possible that the difficulty of being Christian in international relations is greater than that which has to be overcome in any other province of morality. But the difficulty has to be faced, if we are honest Christians; and we need not have the least doubt that those who in this struggle set themselves to find out and do the will of God will have light on their path, and bring down blessings on their country and on mankind.

3. Once more. The English people is made up of its constituencies, of families, of individuals. A steady nation cannot be created out of light-headed citizens. The policy of a country will not bear the marks of noble aims, of high-mindedness, of courage, of care for the weak, of respectfulness, of the fear of the righteous God, if the many whom its authorities

represent are absorbed in anxiety about their petty personal interests or in careless pleasure-seeking, or are moved in crowds without thought by catching sentiments. We, here, are not a very important section of the English people; but we desire, I am sure, to do what in us lies to uphold the honour of our sacred land, and to contribute to its prosperity and greatness. We are thankful for the blessings bestowed upon us in the high character and long life of our Queen, and in the progress and expansion which give distinction to her reign. This thankfulness we cannot show more effectually, we cannot serve our Queen and country more loyally, than by endeavouring to prove ourselves personally good English Christians. Let us be glad that our daily humble efforts to do our duty should be quickened and stimulated from time to time by a joyous breath of patriotism. The sobriety and good sense and sympathy and unselfish devotion to duty that will make good English citizens are the same qualities that will make happy English homes; and these and all precious qualities will grow out of the fear of God and the following of Christ. Let us yield ourselves willingly to the emotions of the day as to thoughts and feelings which our God inspires. As this great Jubilee calls to us to lift up our hearts, let us answer in faith and hope, " We lift them up unto the Lord!"

XXIV

SOME INTERPRETATIONS REVISED[1]

I

"RECKONINGS" IN 2 CORINTHIANS X.

I THINK I may assume that the frequent recurrence of the word λογίζεσθαι in this passage, and the bearing of this recurrence on the interpretation to be given to λογισμοί in verse 5, have failed to attract the notice of expositors. I venture to write without consulting the most recent commentaries on this Epistle, but it can hardly be a work of supererogation to call attention to a feature which was evidently not observed by the Revisers of the English New Testament.

The sentences in which the word occurs are thus rendered in the Revised Version: "I beseech you, that I may not when present shew courage with the confidence wherewith I *count* to be bold against some, which *count* of us as if we walked according to the flesh" (v. 2); "If any man trusteth in himself that he is Christ's, let him *consider* this again with him-

[1] From *The Expositor*.

self, that, even as he is Christ's, so also are we" (v. 7); "Let such a one *reckon* this, that, what we are in word by letters when we are absent, such are we also in deed when we are present" (v. 11). That the Revisers did not render the word uniformly is in any case rather surprising; but it may be taken for certain that if they had thought there was anything pointed in St. Paul's use of it, they would have given the same English for it throughout. "Reckon" is the most obvious equivalent for λογίζεσθαι. And there seems to be no reason why we should not read, "I *reckon* to be bold against some who *reckon* of us," "Let him *reckon* this again with himself," "Let such a one *reckon* on this." And then it would be congruous to render λογισμούς by "reckonings."

The Second Epistle to the Corinthians is full of traces of extraordinary excitement. The whole composition becomes luminous in the light of a partly hypothetical but nearly certain explanation of the circumstances which occasioned it. They seem to have been as follows. Not long before he left Ephesus St. Paul had sent Timothy to Macedonia and Corinth (Acts xix. 22, 1 Cor. xvi. 10). Timothy had found the Corinthian society painfully disturbed. Some persons had arrived at Corinth who brought with them credentials from the Jerusalem Apostles, and had been impugning the authority of St. Paul. Their statements had shaken the loyalty of his converts and friends. One man had stood forward as the leader of the movement against St. Paul. He and others had said many disparaging things about the absent Apostle; they had dwelt on his want of credentials, had spoken lightly of his personal powers, had put wrong constructions on some of his acts, and had charged him with self-seeking. Timothy had hastened back with the melancholy tidings of this revolt, and had met his master at Troas. St. Paul immediately despatched Titus, a disciple of more strength of character than Timothy, with a sharp and threatening letter to Corinth. The letter had not long been gone before St. Paul began to wish he had not written in such anger. But the letter produced its effect upon the Corinthians. Their self-reproachful sorrow was great. They put the chief blame on the leader of the shameful attack, whom they denounced and repudiated (2 Cor. ii. 5-8, vii. 11). Meanwhile St. Paul had come on, in a very restless and unhappy state of mind, from Troas into Macedonia. There Titus met him with the good news of the repentance of the Corinthian believers, and St. Paul poured out his feelings at once in a letter which he sent forward to precede his own arrival — this Second Epistle to the Corinthians.

The letter exhibits a tumult of contending emotions. Wounded affection, joy, self-respect, hatred of self-assertion, consciousness of the authority and importance of his ministry, scorn of his opponents, toss themselves like waves, sometimes against each other, on the troubled sea of his mind, and accordingly the letter abounds in the rhetoric of passion. There are two kinds of rhetoric—the artificial kind, which is cold and tiresome, and that which heated feelings throw out, the foam of agitation. Strong language, not seldom stronger than the occasion seems to warrant, figurative expressions, abrupt turns, phrases seized and flung at his assailants, words made up, iterated, played upon, mark this epistle far more than any other of the Apostle's letters. All these features will show themselves plainly to a reader who is on the look-out for them. Even the calmer parts of the letter are influenced as to their style by the emotion which breaks out in the more vehement.

The tenth chapter begins with a soft note; but, as the image of his assailants presents itself to the writer's mind, his feelings quicken, and he becomes somewhat bitter and defiant. He welcomed back the remorseful Corinthians to his heart, but he was not inclined to spare his detractors. The word λογίζομαι is not an uncommon one with St. Paul; on the contrary, it belongs to the characteristic Pauline phraseology. But there is something obtrusive in the use of it here. The repetition of it in the second verse, and the double defiance expressed in it in the seventh and eleventh verses, seem to show that St. Paul used it in a meaning way. This use of the word will be explained if we suppose that St. Paul was taking up an expression which had been reported to him, and by which he had been displeased. One of his assailants may have said that he "reckoned" this or that to be the case about St. Paul. Some such observation causes St. Paul to fasten on the phrase.

Some of you, I hear, "reckon" of me as if I walked after the flesh, as having the motives and the ways of the carnal man. I for my part "reckon" that I will proceed against such persons with a power which they will not be able to resist. The weapons of my warfare are not carnal.

The power of God is with me to cast down "reckonings" and whatever sets itself up on high against the knowledge of God, and to take every thought captive to the obedience of Christ. Yes, I am prepared to punish all disobedience. If any one is confident in himself that he is Christ's, let him "reckon" that I am Christ's as much as he is. Some one has told you that though my letters are strong my bodily presence is weak and my speech of no account; let him "reckon" on this, that I will act as strongly as I write.

A little farther on, xi. 5, the word occurs again; and it seems probable that we may class this use of it also with those which have just preceded it. "I 'reckon' that I am not a whit behind those superlative apostles (τῶν ὑπερλίαν ἀποστόλων)." It is more doubtful whether a further use of it, in xii. 6, is suggested by any remnant of the irritated feeling: "I forbear, lest any one should 'reckon' as to me (εἰς ἐμὲ λογίσηται, should account of me, R.V.) above that which he seeth me to be, or heareth of me."

There are two other places in this epistle in which the word λογίζεσθαι occurs. In v. 19 it has obviously that simple sense of "reckoning" in which it is so frequently used in the Epistle to the Romans. But this sense has not been usually given to λογίσασθαι in iii. 5. Here it has been commonly supposed to mean the exercise of the mind on spiritual subjects. The Authorised Version has, "not that we are sufficient of ourselves to think anything as of ourselves"; and the Apostle has been generally understood to be protesting that he was not sufficient of himself to do any of the thinking or reasoning of his Apostolic ministry, that his teaching was not his own, but God's. And no doubt λογισμούς in x. 5, rendered "imaginations" or "reasonings," has been held to confirm this interpretation. But the Revised Version has "not that we are sufficient of ourselves, to account anything as from ourselves"; where the comma must be intended to guard the reader against making "to account" depend upon "sufficient." St. Paul, according to this amended translation, says, "not that of myself I am sufficient (for my ministry), that anything I do should be reckoned as from myself." It will be found, I think, that everywhere in the New Testament λογίζεσθαι preserves its proper sense of "reckoning" or "taking account."

XXV

SOME INTERPRETATIONS REVISED

II

ST. PAUL'S "GRACE"

THERE are many places of the New Testament in which the Revisers have made alterations which to most readers it has seemed hardly worth while to make; and there are many in which they have refrained from making alterations which critical readers wish they had made. But I do not know of more than one place in which they seem to me to have altered any rendering of the Authorised Version for the worse through misapprehension.

The place to which I refer is Philippians i. 7; "Even as it is right for me to be thus minded in behalf of you all, because I have you in my heart, inasmuch as, both in my bonds and in the defence and confirmation of the gospel, ye all are partakers with me of grace." So the Revisers give the last clause. But the Authorised Version has, "ye all are partakers of my grace." I shall endeavour to show that the Authorised is right here, and that St.

Paul was speaking of a particular grace bestowed on himself.

The Greek is συγκοινωνούς μου τῆς χάριτος πάντας ὑμᾶς ὄντας. The article before χάριτος is not conclusive, but it agrees better with the Authorised rendering than with the Revised. That St. Paul was accustomed to think of himself as having received a special χάρις is to be inferred from several passages of epistles written at different times. The word χάρις he uses abundantly and in all its senses. Its primary meaning, I suppose, is an act or movement which gives pleasure, something which charms. In its New Testament usage it means (1) kindness, (2) active kindness, (3) beneficent spiritual influence, (4) a gift or boon; and also (5) gratitude or response awakened by kindness, and (6) thanks. The word is sown lavishly over a section of 2 Corinthians, chaps. viii. and ix., in which it occurs ten times, in addition to εὐχαριστίαν and εὐχαριστιῶν. In viii. 1, 9, ix. 8, 14, it has the familiar sense of the Divine goodness acting with spiritual influence upon human souls. In viii. 4 τὴν χάριν is perhaps equivalent to charity, the sympathetic charity of the benevolent; in 6, 7, and 19 this "charity" is more definitely the collection for the poor at Jerusalem. In viii. 16 and ix. 15 χάρις is thanks, "Thanks be to God." When St. Paul is speaking of his χάρις he means by the word a gift or privilege conferred by God upon himself.

He dwells upon this most fully in the Epistle to the Ephesians, which was written in the same year and under the same circumstances as the Epistle to the Philippians, so that the one may reasonably be a guide to the thoughts of the other. In the third chapter we read, " For this cause I Paul, the prisoner of Christ Jesus in behalf of you Gentiles,—if so be that ye have heard of the dispensation of that grace of God which was given me to you-ward ; how that by revelation was made known unto me the mystery, ... to wit, that the Gentiles are fellow-heirs, and fellow-members of the body, and partakers of the promise in Christ Jesus through the gospel, whereof I was made a minister, according to the gift of that grace of God which was given me according to the working of His power. Unto me, who am less than the least of all saints, was this grace given, to preach unto the Gentiles the unsearchable riches of Christ." Nothing could be more explicit than these last words ; but the whole passage sets forth the wonderful· privilege, the grace, that had been conferred upon St. Paul when he was called to be the Apostle of the Gentiles. His particular grace, then, was his Apostleship, his commission to proclaim the good news of Christ to the Gentiles.

When, some years earlier, he was writing to the Romans, he was already accustomed to speak of the commission given to him as his grace. There is a not quite definite use of the term in i. 5, "Jesus Christ our Lord, through whom we received grace and apostleship, unto obedience of faith among all the nations." In xii. 3, "I say, through the grace given unto me, to every man that is among you, not to think of himself more highly than he ought to think," it is tolerably certain that St. Paul is referring distinctly to the authority with which his commission invested him. This is still plainer in xv. 15, "I write the more boldly unto you in some measure, as putting you again in remembrance, because of the grace that was given me of God, that I should be a minister of Christ Jesus unto the Gentiles." In the Epistle to the Galatians, written at nearly the same time, there are two places in which he connects the word grace with his call and commission; but in i. 15 the grace is the Divine will to give rather than the gift itself—" When it was the good pleasure of God, who . . . called me through His grace, to reveal His Son in me, that I might preach Him among the Gentiles"; in ii. 7-9 it again means distinctly the Apostolic commission, "When they saw that I had been intrusted with the gospel of the uncircumcision, even as Peter with the gospel of the circumcision; . . . and when they perceived the grace that was given unto me, James and Cephas and John . . . gave to me and Barnabas the right hands of fellowship, that we should go unto the Gentiles, and they unto the circumcision."

We see, then, that it was habitual to St. Paul to describe his Apostolic commission as a special privilege and favour for which God's goodness had selected him; in a single word he called it the χάρις or grace given to him. To the Philippians he feels deeply grateful because they had associated themselves with his Apostolic work. This association is what strikes the note of joy throughout the epistle. It was chiefly by the sending of gifts, first in the beginning of the Gospel, and then during the imprisonment at Rome, that the Christians of Philippi had made themselves his partners in the work of spreading the Gospel; but the gifts of money had been consecrated to him by their being thus devoted to the cause of the Gospel of which he was the commissioned preacher. And he pours forth his gratitude in those cordial words, "I thank my God upon all my remembrance of you, always in every supplication of mine on behalf of you all making my supplication with joy, for your fellowship in furtherance of the gospel from the first day until now; being confident of this very thing, that He which began a good work in you will perfect it until the day of Jesus Christ: even as it is right for me to be thus minded on behalf of you all, because I have you in my heart, inasmuch as, both in my bonds and in the defence and confirmation of the gospel, ye all are partakers of my grace." They had proved their fellowship with St. Paul in the furthering of the Gospel; they had made themselves partners of his Apostleship—of his special grace—in the imprisonment and in the defending and establishing of the Gospel. If grace in this passage is taken to mean the spiritual influence shed on all believers, the preceding words lose their point. How had the Philippians shown themselves to be partakers of Divine grace in St. Paul's imprisonment? The share in furthering the Gospel, the association with the imprisonment, and with the active work on behalf of the Gospel, involved in the sympathetic assistance they had given him, made the Philippians his partners, not only in the general Divine grace bestowed on all Christians, but in his Apostleship. And St. Paul so cherished the office entrusted to him that to claim a partnership in it was the surest way to his heart.

XXVI

SOME INTERPRETATIONS REVISED

III

THE "MANY MANSIONS" AND THE "RESTITUTION OF ALL THINGS"

THE interpretations of these two phrases which I am about to advocate have this in common—that they bring into this life and into the past and the present what has generally been put off into another life and the future.

"In My Father's house are many mansions; if it were not so, I would have told you; for I go to prepare a place for you" (St. John xiv. 2). Every one would admit that the word "mansions" is not a happy rendering of μοναί. Etymologically, indeed, it is an exact equivalent; *mansion* means an abiding or abode, as μονή does. But it has acquired in common use a different sense from that which it first bore. But what are the μοναί or abiding-places in the Father's house? I think it is assumed in all comments on the passage that they are the places to be occupied in the future world by the faithful disciples of the Lord. Bishop Westcott in his note on the verse expounds the words as relating to "the future being of the redeemed," to "future happiness."

The nature of the μοναί will depend upon the nature of "My Father's house." In Bishop Westcott's words, this is "the spiritual and eternal antitype of the transitory temple"; "Heaven is where God is seen as our Father." There are many references to the house of God or of the Father in the New Testament, and none of them obliges us to think of the future life. The material house is so natural an image of the spiritual or domestic house, that in some passages we cannot distinguish sharply between the two senses of the word. Where St. Paul speaks of the Gentiles being brought into the Divine family, he makes large use of the double significance of οἶκος. "So then, ye are no more strangers and sojourners (πάροικοι), but ye are fellow-citizens with the saints, and of the household of God (οἰκεῖοι τοῦ θεοῦ), being built upon the foundation of the apostles and prophets, Christ Jesus Himself being the chief corner stone; in whom each several building, fitly framed together, groweth into a holy temple in the Lord; in whom ye also are builded together for a habitation of God in the Spirit" (Eph. ii. 19-22). St. Peter uses the image in the same manner, remembering, it would seem, that saying of his Lord of which his name (stone) was a witness—"unto whom coming, a living stone, ye also, as living stones, are built up a spiritual house" (1 Peter ii. 4, 5). In a passage of the Epistle to the Hebrews, where the word rendered "built" is κατασκευάσας, it is doubtful whether the writer is thinking at all of the construction of a material house, or only of the founding of a human house; but God's house is to him what it is to St. Paul and St. Peter. "He [Jesus] has been counted worthy of more glory than Moses, by so much as he that built the house hath more honour than the house. . . . And Moses indeed was faithful in all His [God's] house as a servant, for a testimony of those things which were afterwards to be spoken; but Christ as a son, over His [God's] house; whose house are we, if we hold fast our boldness and the glorying of our hope firm unto the end" (Heb. iii. 3-6). The Apostolic writers always assume that the Father's house was the home of themselves and their fellow-believers whilst they were still living on the earth.

Christ went, He tells the Apostles, to prepare a place for them. He "went," through His death and departure into the unseen world. But He adds, "If I go and prepare a place for you, I come again, and will receive you unto Myself; that where I am, there ye may be also." The natural sense of these words is, not that the disciples when they severally died should go to Jesus and be with Him, but that He would come to them. This return of His began with the Resurrection and was fulfilled on the Day of Pentecost. Jesus promised that the Spirit should be given; and the Spirit would construct a Divine home. "I will not leave you desolate (or bereaved): I come unto you. Yet a little while, and the world beholdeth Me no more; but ye behold Me: because I live, ye shall live also. In that day ye shall know that I am in My Father, and ye in Me, and I in you.... If a man love Me, he will keep My word: and My Father will love him, and we will come unto him, and make our abode with him." Here *abode* is μονήν. This is the only other place in which μονή occurs in the New Testament, though μένω, abide, is almost the key-word of St. John's spiritual teaching.

The Apostles evidently understood their Master to promise that, when He had gone out of their bodily sight, He would come to them again in spiritual presence, and they would dwell with Him and the Father in a spiritual home; and after the Day of Pentecost they were accustomed to assume that the promise had been fulfilled, and that they were living as the Father's children with the other members of the Divine family, looking up to the Divine Son as their head. The "many mansions" are places in this household, occupied by the οἰκεῖοι τοῦ θεοῦ. The kingdom of heaven is opened to all believers, the home of God is established on the earth; and Christians are to know themselves as fellow-subjects of the kingdom, as fellow-inmates of the home.

The phrase "restitution (or restoration) of all things" occurs in the following passage of St. Peter's address, spoken in explanation of the cure of the lame man at the Beautiful Gate of the Temple— "Repent ye therefore, and turn again, that your sins may be blotted out, that so there may come seasons of refreshing from the presence of the Lord; and that He may send the Christ who hath been appointed for you, even Jesus: whom the heaven must receive until the times of restoration of all things, whereof God spake by the mouth of His holy prophets which have been since the world began" (Acts iii. 19-21).

The Apostolic expectations with regard to the future form a constantly recurring ·difficulty in the New Testament. Commentators are apt to assume that when they have adopted the belief that the Apostles expected what did not come to pass the difficulty is disposed of. But that is not so: it remains difficult to know what the expectations were. That difficulty confronts us in this passage. Leaving out of account what actually occurred in the Apostolic age, what are we to suppose that St. Peter meant, and that the author of the Acts understood him to mean? The Apostle seems to say that, if his hearers turned to God by believing in Jesus as the Christ, the Christ would be sent to them from heaven, and there would be a happy spiritual time ; but that the Christ would remain shrouded in heaven "until the times of restoration of all things"—or, in other words, until they, the Jews who heard Peter speaking, should repent. That restoration of all things had been the subject of all the prophets. All the prophets, from Samuel onwards, had "told of these days," κατήγγειλαν τὰς ἡμέρας ταύτας. St. Peter expressly associates the sending of Christ, the blessed time, the restoration of all things, with those days, with the age in which he and his hearers were living. And it is remarkable that the address closes with the statement that the Christ who was to be sent to the people on their repenting, had been already sent to them after His death that they might repent. "Unto you first God, having raised up His Servant, sent Him to bless you, in turning away every one of you from your iniquities." In the Divine history, it would appear, Christ had come. To those who, through repentance, had eyes to see Him, He was present, and had brought His blessings with Him ; but those who still had a veil on their hearts could not see Him or enter into those blessings : for these He had yet to come. The restoration of all things was then taking place in the Divine history, and would be actually accomplished —all things would be put in their right order—in the general recognition of the Christ who had come.

The restoration of all things, ἀποκατάστασις πάντων, cannot be separated from that remarkable saying of our Lord's recorded in Matthew xvii. After the vision of Moses and Elijah talking with Him, Jesus commanded His disciples, " Tell the vision to no man, until the Son of man be risen from the dead. And His disciples asked Him, saying, Why then say the scribes that Elijah must first come ? And He answered and said, Elijah indeed cometh, and shall restore all things (ἀποκαταστήσει πάντα): but I say unto you, that Elijah is come already, and they knew him not, but did unto him whatsoever they listed. . . . Then understood His disciples that He spake unto them of John the Baptist." And ἀποκαταστήσει is the word used in the Septuagint version of Malachi, where the Hebrew is rendered "turn." " Elias shall restore the heart of father towards son, and the heart of a man towards his neighbour" (iv. 5). These coincidences can hardly be accidental.

It was the establishment of the Messianic kingdom, the turning of mankind into the Divine family, that the prophets and our Lord and St. Peter had in view. The coming of the kingdom would put all things right. In being the herald of the Messianic kingdom, John the Baptist, that other Elijah, brought in this restoration. The essence of the right establishment of all things was the fulfilment of true spiritual relations. To put hearts right was to put all things right. When men, repenting and turning to God, saw and confessed the Son of man reigning at the Father's right hand, all would be right with them; family life, social life, would be perfected in the acknowledging of Christ. When St. Peter spoke, he knew that the Christ was reigning; and he knew that the blessings of His reign were enjoyed by His true spiritual subjects; and he was convinced that for his countrymen their Messiah was come and all was put right—if only they would turn to Him with their hearts and acknowledge Him as their Lord.

THE END

BY THE SAME AUTHOR.

ORDER AND GROWTH AS INVOLVED IN THE SPIRITUAL CONSTITUTION OF HUMAN SOCIETY. Crown 8vo. 3s. 6d.

SOCIAL QUESTIONS FROM THE POINT OF VIEW OF CHRISTIAN THEOLOGY. Crown 8vo. 6s.

THE EPISTLES OF ST. PAUL TO THE EPHESIANS, THE COLOSSIANS, AND PHILEMON. 8vo. 7s. 6d.

THE GOSPEL AND MODERN LIFE. Extra fcap. 8vo. 6s.

THE CHRISTIAN CALLING. Extra fcap. 8vo. 6s.

WARNINGS AGAINST SUPERSTITION. Extra fcap. 8vo. 2s. 6d.

BAPTISM, CONFIRMATION, AND THE LORD'S SUPPER. Fcap. 8vo. 1s.

MACMILLAN AND CO., Ltd., LONDON.

A SELECTION FROM

MACMILLAN'S THREE-AND-SIXPENNY LIBRARY.

Crown 8vo.   3s. 6d. each.

By Archdeacon FARRAR.

SEEKERS AFTER GOD. THE LIVES OF SENECA, EPIC-TETUS, AND MARCUS AURELIUS.
ETERNAL HOPE. Five Sermons preached in Westminster Abbey.
THE FALL OF MAN, and other Sermons.
THE WITNESS OF HISTORY TO CHRIST. Hulsean Lectures for 1870.
THE SILENCE AND VOICES OF GOD. University and other Sermons.
IN THE DAYS OF THY YOUTH. Sermons on Practical Subjects preached at Marlborough College.
SAINTLY WORKERS. Five Lenten Lectures.
EPHPHATHA: or the Amelioration of the World. Sermons preached at Westminster Abbey.
MERCY AND JUDGMENT: a few last words on Christian Eschatology.
SERMONS AND ADDRESSES DELIVERED IN AMERICA.

By FREDERICK DENISON MAURICE.

SERMONS PREACHED IN LINCOLN'S INN CHAPEL. 6 Vols. 3s. 6d. each.
CHRISTMAS DAY, and other Sermons.
THEOLOGICAL ESSAYS.
PROPHETS AND KINGS.
PATRIARCHS AND LAWGIVERS.
THE GOSPEL OF THE KINGDOM OF HEAVEN.
GOSPEL OF ST. JOHN.
EPISTLE OF ST. JOHN.
LECTURES ON THE APOCALYPSE.
FRIENDSHIP OF BOOKS.
SOCIAL MORALITY.
PRAYER BOOK AND LORD'S PRAYER.
THE DOCTRINE OF SACRIFICE.
THE ACTS OF THE APOSTLES.

By CHARLES KINGSLEY.

VILLAGE AND TOWN AND COUNTRY SERMONS.
THE WATER OF LIFE, and other Sermons.
SERMONS ON NATIONAL SUBJECTS, and THE KING OF THE EARTH.
SERMONS FOR THE TIMES.
GOOD NEWS OF GOD.
THE GOSPEL OF THE PENTATEUCH, and DAVID.
DISCIPLINE, and other Sermons.
WESTMINSTER SERMONS.
ALL SAINTS' DAY, and other Sermons.

MACMILLAN AND CO., LTD., LONDON.

www.ingramcontent.com/pod-product-compliance
Lightning Source LLC
Chambersburg PA
CBHW020317240426
43673CB00039B/839